Reading Chubak

Bibliotheca Iranica

Literature Series, No. 10

No. 1

Once a Dewdrop

Essays on the Poetry of Parvin E`tesami

Edited by Heshmat Moayyad

No. 2

Suppressed Persian

An Anthology of Forbidden Literature

Paul Sprachman

No. 3

Reading Nasta'liq

Persian and Urdu Hands from 1500 to Present

William L. Hanawaay and Brian Spooner

No. 4

Conversations with Emperor Jahangir

"Mutribi" al-Asamm of Samarqand

Richard C. Foltz

No. 5

Welcoming Fighānī

Imitation and Poetic Individuality in the Safavid-Mughal ghazal

Paul E. Losensky

No. 6

Sands of Oxus

Boyhood Reminiscences of Sadriddin Aini

John R. Perry and Rachel Lehr

No. 7

Language and Culture in Persian

Paul Sprachman

No. 8

Persian Literary Influence on English Literature

With Special Reference to the Nineteenth Century

Hasan Javadi

No. 9

A Conversation with Modern Persian Poets

Girdhari Tikku

Reading Chubak

M. R. Ghanoonparvar

MAZDA PUBLISHERS, Inc. ♦ Costa Mesa, California ♦ 2005

Funding for the publication of this volume
was provided in part by a grant from

The Iranica Institute at *www.iranicainstitute.org*,
and by A. K. Jabbari Family Trust Fund

Mazda Publishers, Inc.
Academic Publishers since 1980
P.O. Box 2603
Costa Mesa, California 92628 U.S.A.
www.mazdapub.com

Library of Congress Cataloging-in-Publication Data

Ghanoonparvar, M.R. (Mohammad Reza)
Reading Chubak / M. R. Ghanoonparvar.
p.cm.—(Bibliothca Iranica. Literature Series, No, 10)
Includes bibliographical references and index.

ISBN: 1-56859-181-0
(paper, alk. paper)

1. Chubak, Sadiq—Criticism and interpretation. 2. Persian fiction—20th century—History and criticism. I. Title. II. Series.
PK6561.C45Z64 2005
891'.5533—dc22
2004061101

Cover photo by Diane L. Wilcox

انتشارات مزدا

To Faridoun and Cindy Farrokh
Kindred Spirits

Contents

Preface and Acknowledgments

I began this project over 25 years ago while I was translating *Sang-e Sabur* [The Patient Stone] (1966) published by Mazda publishers in 1989. In the course of these years, at various intervals, whenever I wanted to continue the project, another project that I found to be more relevant and crucial to my research and teaching took priority.

With the title, *Reading Chubak*, I mean to present a descriptive analysis of each and every story by Sadeq Chubak. In this book, in addition to providing detailed descriptive analyses of the first collection of Sadeq Chubak's short stories, *Kheymehshabbazi* [Puppet Show] (1945), I have discussed, in chronological order, every short story Chubak wrote in his other short story collections, namely, *Antari keh Lutiash Mordeh Bud* [The Baboon Whose Buffoon Was Dead] (1949), *Ruz-e Avval-e Qabr* [The First Day in the Grave] (1965), and *Cheraq-e Akher* [The Last Alms] (1966), including his two plays, along with his first novel, *Tangsir* (1963). A major portion of this book is also devoted to Sadeq Chubak's last novel, *The Patient Stone*, which he considered his *magnum opus*, and which many critics consider the same. In the section on *The Patient Stone*, I examine this work in the light of the definitions of the stream of consciousness novel and literary devices in this genre. I also provide detailed analysis of this novel within the context of Iranian history and literature. In the conclusion, I address certain issues regarding the *Zeitgeist* when all of Chubak's work was written, and then I discuss certain unpleasant traits in the work and the views of writers like Chubak regarding their attitude toward Iranian religious and ethnic minorities and non-Iranian Arab neighbors, since I believe that such an attitude was nurtured subconsciously, or perhaps because of the *Zeitgeist*, particularly xenophobia and nationalism, characteristics of the 20th century. With this, I hope to at least question the sanctification of certain literary artists by critics and their compatriots who deify such figures, by placing Chubak in the historical, social, political, and cultural milieu in which he created his work, in contrast to the global climate in which readers in the ensuing generations read his work.

As always, I consider this project partial repayment to the culture and the people of my birthplace, wishing for a better future for that country. But most importantly, I am indebted to my friends, colleagues, and family, for their support during the completion of this work. They enabled me with their encouragement to devote the time needed to the completion of this long-delayed project.

I would like also to express my admiration and gratitude to Dr. Ahmad Kamron Jabbari of Mazda Publishers for his unceasing effort to promote and make more widely available books on Persian literature and Iranian culture.

All translations of stories in this volume are my own unless otherwise indicated in the "Chapter Notes" that appear immediately after the conclusion.

CHAPTER 1

Introduction

In 1946, the Persian literary scholar P. N. Khanlari made a now often quoted statement declaring the modern era of Persian literature as "the age of prose."[1] Kanlari's statement appeared at that time a rather daring declaration, since by implication it also meant that the centuries-old tradition of verse as the established and prominent vehicle for literary expression had now given way to prose, and more specifically to prose fiction. Today, although Persian poetry has not by any means given way completely to prose fiction, and modern Persian poetry has developed into a mature literary kind, the importance of prose fiction in the arena of modern Persian literature cannot be challenged. Thus, some twenty years after Khanlari's declaration of "the age of prose," one critic confidently remarked that "undoubtedly today's literature in Iran moves towards fiction,"[2] and in a recent survey in the latter decades of the 20th century, other critics view modern Persian fiction as a reflection and conscience of modern Iran, and representations of historical events do indeed mirror the strongly felt presence of Iran's past history in that country's contemporary society.

I

Sadeq Chubak's work is a landmark in the development of modern Persian fiction. As such his short stories and novels obviously deserve attention for their literary merit. But they should also be considered in terms of their relation to the society and the literary context from which they derived, since any work of art cannot be fully understood without taking into account the soil in which and the climatic conditions under which it was cultivated. As M. A. Jazayery puts it:

> Taken as a whole, a national literature is one of many institutions that reflect a social order and are reflected in it. As one of many components, it cannot be accurately understood in isolation because it does not exist in isolation. Any serious interpretation, any critical analysis of literature, must consider the features that make a piece of writing essentially *literary*, uniquely personal; but if such interpretations and analyses are to be reasonably reliable and valuable for others, they must also consider the literary product in terms of the complex network of multilateral social relationships of which it is a part.[3]

The development of modern Persian fiction has not occurred in literary isolation; rather, it has been directly linked with and influenced by social and political trends. As Hassan Kamshad observes:

> Perhaps in no other country has the development of literature been so closely associated with social and political fluctuation as in Persia during the present [20th] century.[4]

Social and political factors have indeed been of vital importance to virtually all modern Persian writers and have had substantial effects both on their work and the reception of their art in Iran. It follows, then, that to appreciate Chubak's work, considerations both literary and extra-literary must be taken into account. In this chapter, I will investigate three extra-literary areas. I will survey the development of modern Persian fiction in the context of political change in twentieth century Iran, I will provide a brief review of Sadeq Chubak's life and literary career, and finally, I will discuss the socio-political and literary factors influencing the reception of Chubak's work in Iran.

II

The Iranian socio-political events of concern to this discussion begin with the Constitutional Revolution of 1906-1911, a challenge to the autocratic reign of the Qajar dynasty that had ruled the country for more than a century. In 1921, Reza Khan, a general in the Iranian army, came to power with a coup d'état that overthrew the Qajars. The Pahlavi dynasty began with the election of Reza Khan as shah by the Iranian Parliament in 1925 and his subsequent coronation in 1926. With his accession to power, Reza Shah Pahlavi attempted to establish a strong central government by suppressing local and tribal rulers and decreasing the power of the clergy, previously strongly influential in the political arena. He also strove to "modernize" the country. Gradually, however, he established an authoritarian dictatorship that came to an end when he was forced by the Allied powers to abdicate in 1941 because of his sympathetic policies toward Nazi Germany. His son, Mohammad Reza Pahlavi, assumed the throne. With the resultant loosening of government controls mainly due to the Allied occupation of the country, many political parties came to the fore during the 1940s, some with communist and socialist ideologies. After a series of violent political events, in 1953, Mohammad Reza Shah Pahlavi was pressured by Prime Minister Mohammad Mosaddeq (1880-1967) and his nationalistic government to leave the country. However, one week later he returned to Iran, after his military supporters, with the backing of the British intelligence forces and the American CIA, had overpowered Mosaddeq. Mohammad Reza Shah Pahlavi then began to rule the country with increased consolidation of power, suppressing all opposition, until his eventual overthrow in 1979 by the supporters of the religious leader, Ayatollah Ruhollah Khomeyni.[5]

The above brief outline should clarify a number of references made in the following pages to socio-political events during the twentieth century in Iran as they relate to the present discussion of modern Persian fiction.

III

Fiction in the form of short stories and novels as exists in the West is a relatively new art form in Persian literature, although stories and the telling of tales are probably as old as Iran itself. In the millennium of imaginative literature in the neo-Persian language, narrative tales, fables, anecdotal stories, and romances have been produced in prose and verse, verse having been the predominant mode until the 20th century. The birth of modern prose fiction and the modern Persian short story in Iran is commonly regarded as corresponding with the publication of Mohammad Ali Jamalzadeh's (1895-1997) collection of stories, *Yeki Bud Yeki Nabud* [Once Upon a Time] in 1921.[6] The predominance of poetry in Persian literature at this time is evident in Jamalzadeh's emphasis on and defense of the writing of prose fiction in his preface to *Once Upon a Time*, which is considered a sort of manifesto for modern Persian literature. For Jamalzadeh, the function of prose fiction is two-fold: first, to educate the masses and second, to preserve the common expressions of the people. Influenced by his contact with Western culture and literature, he reacts to what may be called a sort of dictatorship in the literature of his time, and he calls for "literary democracy." He claims:

> The very substance of Iranian political despotism, which is well known throughout the world, can be detected in the matter of literature, that is, when a writer takes up his pen, his attention is solely directed to the small group of the learned and literati.[7]

Jamalzadeh's call for "literary democracy" in 1921 was very much in tune with the political and social events of the time. The Iranian Constitutional Revolution of 1906-1911 was part of the recent past, and the post-revolutionary spirit was still much in the air.[8] The year of the publication of Jamalzadeh's collection also coincided with the coup d'état of Reza Khan, later Reza Shah Pahlavi, which put an end to the weakened central government of the Qajar dynasty, challenged the open influence of foreign powers, and initiated a new era of self-conscious nationalism in Iran. Thus, from an Iranian literary-historical standpoint, Jamalzadeh's *Once Upon a Time* with its "manifesto" for Persian prose fiction was neither an unexpected nor, for that matter, a wholly unprecedented event. Thematically, the stories of *Once Upon a Time* involve types of social criticism that were favorite subjects of both the newspapers and a few popular fictional works of the time. In 1902, for example, *Siyahatnameh-ye Ebrahim Beyg* [The Travel Diary of Ebrahim Beyg] was published anonymously in Cairo, telling the story of an Iranian born and brought up in Egypt who yearns for his "paradise" of a country only to find his dreams shattered when he actually visits his fatherland, where he records finding a country full of wretchedness, poverty, religious hypocrisy, and political oppression.[9] Along with *The Travel Diary of Ebrahim Beyg*, the 1905 Persian translation of James Morier's *The Adventures of Hajji Baba of Ispahan* (1824) caused much apprehension in the country.[10] This work tells the story of the son of a barber from Isfahan who learns his father's trade as well as many Persian tales and quotations which, along with his training in thievery and trickery, eventually prepare him for a career of diplomatic intrigue at the court of the shah. Through the adventures of this Persian picaro, Morier draws a grim picture of Iranian life, especially that of the corruption of its political and religious institutions.[11] Not only thematically, but also to some extent stylistically, these two books paved the way for Jamalzadeh's *Once Upon a Time* stories, each in its own way parodying the pompous prose of conventional writers and attempting to introduce a prose style close to spoken Persian, a practice uncommon in traditional Persian literature. In a discussion of precedents for Jamalzadeh's *Once Upon a Time*, mention should also be made of a series of satirical articles called "Charand Parand" [Fiddle-Faddle] by Ali Akbar Dehkhoda (1879-1956), appearing in the newspaper *Sur-e Esrafil* in 1907.[12] In addition to their importance as commentary on social and political issues, the "Fiddle-Faddle" articles contributed much to the development of fictional prose in their use of colloquial language and particularly of popular proverbs and expressions.[13] In the rural character he created for these articles, Dehkhoda found a medium through which he could employ a lively, colloquial style in writing on various social issues. In a sense, then, in his articles he had exemplified one of the "advantages" of fictional prose which Jamalzadeh was later to set down in his celebrated preface, the idea that fictional prose can serve as a "phonograph" of the "words, expressions, proverbs, idioms, different structures of speech, and dialects...of various classes and groups of a nation."[14]

An important issue during the revolutionary period of the first two decades of the twentieth century, a period instrumental in giving birth to the writings discussed above, was patriotism. With the rise to power of Reza Khan in 1921 and his subsequent coronation as Reza Shah Pahlavi in 1926, this patriotism of the revolutionary years was channeled by the government into secular nationalism. In fact, it served as a key element for Reza Shah Pahlavi in creating a strong central government in a country which was on the verge of disintegration as a result of the weakness of the Qajar dynasty in its final years and of the direct intervention of foreign powers in its internal affairs.[15] Along with this spirit of secular nationalism, Reza Shah instigated a series of programs to "modernize" the country, and these two factors, nationalism and modernization, found their way into the literature of this period. Thus, pertinent social themes and interest in the historical heritage of Iran are reflected in the popular literature of the time: on the one hand, sentimental novels full of social commentary on such themes as conventional marriage customs or prostitution and its causes, including the novels *Tehran-e Makhowf* [The Horrible Tehran] (1922) by Moshfeq Kazemi, *Ensan* [Mankind] (1924) by Abbas Khalili, and *Jenayat-e Bashar* [The Crimes of Mankind] (1930) by Rabi' Ansari; on the other hand, historical novels written to foster a sense of national pride and identity, such as *Damgostaran ya Enteqamkhahan-e Mazdak* [The Plotters or Avengers of Mazdak] (1921) by Abdolhoseyn San'atizadeh, *Dastan-e Bastan* [The Story of Yore] (1921) by Hasan Badi'i, and *Shah-e Iran va Banu-ye Arman* [The Shah of Iran and the Armenian Lady] (1927) by Zabih Behruz. This era of nationalism and social self-awareness also produced Iran's most famous twentieth century author, Sadeq Hedayat (1903-1951), whose works do not conform to the popular trends mentioned above. However, his nonconformity, which appears to place him out of the mainstream, should not lead to the conclusion that he completely escaped the current trends of nationalism and sentimental social criticism found in contemporary fiction. These elements appear in Hedayat's works, but in a different light. While the historical novelists expended their efforts in transforming historical figures from the Iranian past into romantic, glorious heroes, Hedayat's interest was drawn to Iran's cultural heritage. And while those novelists interested in portraying the social ills of their time preached their way through sentimental fiction, Hedayat displayed the ills of his society with more realistic presentations of characters as seen by a more sympathetic, less aloof eye than his contemporaries had possessed. Like Jamalzadeh, Hedayat was stimulated by his contact with Western culture and literature. Having gone to France on a government scholarship in the mid 1920s, and after several aborted efforts at studying various sciences, Hedayat became interested in pre-Islamic Iranian languages and the ancient culture of his country. As he was an avid reader of both Western and Eastern literatures, his interests then focused on creative writing, and he produced a number of fictional works that mark for Persian prose fiction a significant break from the anecdotal tales of Jamalzadeh. Hedayat's literary output can be considered a second phase in the development of modern Persian fiction following Jamalzadeh's contributions. Hedayat greatly influenced the following generation of writers and his work is said by some critics to have had a lasting effect on many new writers even today. As Ehsan Yarshater noted in 1971:

> Although Hedayat died before the 1960s, he is still a very live figure on the Persian literary scene. He is widely published and read, and maintains to this day a formative influence on developing writers.[16]

Some of the most influential aspects of Hedayat's fiction are his attempts to portray more true-to-life characters than had previously appeared in Persian fiction and his simplification of the language used, both in his realistic short stories and in his psychological works, such as his most famous work *Buf-e Kur* [The Blind Owl] (1937).[17] But perhaps even more pervasive was Hedayat's personal philosophical worldview, his subjective, fatalistic vision of humanity epitomized in his enigmatic novel *The Blind Owl*, which captures the imaginations of ensuing generations of writers, opening up new possibilities for experimentation in Iranian fiction.[18] This novel, however, was first published in India in a limited edition, since during the latter part of Reza Shah's dictatorship strict government control and censorship were enforced, allowing publication only of those works that were considered by the censors not to clash with the interests and policies of the state. But as mentioned above the tight control came to an end with the occupation of Iran by the Allied forces and the abdication of Reza Shah in 1941.

During the first four decades of the twentieth century, Persian literature had undergone the early phases of what some literary historians regard as a "renaissance,"[19] with manifestations both in prose fiction, of which the foundation was laid in this period, and in poetry, revitalized into a creative rather than conventionally imitative medium as "new poetry."[20] However, this so-called literary renaissance or literary revolution was not brought about in a state of literary isolation. The political atmosphere of the revolutionary years, indeed that of the early decades of the century, the zeal for modernization of the country first appearing in the nineteenth century and accelerating during the reign of Reza Shah, and the assimilation of European and later American values that began about 1800 with Iran's involvement in European power politics all contributed to this change.[21] Even more direct factors influencing this new era in literature include the European educations of many of the writers of this period, among them Jamalzadeh, Hedayat, and Bozorg Alavi, and their familiarity with the literature of the West in the original languages, as well as the availability to the Persian reader of many Western books in translation. In the era of relative political freedom of the 1940s, those writers who had not been tolerated during the Reza Shah period found an opportunity to be heard. Jamalzadeh, for instance, who had kept silent for more than twenty years, emerged again with several new works in the span of a few years. And

Hedayat's *The Blind Owl* was published for the first time in Iran in 1941. Perhaps most directly affected by this new-found freedom were those politically active writers who had previously been suppressed by the government. They are represented by Bozorg Alavi (1904-1997), who had been incarcerated for four years during Reza Shah's reign because of his Marxist views. Directly involved in politics, especially that of the communist Tudeh Party founded in late 1941, Alavi advocated a "committed" literature in the service of political ideology dedicated to the service of the masses. It follows that for him the duty of the writer is to lead the people, since he is in the best position to point out what the masses cannot clearly express themselves.[22] Illustrative of Alavi's "commitment" is his one novel, *Cheshmhayash* [Her Eyes] (1952), which tells the story of a young aristocratic woman involved with a famous painter, an organizer of a socialist anti-government movement during the reign of Reza Shah.[23] The painter's life is saved when the woman consents to marry the chief of police, a man she claims to despise.

With the opportunity for free expression in the 1940s, new voices began to be heard, some of which became major voices in Persian fiction in the following decades. Most prominent among them were Jalal Al-e Ahmad and Sadeq Chubak. Al-e Ahmad (1923-1969), who published his first work *Did-o Bazdid* [Exchange of Visits], a collection of short stories, in 1946, was like Alavi at one time affiliated with the Tudeh Party. Later, however, he disassociated himself from organized political groups (except for a short involvement in politics in 1953), yet remained an engagé writer to his death, consistently addressing political and social issues. Al-e Ahmad was a leading spokesman in the 1960s for the Iranian non-establishment intelligentsia. His best-known novel in Iran, *Modir-e Madreseh* [The School Principal] (1958), typical of his work, deals mainly with social ills and bureaucratic corruption as they affect students and teachers in an Iranian elementary school.[24] His most well known non-fictional work, *Gharbzadegi* [Plagued by the West], published in 1962, a polemical essay addressing the negative aspects of Western cultural influences and Western exploitation of Iran and other so-called Third World countries, had an impact on many educated Iranians.[25] The social critical content of Al-e Ahmad's work has gained him a distinguished status among modern Iranian writers, even though from a literary viewpoint his short stories and novels suffer from technical shortcomings. These shortcomings in technique along with Al-e Ahmad's didactic tone have often been a deterrent to an appreciation of his unique prose style, characterized by direct, biting, short sentences, a style considered by some as unmatched in modern Persian literature.[26]

Another new writer to appear during this period, Sadeq Chubak, made his literary debut with a collection of short stories, *Kheymehshabbazi* [Puppet Snow] (1945), which focuses mainly on various aspects of the lives of individuals from the lowest classes of society. With his choice of characters and his use of colloquial speech, he was recognized as an artist following in the traditions of Jamalzadeh and Hedayat. However, most critics did not fail to recognize in Chubak an original artist and a careful craftsman, specifically noting his carefully drawn sketches of Iranian life and his success at transliterating the colloquial language of his characters.[27] In a broad sense, some of the traits mentioned above place Chubak in the mainstream of the fiction writing of the mid-1940s in Iran. One aspect, however, sets him clearly apart from his contemporaries, that is his comparatively impersonal and objective worldview, his ability to represent the emotional and mental aspects of each of his subjects in order to create a variety of vivid, believable characters. Unlike most of his contemporaries of this period who used literature as a vehicle for extra-literary purposes, such as Alavi's use of literature for the propagation of his socialist ideologies and Al-e Ahmad's social criticism, Chubak concerned himself primarily with the art of fiction writing itself. The limited perspective of these "committed" writers resulted in a limitation of time, space, and subject matter in their stories, and their characters often remain confined to their specific social and cultural circumstances. On the other hand, although Chubak's characters are palpably Iranian, in an Iranian social milieu, his stories constitute a microcosmic reflection of the universe. In this respect, perhaps, he follows most faithfully Hedayat's legacy. Of the important literary voices of the

1940s, Jalal Al-e Ahmad and Sadeq Chubak alone retained leading positions as writers of fiction in the 1950s and 1960s, while a number of new faces began appearing on the scene, notably Ebrahim Golestan (b. 1922), Gholamhoseyn Sa'edi (1935-1985), and Hushang Golshiri (1937-2000).[28] Golestan, perhaps best known in Iran as a cinematographer, with four collections of short stories and a novel, *Asrar-e Ganj-e Dar-reh-ye Jenni* [The Secrets of the Treasures of the Haunted Valley] (1974), is especially noteworthy for his experimental use of a rhythmic, even musical, prose style, attempting to create a harmony between thought, feeling, and mood and the aural aspects of language. By profession a psychiatrist, Gholamhoseyn Sa'edi, a prolific writer and perhaps the most important playwright in Iran, produced seven books of fiction as well as other works. His fiction can be characterized as basically psychological studies of lower classes, employing an abundant use of dialogue as opposed to straight narration. Hushang Golshiri, although the author of a number of short stories, gained recognition particularly for one work, *Shazdeh Ehtejab* [Prince Ehtejab] (1968/69), a story which deals with one of the descendents of an Iranian ruling family whose conscience is burdened with the guilt of his ancestors' tyranny. A stream of consciousness narrative, the book is noteworthy for its often illusive shifts in the presentations of the consciousnesses of various characters, much in the vein of Virginia Woolf's *Mrs. Dalloway*.

The most prominent fiction writers of the 1970s remain those appearing in the preceding two decades. Nevertheless, mention should also be made of Reza Baraheni, primarily a literary critic, whose monumental novel *Ruzegar-e Duzakhi-ye Aqa-ye Ayaz* [The Infernal Times of Aqa-ye Ayaz] (1972), a haunting tale of violence, bloodshed, and sex and a portrayal of Iran's history as a nation in which the Iranian people are raped symbolically and actually by their rulers, is in its sexual explicitness and naturalistic, detailed descriptions reminiscent of Chubak's work, especially *The Patient Stone*.

Of the generation of writers mentioned above who had become recognized literary figures in the first half of the twentieth century, Chubak alone remained a prominent figure of the 1970s, Hedayat and Al-e Ahmad having died, and

Jamalzadeh and Alavi, though still alive at the time, neither having kept up direct contact with Iran (both lived outside the country for many years) nor remained influential fiction writers in ensuing decades. In effect, Chubak was able to link the previous generation of writers with the future generations and remained perhaps the most important short story writer and novelist of the 1970s.

To sum up, Persian fiction has undergone several phases since its beginning in the early 1920s with Jamalzadeh's anecdotal stories spiced with colloquial Persian expressions. The most notably influential figure in twentieth century Persian prose fiction, Hedayat, in the 1930s, follows Jamalzadeh in his interest in various aspects of Persian culture and language. However, his impact on the development of Persian prose fiction arises basically from his artistic sensitivities as well as his hauntingly personal, subjective worldview. Still another phase, in the 1940s, is marked by the works of writers with primarily socio-political concerns, and with only secondary interest in the artistic aspects of fiction, among whom the most widely recognized were Alavi and Al-e Ahmad. From a literary, artistic viewpoint, however, the works of Chubak from the 1940s to the 1960s, with his particular attention to the formal aspects of fiction, his craftsmanship, and his objective, impersonal worldview, have greatly influenced the development of modern Persian fiction, as they have opened the way for experimentation. And the fiction of the last five decades reflects the impact of the earlier phases, both in its artistic development or form and in its social content, as exemplified in the works of such writers as Hushang Golshiri and an increasing number of talented new writers, including many women who have taken the lead, such as Moniru Ravanipur and Shahrnush Parsipur, with the publication of outstanding novels.[29]

IV

Born the son of a bazaar merchant in the port town of Bushehr on the Persian Gulf in 1916, Sadeq Chubak spent his formative years first in the town of his birth and later in nearby Shiraz, where he moved with his family. The impressions of these years, of his early schooling, of his parents, of the atmosphere of the times, remained with Chubak, many of them appearing vividly in his autobiographical poem "Ah-e Ensan" [The Sigh of Mankind] in which he reflects:

> My childhood,
> My youth,
> And my life
> Are asleep with me under my pillow
> And whenever I wish
> I suck on
> Their poisonous gem.[30]

And these memories provide Chubak with much of the material that later appears in his stories. In a number of stories such as "Omarkoshun" [Omar Killing], for instance, Chubak seems to draw on his recollections of early childhood experiences in Bushehr. Bushehr also becomes the backdrop for his first novel, *Tangsir* (1963), in which he depicts incidents he witnessed as a child. And Shiraz becomes the locale of his last novel, *The Patient Stone* (1966), in which he fictionalizes an actual series of murders that took place there in the 1930s. In 1937, Chubak completed his formal education, graduating from the American College of Tehran. He taught in the public schools in Khorramshahr, another port town on the Persian Gulf, until he joined the Iranian army in 1939. By 1940, he had become a cadet officer and English translator for the General Staff in Tehran, a post he kept until shortly after the publication of his first book *The Puppet Show* in 1945, when he became employed as a translator for the British Embassy Information Department.[31]

With two books published, Chubak became established as a short story writer, and in 1955 he took part in an international summer seminar for writers at Harvard University as a representative from Iran. But the period between 1950 and 1962 was for Chubak a period of literary silence. As a result of the political turbulence of the early 1950s, with the rise to power and ultimate downfall of Prime Minister Mohammad Mosaddeq and the years of military control over the government, a renewed impetus was given to writers. However, until the early 1960s, during which some sort of political "stability" was in its formative stages, Chubak published no new works. In 1963, however, Chubak's first novel, *Tangsir*, was published, which by and large did not have a good reception.[32] Two years later, a third collection, *Ruz-e Avval-e Qabr* [The First Day in the Grave] (1965), appeared, followed seven months later by *Cheraq-e Akher* [The Last Alms] (1966), another collection of short stories. In *The First Day in the Grave*, Chubak once again concerns himself with the seamier side of Iranian life. The stories focus for the most part on various aspects of the lives of unfortunate individuals and underprivileged classes. But two of the longer pieces of this collection, Chubak delve into the psyches of socially and financially rather successful characters who seem haunted by the voice of conscience. The majority of the stories in these two collections, however, deal with the sordid lives of the unfortunate and poor.[33] Perhaps for this reason many critics believed that Chubak had returned to the style and subject matter of his work before *Tangsir*, a grimmer picture of the poor in shorter sketches.

In 1966, Chubak published his last work, *The Patient Stone*, a novel that marks a turning point in his career as a writer. The complex structure of the novel and some of its more esoteric elements precluded its appreciation by the general public, and in this respect the novel seems to have been addressed to a more elitist literary audience. But at the same time, *The Patient Stone* may be the epitome of all Chubak's literary output in that it is a potpourri in which he brings together all those elements of his earlier works that marked him as a writer of distinction in Iran, particularly his choice of low-life characters, his use of colloquial language, his themes and worldview, and his attention to the formal aspects of fiction.

Although the characters in Chubak's works are drawn from all walks of life, are infinitely varied as to age and social standing, and even include a handful of animals, most of them can be placed in one of two categories, oppressor and oppressed. His oppressors include, among others, a king who mobilizes his entire nation against all crows, since one of them had defiled his statue with excrement; a state official, in a psychological study, whose life of mistreatment of others is threatened in a series of anonymous letters; and a cruel, wealthy husband who casts off his wife and disowns his child, forcing the mother into a life of religiously sanctioned prostitution. By far the largest category of characters consists of the oppressed, the majority of whom belong to the lowest strata of society, chosen from among the poor, the wretched, the downtrodden, and the forgotten. They include sexually frustrated females, opium addicts, young girls driven to prostitution, abused and abandoned children, and dying, lonely, aged men and women. But although many of his characters share common problems, even common fates, each has an individual identity. The credit for the initiation into Persian literature of characters chosen from lower classes must, of course, be given mainly to Jamalzadeh and Hedayat who, partly as a result of their familiarity with Western literature and partly as a reaction to the political and literary dictatorship in Iran concurrent with the revolutionary atmosphere in the country at the time, strove to "democratize" Persian literature by breaking with the tradition that focused its attention almost exclusively on the nobility. This process of democratization also involved a concern on the part of these writers with the use of colloquial language in their fiction. Jamalzadeh's main interest in the language of the people was reflected in his recording of colloquial expressions and popular proverbs, while Hedayat focused for the most part on collecting folklore and describing the mores of the people. Hedayat, however, contributed much to the simplification of the language of fictional prose. But neither Jamalzadeh nor Hedayat could completely accomplish the almost unprecedented task of bridging the gap between colloquial and written Persian, both because of the difficulties inherent in transliterating the spoken language and because of the differences in syntax and vocabulary between the spoken and written forms of Persian. [34] This task was left to Chubak. As one critic points out:

> Both Jamalzadih and Hidayat had a rather narrow conception of spoken language. They picked up colloquial words and phrases and put them in sentence patterns which were those of "written" language. Chubak, on the other hand,

> not only paid attention to the "lexical items," but tried to employ the pattern and rhythm of the spoken language in his work.[35]

Chubak's particular attention to the technical aspects of language reveals merely one aspect of his craftsmanship. His ability to create harmony between the various elements of his stories, between characters and language, form and content, theme and mode of expression, has often been noted. Perhaps one critic's observation concerning Chubak's short stories may stand as an assessment of the author's craftsmanship in general:

> His feeling for this form is illustrated by his economy of incident, ...with a minimum of descriptive apparatus. His treatment of detail suggests the intricacy, combined with boldness of conception, of the Persian miniature painting. Chubak keeps his picture balanced and spare; and yet a whole pattern of emotion and situation is revealed within it. The result is generally convincing and shows a moving insight into human nature.[36]

But this insight, which Vera Kubičková terms "somewhat rare in modern Persian literature,"[37] reveals a grim picture, Chubak's grim worldview as it is reflected in the themes of his stories, which include poverty, death, oppression, sexual deprivation, the victimization of women and children, fatalism, alienation, loneliness, and the degeneration of the individual and society in the grip of religious superstition. This vision is presented most intensely in the gloomy lines of his poem, "The Sigh of Mankind":

> The foul pinion of the vulture of hunger, sickness, and death
> Has spread its shadow over city and village
> Over hearth and home
> Over mountain and sea
> Breaths in throats have been nailed to the rack
> Eyes have befriended darkness
> Tongues have been paralyzed

And the warmth of the sun has waned
And the root of the mandrake has dried
And water has died and the cloud is despondent
And the squalid, scurvy hearse
Waits at house doors
And the gaunt, worn horses
Restlessly
Stomp the ground.[38]

V

In the post-Mosaddeq era, during which Mohammad Reza Shah Pahlavi (reigned 1941-1979) was able for the first time since his father's abdication in 1941 to tighten monarchical control and impose gradually increased censorship, and during which most of Chubak's work was published, writers, literary critics, and educated readers demanded that the writer be explicitly non-establishment and even antiestablishment. However, this was not a new demand. As early as 1946, in the First Congress of Iranian Writers, Alavi had stated, "We must know the purpose of art and the duty of the artist"; he advocated a revolutionary position for the writer, who must "move in front of the people and guide them" in their struggle.[39] This attitude, shared by most writers and their audiences even as far back as the Constitutional era (1906-1911), never having completely faded away, once again became a special focus of attention during the 1960s. Social commitment in literature and other extra-literary concerns then became major factors in the evaluation of literary works and the popularity of the writer, allowing Al-e Ahmad, for example, to become more popular in spite of (or perhaps because of) a number of his works having been banned. Similar criteria were decisive in the popularity of the new writers of these years as well, such as Samad Behrangi (1939-1968), whose stories lack sophistication and fail as literary pieces but were popular after his sudden death, allegedly due to political activities, and who became a popular, almost cult figure among the antiestablishment and dissident forces. In such an atmosphere, Chubak's only two novels, *Tangsir* and *The Patient Stone*, were published, and subsequently received harsh attacks from a number of critics in Iran.[40] With no taste for filling his work with direct political slogans and no inclination toward any personal participation in antiestablishment sociopolitical issues, Chubak was judged negatively by the Iranian intelligentsia, consisting mainly of dissident university students, poets, and writers (some of them critics trying to gain the approval of their literary audiences). These individuals had unwritten rules dictating the condemnation of those writers who did not openly and publicly conform to the norm of the writer as a "leader of society."[41] In addition, with the increased government control of the 1970s, almost every writer of some distinction underwent a period (however short) of incarceration, a very visible criterion in his evaluation as "committed."[42] Chubak did not. Since the "committed" subject matter of Chubak's two novels as well as his short story collections, with their rather harsh criticism of Iranian society and its institutions, including its political institutions, cannot be overlooked by the objective reader, it would seem then that the "committed" nature of a work alone was not a satisfactory criterion for the favorable reception and critical praise of that work during the latter two decades of the Pahlavi rule. Rather, the personal involvement of a writer in antiestablishment political activities seems to have been a decisive factor in the overall acceptance of his works. But it would seem simplistic to assume that Chubak's politics alone was a source of displeasure for the Iranian literary public. During this same period, in the wake of the continuous bombardment of the country with Western ideas and influences, a new reactionary, xenophobic nationalism began to arise, one that condemned these influences as having "demolished" Iranian values. These Western influences, which began prior to the Constitutional Revolution, continued through the first half of the 20th century, gradually increasing in the second half, clashed with national and historical traditions. In the losing struggle of tradition against the forces of modernity, as one historian observes, "Iranian society began to perceive certain at least potentially true benefits, certain advantages, certain pleasures." He also believes that:

> A tremendous sense of guilt haunts Iranian society for having profited in the abandonment of its

> traditions, and ... this is the reason for the present misadjustment of the Iranian people to their new Westernized ideals and aims.[43]

Perhaps this guilt best justifies the nationalism that gave rise to an essay such as Al-e Ahmad's *Plagued by the West,* mentioned above, with its cry for a reassessment of Western values that have been so blindly accepted. In the wake of the nationalism epitomized in Al-e Ahmad's *Plagued by the West*, a novel such as *The Patient Stone*, for instance, that ridicules many of Iranian society's institutions and traditions, including its religion and even its cherished literary heritage, was not surprisingly an object of reactionary scorn. Thus, one critic, for example, was compelled to condemn Chubak on the basis of his portrayal of Belqeys, a principle female character in *The Patient Stone*, for to him she could not possibly represent "the Iranian woman." To illustrate the "validity" of his view, he compares Belqeys with another female character in a popular Persian novel, *Showhar-e Ahu Khanom* [Ahu Khanom's Husband] (1961). The critic hails this latter heroine, a wretchedly humiliated wife of a baker infatuated with a local wanton whom he brings home, as a true representative of the Iranian woman, citing her reaction to her plight:

> I do not resent my husband in the least, nor do I have any grievance against him. If there were one man in the world for me, it would be none but him. Man is the wife's little god, and whatever he does cannot be objected to. Abraham the prophet also took another wife while married to Hagar. And all the wives of the Prophet [Mohammad] had co-wives.[44]

And for contrast, he continues his argument with a quote from Belqeys, the sexually frustrated wife of an impotent opium addict, illustrating, in his opinion, "the picture that Chubak gives of the Iranian woman":

> If I go be a wife to a dung farmer, at least he might be a man. He'd grab me, hug me tight at night, and squish the shit out of me .... If I don't find no husband, I can go to Mordessun District and be a whore, so I get ten fellas riding me every night.[45]

Women's sexuality, as depicted in *The Patient Stone* through the character of Belqeys and other stories by Chubak, seemingly threatened the traditional Islamo-Iranian family institution in which a woman, such as Ahu Khanom, remains a self-sacrificing wife and mother under all circumstances. Although female sexuality was not a new subject in modern Persian literature, it had generally been restricted to that of young upper class women, who could easily be blamed as having been "corrupted" by Western influence.[46] But the sexuality of a lower class woman could not be so easily rationalized and accepted, since it was highly unlikely that she had been "corrupted" by Western ideas. And this aspect of Chubak's work seemed a direct affront to the pride of the chauvinistic Iranian male.

But Chubak's treatment of female sexuality is not the only source of the criticism he received. His use of sexual explicitness in general doubled with his use of "obscene" language provided critics with additional grounds for the condemnation of his last novel in particular. Even though in his earlier stories Chubak had occasionally employed "obscene" words, he did not receive the harsh criticism he later did for *The Patient Stone*. Concerning Chubak's first two collections of short stories, one critic, for instance, had observed in 1957, "He might be blamed for having a freedom of expression which does not always suit readers of all ages."[47] On the other hand, with the publication of *The Patient Stone*, Chubak was actually accused of loving "obscenity for the sake of obscenity."[48]

Another factor contributing to the unfavorable reaction of the reading public to much of Chubak's work may be his critical view of the institution of Islamic religion in Iran. Modern Persian literature has from its beginning served as an arena for the criticism of Islam. In fact, in a survey of the established writers and poets of the 20th century, one would be hard pressed to find one writer who has not indulged in the criticism of religion, many having been condemned for this aspect of their work. But the political upheaval of 1978 and beyond, with a religious leader as its central figure, events whose momentum was building during the late 1960s and early 1970s, strongly suggests that religious fervor was gaining ground in the 1960s when most of Chubak's stories were published. Therefore, even though the criticism of religion has been a common practice in modern Persian literature, this aspect of Chubak's work could not have been overlooked by a significant portion of its reading public. What seems to have been overlooked in Chubak's work is that he provides his readers with a new window through which they can view their society, culture, beliefs, and their lives and see the truth, a new truth, as it were. As William James observes:

> New truth is always a go-between, a smoother-over of transitions. It marries old opinion to new fact so as ever to show a minimum of jolt, a maximum of continuity.... We say this theory solves it on the whole more satisfactorily than that theory; but that means more satisfactorily to ourselves, and individuals will emphasize their points of satisfaction differently.[49]

As "new truth," a go-between in the development of modern Persian fiction, the works of Chubak bridge the gap between old and new, as the works of Hedayat and Jamalzadeh before had done. In the words of one Persian critic:

> The road that [Chubak] has taken here is a road which no one has trodden before him in our literature: the grafting of ideas with the portrayal of life, the grafting of the recognition of realities with a look into the future. This is a road unknown and unsmooth. Chubak has taken the first step and with this step he has opened a new way for our fictional literature.[50]

Although unconventional in terms of its new treatment of old issues, Chubak's literary output is, nevertheless, the "legitimate" offspring of its social and literary heritage. As works of art, however, his novels and short stories must be considered in literary critical terms, which will be the subject of the following chapters.

CHAPTER 2

Social Puppets

Sadeq Chubak's first collection of short stories, *Kheymehshabbazi* [The Puppet Show], was published in 1945, even though some of these stories were published in literary journals earlier. The first edition contained eleven short stories and dealt mostly with the lives of oppressed and lower class individuals and their dreams and aspirations.[1]

The Puppet Show collection shows many of the characteristics of Chubak's later work, especially his choice of characters from the lowest strata of society, his careful reproduction of colloquial Persian, and his attention to detail in describing scenes and the external behavior and movements of characters. Some of the sketch-like shorter pieces of this collection, which have been described by an early reviewer as "instant photographs,"[2] along with the longer pieces that deal with the ills of society and the lives of friendless individuals, illustrate a remarkable aspect of Chubak's work, that is, the author's objective detachment from the story he tells, an aspect rarely found in the works of many of Chubak's predecessors.

In "Nafti" [The Kerosene Man], the first story in *The Puppet Show*, we find a foreshadowing of many of the elements that Chubak uses in his later short stories and novels. Ozra is a young woman whom the reader finds in the beginning of the story in the holy shrines pleading for a husband:

> Ay, Aqa. Oh son of Moses, son of Ja'far, grant me my desire. Do not hold me any longer in shame before my friends and neighbors. Work something out, ay Aqa, that I might reach the end of my misery and procure a permanent household of my own. Grant me

> as my portion a compliant husband who will take me out of my father's house, take me anywhere he wishes. I ask nothing else of you. The one husband will be enough. Would granting this little thing take something away from your holiness? Is there something wrong with me for God's sake! How come you gave such a good husband to Aziz Khan's daughter, and her with that big ugly boil on her nose? Ay, Aqa, I will sacrifice myself to you out of gratitude. I will make a pledge to God to sacrifice a lamb if you will grant me my desire.[3]

Ozra is totally obsessed with the thought of finding a husband. This thought is so overriding in her mind that even while tying a piece of cloth to the sepulchre of the shrine and noticing a lead-grey piece of cloth tied by a previous pilgrim obviously with a wish, she begins to daydream about the man—for she is sure the wish knot belongs to a man—who is also looking for a mate. In fact, Ozra's entire life has consisted for some time of her obsession, particularly since a pilgrimage to the holy city of Qom when a bus driver helped her onto the bus, holding her under her arms next to her breasts. The memory of this incident remains alive for her, and is even triggered by the smell of gasoline that reminds her of the bus driver.

"The Kerosene Man" concludes in a note of despair for Ozra whose dreams of finding a husband end in disappointment. In the final scene of the story, we find her trying to interest a kerosene peddler in a new wife, herself, in addition to the three wives he already has, but the man responds that he has no use for her, since he is even unable to take care of those he already has.

As the first story in Chubak's first collection of short stories, "The Kerosene Man" is significant in that it contains some of the basic ingredients of Chubak's later work. These elements include character, subject matter, themes, and language. The character of Ozra, for instance, is a brief sketch of several other women in Chubak's later stories, including Belqeys, in particular, in *The Patient Stone*. Contrary to what was often the case in the work of earlier writers who wrote about the poor, Ozra is not depicted as a noble and morally impeccable woman, or a simple young girl suffering the pains of romantic love, but as an ordinary woman with sexual desires and needs. In fact, her plight for a husband is expressed mostly through her lust, so much so that it even transforms her religious performance at the shrine into an expression of her lustful desire for the holy man buried in the tomb:

> But remembering that what she wanted of a man was that he be a husband, she was seized with shame, and she blushed. Hurriedly, yet with agility, she leapt up from her place and fastened several kisses, sticky-sounding, passionate kisses on the screen, out of the fullness of her heart.[4]

Despite the emphasis in the story on Ozra's lustfulness, she is not meant to be taken as a fallen or falling woman, a common practice among writers who dealt with women's sexuality and who punished such characters who violated the norms of chastity. In fact, the reader empathizes with Ozra and her situation. This sense of empathy is particularly reinforced since Ozra is portrayed as a lonely being, and her yearning for a husband is the only way that she believes will ameliorate the situation:

> Ozra was terrified of being alone in this deceitful mortal world. Everyone thought only of himself; no one knew of an Ozra languishing in desperation out of her terror of loneliness and her desire for a husband. There must be a thousand times a thousand men longing for a wife, who, should they come to know of the desire that lay in the heart of Ozra, might sacrifice life and limb to have her. But what did people know? How many men and women of similar desire bed down alone for the night and know nothing of each other. Beware the day that their sleeping mats and blankets should find the tongues to speak, for then people would truly be terrified of each other.[5]

A fascination with the social outcasts, the addicts, the prostitutes, and in general the street people predominates most of Chubak's earlier stories. The second story in *The Puppet Show*, "Golha-ye Gushti" [Flesh Flowers],[6] focuses on a few hours in the life of Morad, a wretched addict who has just sold his jacket in order to buy some opium. Chubak's character choice is a conscious one that is apparent in his rather graphic description of the protagonist and which is characteristic of much of his later work, in which he is more inclined to "show" than to "tell" his stories. Morad is described as a man who "had nothing in life, he was a bunch of moving bones."

This individual was an ill-matched patch on the rotten pants crotch of the society who had an existence of sorts in the lines and seams, like a louse; but he did not live at all. For this reason, he could not be like other people. His pleasures, suffering, and thoughts were as different from others as night and day.[7]

Chubak reduces Morad to the level of an animal that can only survive by instincts. He cares for nothing but his immediate physical needs. When his body is in need of opium, his instincts guide him to find it, and when he is faced with a threatening situation, again his instincts help him escape danger. In fact, the remainder of the story revolves around this creature's physical needs and instincts.

With Morad's instincts all concentrated on reaching a place where he might buy some opium and a drink with the money from the sale of his jacket, his next instinct is to avoid the creditor who is waiting "like a vulture" across the street, ready to deprive him of his money. Meanwhile, Morad's eyes catch sight of a sensual, beautiful, young, aristocratic woman, the scent of whose perfume, reminiscent to Morad of the "scent of morphine," arouses in him another instinct. Drowned in his own thoughts about never being able to possess such a female who is not even aware of his existence, and totally absorbed in the movements of her voluptuous body wrapped tightly in a dress with poppy-flower prints, Morad realizes that the creditor has spotted him and is rushing across the street to collect his money. But in a matter of a few seconds, the creditor is hit by a fast-moving truck, and in a moment he is reduced to a nauseating mass of minced flesh and bones.

Faced with this new situation, Morad's immediate reaction is a sigh of relief for having become free of the pestering creditor. At the same time, however, the sight of the victim's body affects his yearnings for the woman; this time the smell of her perfume only reminds Morad of the "smell of dung, smashed skull and brains and the coagulated blood of a human being."[8]

Chubak's attention to basic animalistic instincts in these early stories is often coupled with his presentation technique, which has been described by critics as naturalistic instant photographs of scenes, often gruesome and generally vivid, to the smallest details. The scene immediately following the accident in "Fresh Flowers" provides such an example:

> A mass of blood and skull, bits and pieces of which were stuck to the pot-bellied truck tires, was scattered on the ground. Black coagulated blood was spread out on the pavement and had soaked into the seams between the stones where they had sunk down. A white blood stained substance, like soft boiled egg whites in which lines of blood were coagulated, mixed with a bunch of smashed bones provided the nauseating sight.[9]

Chubak's preoccupation with the photographic sketches of usually gruesome scenes, and his attention to minute details in recreating such scenes, reveal his awareness of the art of "showing" rather than "telling" in his fiction. Earlier writers, including Mohamamd Ali Jamalzadeh, Sadeq Hedayat, and Bozorg Alavi, can be characterized in most of their writing as storytellers. For instance, in these writers' works, the narrators' presence is felt as an authority with certain views with which the reader may agree or disagree. In other words, in the works of Chubak's predecessors, there is, consistently or perhaps subconsciously on the part of their creator, a degree of direct interference by the author in the form of commentary on a particular situation or character. By way of contrast, in his "photographic sketches," Chubak makes an attempt, and succeeds to a great extent, at removing the narrator-author almost totally from the story and functioning outside the story like a camera. "Adl" [Justice] consists almost entirely of such a photographic sketch. It begins with a vivid picture of a horse with a broken leg:

> A carriage horse had fallen into a wide street gutter and its front leg bone and its kneecap had been crushed. It could be seen clearly that the bone of one of its front legs had been broken under its brown skin and was bleeding. Its other kneecap had been completely disjointed and was only connected to a few veins that had not lost their loyalty to its body to the last moment. The hoof of one of its front legs—the one which had been broken—had turned backward,

> and on it the worn out shiny horseshoe that was hanging on with three nails could be seen.[10]

This detailed description continues for another paragraph, and the remainder of the story is basically comprised of a realistic reproduction of the comments of the onlookers who give their opinions concerning the fate of the poor animal.

On one level, in "Justice," Chubak's choice of the injured animal seems to be a ploy to show the attitude of Iranians in general, represented in the comments of the bystanders, toward a given event. In other words, this story can be seen as an exploration of the concept of justice in the minds of the people in a situation in which they have no personal interest. One bystander advises, for instance, that the horse should be given treatment, and another suggests that it should be shot and put out of its misery. On the whole, however, despite the title of the story, justice as a theme does not seem to be a major concern in the story. What is of concern, on the other hand, is Chubak's experimentation with the techniques of fiction writing, i.e., an effort to bring a scene to life for his audience in the best possible way through the medium of writing, and also in the same vein to reproduce colloquial Persian speech accurately and realistically. In this respect, "Justice" is among a number of Chubak's early stories that serve as the first stage in his experimentation in fiction regarding the art of showing, whereby his effort is to remove himself as a narrator from the story he writes, and to appear as an impartial observer.

Chubak's concern regarding the art of showing in fiction in *The Puppet Show* is also evident in the next story of the volume, "Zir-e Cheragh Qermez" [Under the Red Light], on the first and the last pages of which appear a sketch of a figurine. In the context of the story, this sketched figure serves as a visual device, punctuating the beginning and end of the story, as well as a temporal marker in the flow of the thought processes of one of the two main characters. At the same time, this sketched figure indicates the writer's consciousness of the difficulties inherent in attempting to use the medium of writing to emulate, or rather to achieve a similar effect, as in the pictorial arts.

Similar to the previous stories, Chubak's subjects are social outcasts, this time the prostitutes in a house of ill repute in Shahr-e Now, the infamous red-light district in Tehran at the time. The story revolves around the thoughts and conversations of Afaq, an older woman, and Jiran, a less experienced prostitute. The death of another prostitute in the household affects both the older and the younger woman. On Jiran, the effect is a combination of sorrow and fear. It is the first time that she has experienced the death of someone she has known closely, and she feels sorry for the dead woman who is carried away by municipal porters to be buried in an unmarked grave. Afaq sees in the death of her colleague a reflection of her own future, as she will, she is sure, die prematurely of some sort of disease and will be disposed of as a piece of trash.

Like much of the fiction written in Iran in the 1940s, and all the other stories included in this collection, "Under the Red Light" is a bit sentimental in its depiction of the downtrodden and their lot in comparison to the rich. In this story, Chubak even goes so far as to compare the morality of the rich and the poor, finding that certain moral deviations that bring about misery to the poor can have no ill effect on the rich. Afaq recounts her own story as a maidservant to a wealthy family in which both the husband and wife committed adultery without having to suffer any consequences like those Afaq has come to experience, and comments:

> If you really want to know the truth, I learned to do these things when I was in their home. God knows that my eyes and ears opened in their house. I thought it was good. But later I realized that it was good for them. They have other things that can cover up their greatest faults. The fornication of the rich and the dying of the poor are done without a sound.[11]

As social puppets, the poor have no control over their fate. Chubak expresses this notion through the words of Afaq, who contemplates of her past and present life and actions observes that "she had to do it then and she has to do it now as well."[12] In other words, not unlike puppets, Afaq is presented as a creature whose actions are controlled by someone else, a puppeteer, as it were, who holds the ends of the strings and determines every movement and action of the puppets.

The puppet show metaphor is employed in the next story of the volume, "Akher-e Shab" [Late Night], a short pictorial sketch with no other obvious purpose but to show the mechanical movements of a few characters. The brevity and simplicity of the "story," which contains no apparent plot or character development and action, is reminiscent of the work of a sketch artist who is able to render his or her subject matter with a few calculated strokes. The scene is that of a bar and liquor store with the proprietor sitting with his cat on his lap contemplating his business transactions of the day while his apprentice is closing up shop for the day. At this time, two customers, apparently construction workers, walk in asking for a bottle of liquor. The final scene in the story is when the older customer offers the bottle of liquor to the younger one, who, without any apparent reason and without even taking the bottle, first sits cross-legged and then passes out on the floor.

From the viewpoint of the puppet show analogy, what is interesting in "Late Night" is the puppet show like movements of the characters, who seem not to stem from any particular initiative on their own parts. Examples of the descriptive details of their appearance and the movement of the characters reinforce this notion. The two customers who enter the store are described in the following manner:

> Two persons entered the store. A light layer of snow covered their heads. Neither was wearing an overcoat. Spots of dried up plaster and mud with various shapes could be seen on their clothes. The one who entered first had his hands in his pockets, wearing a muddy black cap with the trowel sticking out of the pocket of his jacket.
> His friend who was bareheaded and had not yet grown hair on his face stood right behind him, looking with an open mouth and with lustfully rolling eyes at the bottles of liquor and cans on the shelves.[13]

The movements of the shopkeeper after having heard the order are also puppet like:

> Still holding his hands over the Primus burner, Aram [the proprietor] glanced at the man with the black cap and then at his friend. Then without troubling himself to remove the cat that was sleeping and snoring on his lap, he stood up stiffly.[14]

"Late Night" can be viewed as one of the experimental pieces in Chubak's early work, in which he attempts to stay outside the story and present his subject matter as objectively as possible. But perhaps for the same reason, it merely functions as a sketch, and not necessarily as a successful short story. It is simply a static picture, almost a photograph, in which insufficient information is provided to help the story serve either as a meaningful, aesthetic, artistic creation, or a revealing social document. As discussed earlier in the context of *The Puppet Show* collection, it may help reinforce the overall puppet show metaphor that is a common thread running through this collection of short stories. Are we as readers supposed to take the characters in this sketch precisely as puppets that are generally typecast and whose personal history and life outside the puppet show are of no significance? If the answer is in the affirmative, with "Late Night," Chubak goes a step even further than he does in the other stories in this collection, and by depriving the characters of meaningful human traits, he presents a picture of these Iranian social puppets even more pessimistically than those he has offered in "The Kerosene Man," "Fresh Flowers," or "Under the Red Light."

Sketch-like stories such as "Late Night" and "Justice" are obviously experimental attempts, perhaps to the extreme, in the art of showing as opposed to telling in Persian fiction. On the other hand, in perhaps all the other stories of this first collection, although still conscious of his preference for an objective representation of the realities of the society, Chubak resorts to the conventional methods of "storytelling." More in line with conventional short stories in terms of both form and content is the next selection in the volume, entitled "Mardi dar Qafas" [A Man in a Cage].[15]

Seyyed Hasan Khan is the sole survivor of a prominent wealthy family. His grief from having lost all his relatives as well as the loss of one leg leaves him with no desire to go on living and nearly drives him mad, until he falls in love and marries a thirteen-year-old girl. His love for his wife, Sudabeh, helps wipe the grief over the loss of his family from his heart, and even rekindles a new interest in life in him. This newfound happiness, however, does not last long, and within three months Sudabeh suddenly dies of asphyxia.

Sudabeh's death is the final blow to Seyyed Hasan Khan. He retreats to his ancestral home, now spending his days in isolation, drinking and smoking opium in an attempt to forget the tragic events of his life. A maidservant, Yasaman, who has been in the family for many years, takes care of Seyyed Hasan Khan's daily needs of food and opium while he spends his days and nights suffering from both physical and psychological pain. In recent years, however, another creature has entered Seyyed Hasan Khan's life. This new companion is a female Irish setter he has named Rasu that he found two years earlier in the courtyard garden of his house, and who, despite Seyyed Hasan Khan's initial reluctance, has found a place in his life. Rasu not only shares his master's isolated life but also has become addicted to the fumes of his opium. With time, these companions become so accustomed to each other that they spend almost all their waking and sleeping hours together. Seyyed Hasan Khan, who shuns the companionship of people, is happy with Rasu, for she is not human and does not have the usual needs of "civilized people" who, for instance, "want to leave their offspring behind in the world to inherit their wealth."[16]

Like everything else for which Seyyed Hasan Khan develops a fondness, Rasu's companionship comes to an end when he realizes that the dog is ready to leave him for the male dogs that have for several days been barking and beckoning Rasu. He scolds the dog:

> My Rasu, my pretty little girl! You are so disloyal. You are not a human being, are you? You didn't used to be. When did you start to act like humans?[17]

Finally, when neither his scolding nor shutting Rasu up with him in his room helps persuade the dog to abandon her natural instincts, Seyyed Hasan Khan is forced to act as a merchant of love for his dog. With a great deal of physical effort due to his handicap and failing health, he manages to go to the garden gate and let in one of the street dogs that have been barking in a frenzy behind the garden gate. At dawn the next morning, we find Seyyed Hasan Khan:

> Crouched up behind the garden gate, his body soaking wet from the rain, his head dropped on his chest

> hiding his face. Two steps away before him was Rasu, muddied with a pitiable beaten up look on her face, and locked bottom to bottom with the strange dog. They were not ashamed at all of the crouched up human being two steps away from them.[18]

In respect to the choice of the main character, "A Man in a Cage" belongs to a group of characters in Chubak's later stories such as "Ruz-e Avval-e Qabr" [The First day in the Grave], in which he provides a psychological portrayal of financially well-to-do individuals. However, from the standpoint of the overall theme of the collection, "A Man in a Cage" shares some of the characteristics of the other stories in *The Puppet Show*. Similar to Ozra in "The Kerosene Man," Morad in "Flesh Flowers," and the prostitutes in "Under the Red Light," Seyyed Hasan Khan is a lonely individual who has a marginal relationship with the society. Whereas Ozra's handicap is her lack of a husband, Morad's is poverty and addiction, and the prostitutes' both poverty and their violation of social morality for which they are rejected from the social mainstream, Seyyed Hasan Khan's is not only a handicap that is physical but also emotional and psychological.

Unlike "A Man in a Cage" with its psychological probing of its protagonist, in "Pirahan-e Zereshki" [The Maroon Dress], once again Chubak depicts the animalistic and instinctive aspects of human beings. Even the deepest emotions of the two characters in this rather bizarre and haunting story stem from their physical needs, whether lust or greed.

"The Maroon Dress" is perhaps the most gruesome picture Chubak presents in *The Puppet Show* collection. The scene is a mortuary where two women, Saltanat and Kolsum, are engaged in the Moslem ritual of washing the dead in preparation for burial. The story consists of a combination of detailed description of the corpse the women are working on and the conversation between them, interjected with private thoughts of each character trying to outfox the other. The opening passage of the story both sets the gloomy atmosphere and introduces the despicable characters:

> As Saltanat and Kolsum lifted the corpse by her head and feet, lying there down on the slab, hurriedly Saltanat removed the corner of the cover and quickly

> examined her clothes with her wet, shriveled hand. She rubbed the material of the dress between her short, thick fingers with a covetous look, a crooked smile covering her pockmarked shriveled face. With her harelip, Kolsum was standing akimbo next to her. She was also checking out the clothes of the corpse with a greedy look on her face. The smell of the camphor mingled with the steam, stale cigarette smoke, and ground lotus that filled the air of the mortuary. A dim light bulb with a reddish light twinkled, dangling in the middle of the ceiling, its light barely passing through the steam and becoming dimmer and more invisible the farther it traveled.[19]

What Saltanat has in mind is to take the maroon dress of the corpse for Shamsi, a young girl apparently under nine years of age whom she has set up as a prostitute. Her mind is totally preoccupied with the girl, the dress, and the profits she will bring her:

> The dress will be perfect on Shamsi. When she puts it on, she will have customer after customer. After all, she looks better than this one here. Poor naked girl! Who would want to sleep with a woman like this? Everybody thinks she is a beggar. If Sadiqeh gets her hands on her, she will take her straight to the Shahr-e Now red light district. She will do it even to take revenge. But the good thing is that she's not of age yet. Before her eyes and ears open, the money for the mortgage of Kal Abbas's house will be made. Nobody knows what's going on, it is both business and pleasure, and I might even find somebody among those who come for her.[20]

Nevertheless, Saltanat does not want to give Kolsum a share of the dress, and eventually dupes her partner with some black magic potion that she promises to give her in exchange for her share of the dress.

All this scheming is carried out by the two women with total indifference to and even irreverence for the corpse before them. In fact, Chubak creates a contrast between the two women and the lifeless body they are washing:

> The corpse was that of a woman of twenty-seven or twenty-eight years of age, with massive auburn hair and skin that had been white when she lived but now had turned the color of sweet lemon. Her grey half open lips were pressed together, and her old violet-colored lipstick had caked up. Her belly was swollen. On the right side of her navel one could see a long stitched up incision of an old wound. Her skin was shiny and drawn. Her eyes were closed and her eyelashes pressed together, like those of a doll, were locked together tightly.
>
> Her face was calm, with a smug look. On her face, some sort of begrudging stubbornness was frozen, as if she had not yet given up. The most serious and realistic image of an artificial and ridiculous life was imprinted on that face, and the last sad act of a deceptively sad comedy was left on it. Now, that face had abandoned all lust, hatred, lies, and selfishness, and was devoid of all the ridiculous games of life. This was the sad last act of life that continued to make faces, and its players, lifeless and unceremoniously, were frozen in place. She was in a sleep that was not even disturbed by the movement of breathing.[21]

The contrast is between the petty concerns of the two women and lack of all concern on the part of the dead woman who has left behind all the "ridiculous games of life" and whose eternal peace is now disturbed, only for a short period of time, by Saltanat and Kolsum. The macabre setting of "The Maroon Dress" provides Chubak with a suitable background to enhance his portrayal of the pettiness and gruesomeness of human life. The lifeless corpse the two women are preparing for burial is not by any means a reminder to the mortuary workers of the futility of their petty concerns. Oblivious to the nature of what she does, as if she were merely engaged in a chat with an acquaintance, Saltanat feels like smoking a cigarette, and even though she has her own packet of cigarettes in her pocket, she decides to use the opportunity to try to bum a cigarette from her fellow worker. Kolsum, on the other hand, is quite aware of Saltanat's ruse, and while cursing her under her breath and thinking about how Saltanat has managed to have a thriving business for herself by doing anything including setting up a young girl as a prostitute, she swears on her life that she has none.

In the context of modern Persian literature, in which a favorite subject matter has been the lives of the members of the lowest classes in the society, Chubak's work is not unusual. Other writers had used such characters in their work. The focus on the lives of the lower classes, of course, has been coupled with the criticism of the social and political system that has caused the deprivation of those classes. For this reason, much of Persian fiction and other genres of modern Persian literature often when dealing with lower class characters present them in a positive light as noble, honest, and hard-working people. In stories such as "The Maroon Dress," Chubak essentially strips such characters of those positive traits. Nevertheless, there is an implicit criticism of the society for having failed to provide a better life for its less fortunate citizens, and hence, not only their circumstances in life but their character traits, including lying, dishonesty, immoral actions, hardheartedness, and crass behavior, may also be implicitly suggested to be the result of the system. In other words, Saltanat and Kolsum in "The Maroon Dress" are merely puppets, every action and behavior of which is determined and controlled by the social puppeteers.

Social control and determinism regarding the fate of the poor is also the theme of the next story in this collection. "Musiyu Elyas" [Monsieur Elyas] is a story with a twist.[22] In certain respects, Monsieur Elyas is reminiscent of characters found in the works of Mohammad Ali Jamalzadeh. Amirza Mahmud Khan is an honest, trustworthy, and hard-working clerk in the Department of Finance. He is a caricature of sorts; Chubak merely describes his character and then gives examples of these traits. The tone of the story is also reminiscent of Jamalzadeh's work.

> Between you and me, Amirza Mamud Khan was then an energetic and competent man. He had been everything from storekeeper, supervisor, cashier and an accountant to the Chief of Accounting and Provincial Director of Finance, performing each of these jobs with honesty and probity. There was not a black mark on his record, and, if God had willed it and the fates smiled on you, and if your conduct were such that you became very close friends with him and

> were received in his house, he would produce a worn and faded leather briefcase stuffed full of testimonials, letters of recommendation, orders for transfer, changes of job, notices of pay raises and promotions, and so on and so on which he would spread out before you. These would be signed by various ministers who had flowed past like water over the years, leaving this old denizen of the Ministry like a pebble in the bottom of a stream. I must tell you that even if they were to cut his jugular vein, he would not part with one of these pieces of paper. That's the kind of man he was—what can you do about it?
>
> There are many stories about this Amirza Mahmud Khan of ours, and, God willing, I will tell you all of them at the proper time. Right now I will try to give you a glimpse of his character and habits, and ask if anybody among his co-workers or indeed among all men has behaved so.[23]

The problem with Amirza Mahmud Khan is that while he lives with his wife and two daughters in relative poverty, he is more concerned about the poverty and problems of others than his own. He and his family rent two rooms in a large run-down rental house with fifteen or sixteen rooms that are all rented to various poor, working-class people. Amirza Mahmud Khan sees the extent of his neighbors' poverty and suffering and becomes angry and depressed. He worries about one neighbor not having enough food and another falling into a life of prostitution to feed her family. He even suffers for the stray dogs in the streets that are put to death by the municipal workers. One day another poor family moves into the only room vacant in the house, which is no more than a damp, filthy cellar space next to the sewage well. Amirza Mahmud Khan, of course, is enraged, cursing the greedy landlord for renting even this hole in the wall to a family with small children. But soon he learns that the head of the family in question is in fact the new owner of the house.

In line with stories such as "The Maroon Dress," in "Monsieur Elyas" Chubak challenges the myth perpetuated by many modernist writers that the poor, unlike the rich, do not possess such character traits as greed and dishonesty and that they are honorable and good by virtue of being poor. In this respect, it can even be said that Chubak's attempt is intended to de-stereotype and hence humanize the poor. What is disturbing about the story, however, is Chubak's choice of a Jewish family to show that the poor can also be greedy. In doing so, consciously or subconsciously, he perpetuates another kind of stereotype that has existed in Iranian culture, namely the notion that Jews are greedy. This anti-Jewish outlook is even evident in the writer's description of the family. All the family's possessions are being carried on a cart:

> The belongings on the cart were so shabby and dilapidated that at first glance it was difficult to tell what they were. There was a patched charcoal sack and a *korsi*[24] with several torn pillows, a red cotton *korsi*-quilt with odds and ends crammed into it, a tin samovar, a toilet pitcher lacking a handle, and several empty water-cans. More repellent than these were two sickly six- or seven-year-old boys and a young mother with a nursing baby stuck to her breast like a tick.
>
> The pitiable condition of this family whose father had just alighted from a ramshackle bicycle, immediately reminded Amirza Mahmud Khan of the cellar near the cesspool. He fumed with anger, and at once began to feel sorry for them. Just between us, Amirza Mahmud Khan was perfectly justified in feeling sorry for this family, for they had misery written all over them.
>
> There were two small boys without britches, wearing greasy, spotted shirts that reached just below their waists. Their eyelids were red and puffy from trachoma. They opened only a slit to show clouded pupils that jumped from side to side and looked like the clay beads of a rosary. One boy sucked at a seedy, yellowish cucumber and for salt he licked the drippings from his nose. Their faces were filthy as though they had been playing in soot. Two narrow streams of tears had squeezed from their eyes and washed the dirt from their cheeks. The crooked nose, bulging eyes and cornsilk hair of the mother, the wide staring eyes of the father (like those of a mouse in a trap), his round, fleshy face, fat stomach, high wide forehead and bald head conveyed immediately

> to Amirza Mahmud Khan that this was a Jewish family.[25]

This description is immediately followed by the scene of a quarrel between the head of the family and the cart driver over his fee.

Chubak's preoccupation with the poor and unfortunate classes in almost all *The Puppet Show* stories may have an ideological and certainly a humanitarian basis. This is particularly evident in his portrayal of children as the innocent victims of the society in general, as well as other human beings. Monsieur Elyas's children are obviously a case in point, and so is Asghar, the protagonist of the next story, "Ba'd az Zohr-e Akher-e Pa'iz" [An Afternoon in Late Autumn]. The setting of "An Afternoon in Late Autumn" is a third-grade classroom. The teacher is pacing back and forth in front of the class delivering a lecture on Moslem daily prayers and instructing the students about the Arabic verses and phrases they must memorize to perform their prayers. While most students are attentively listening to the teacher, Asghar's mind wanders; he is looking outside the window at daily life on the street. Suddenly the teacher becomes aware of Asghar's inattentiveness, reprimanding him with:

> Hey, stupid jackass Sopurian! Hey son of a bitch! Where is your mind? What were you watching? I am telling these things to you so that you would not be like a jackass stuck in mud. Stupid jackass! He can see himself that I am trying to teach him something, but he is looking outside in the street. What was in the street that was more important than the words of God? I guess they were raising an elephant in the air, weren't they? Look at his appearance; he looks like a cesspool cleaner. And you think you're going to the fourth grade. In your dreams. Tomorrow you'll come to stand in front of the class and perform your prayers from the beginning. If you make one mistake and recite one word in the wrong place, I will pull your nails.[26]

Asghar is from a poor family. His mother is a washerwoman, his father was a street sweeper who was run over by a car earlier that year and had died. Asghar is aware of being of a much lower social status than most of his classmates, and particularly envies Fereydun, a handsome boy from a rich family who makes fun of him. In contrast to his own lot in life, Fereydun, Asghar thinks, is blessed with all he wishes he could have:

> Fereydun was the cream of the crop in the class. He was most distinguished among all students in that elementary school. He came to school in a car and returned home in a car. During the second recess every morning, the servant brought a bottle of beverage with a big rubber top for him, which he drank and also shared with his friends. The teacher was never angry with him. His skin was white, his hands always clean, and there was never black dirt under his nails. He had special permission from the principal not to have a crew cut, and always his golden hair soft as silk adorned his head. These were things that made Fereydun superior to Asghar, and each of them had created deep-rooted fear and humiliation in him.[27]

While in "Monsieur Elyas" Chubak's portrayal of children is merely a description of their appearance and generally what is told by the narrator about their life of poverty, in "An Afternoon in Late Autumn," there is more of an in-depth, psychological portrayal of Asghar. The latter type of portrayal of children becomes more predominant in Chubak's later work and in a sense culminates in the character of Kakolzari in his last novel, *The Patient Stone*, which will be discussed in detail in Chapter Four. In a sense, many of these early stories may be regarded as experiments for his final work, in which essentially the characters' psychological portrayal is revealed through the narrated monologues of several characters, whereby Chubak basically abandons the method of telling the story for the art of showing. Another experiment regarding the psychological portrayal of children is seen in the next story of *The Puppet Show* collection, "Yahya."

In "Yahya," Chubak presents the dilemma of an eleven year-old boy in facing the changing society in Iran in the first half of the 20th century.[28] Yahya has found a job selling newspapers. The newspaper he is selling is an English language newspaper called *Daily News*. He has to learn the name of the newspaper, which he does not understand. In his mind, the sound of the foreign words is associated with *dizi*, a sort of crock-pot in which a traditional Iranian soup is prepared. For a while on the street he still remembers the name of the newspaper, but before long, preoccupied with selling the paper and giving this customers the exact change, he forgets it. Frustrated and scared that not knowing the name of the newspaper could result in his losing his job, he tries hard to remember the name. He knows that it sounds like *dizi*, but it is a foreign word. What he remembers in the end, however, is another Persianized foreign word, Primus, which is in fact the name for the sort of burner imported into Iran from England at the time.

The story is obviously no more than an anecdote Chubak uses to sketch out the effects of the rapid Westernization of the country on an unsuspecting young boy. But at the same time, Yahya becomes a symbol of many common people in Iran who were bombarded with an array of Western ideas, concepts, technologies, and culture in general, in a sense the victims of a cultural invasion for which they were not prepared and with which they would have to cope.

The puppet-show character of the last story in the collection, "Esa'eh-ye Adab," [Insolence] is a king. Nevertheless, Chubak portrays him not unlike a comic book figure, obsessed and controlled by self-aggrandizement and greed, and indeed the victim of his own self-centeredness. In other words, the king is also a puppet of the social environment.

Using the archaic prose style of the chronicles of kings, Chubak depicts the king in his court smoking his daily dose of opium and suffering from hemorrhoids. After the court physician is summoned to attend to him, and he begins to feel relief from the pain, he asks for a pair of binoculars and begins to watch the workers who are constructing some new buildings for him and the merchants in the city bazaar who are peddling their goods. But he is annoyed when he sees one worker, apparently suffering from fever, to be resting and also the amount of gold in the jewelry shops, for after all, "The subjects have a king, what would they need gold for? Gold is worthy of kings."[29] He decides to order the courtiers to confiscate all the gold, justifying the act by saying, "We are sufficient for them, are we not better than gold?"[30]

Through the binoculars, he also sees a large stone statue of himself that had been erected the previous year. But while he is enjoying the appearance of the statute that towers over his subjects in the capital city and decides that many of these statues must be erected around his kingdom for the people to see in every corner, suddenly a crow appears, circling the statue, then sits on it, pecks at it, and eventually defecates on its hat. The king is outraged. He summons his Minister of War and commands that all the military budget of the country be spent on ground-to-air artillery to kill all crows in the world. The story ends with the migration of the crows, a large number of which have been killed in the war declared against them by the kingdom.

"Insolence" in some respect may not fit the general thematic content of this volume of short stories, in that it does not deal directly or is not written from the perspective of the poor, the downtrodden, and social outcasts. Nevertheless, it resembles "A Man in a Cage," discussed earlier in this chapter. The king, as mentioned, is not dissimilar to the main character in "A Man in a Cage," and not innocent; nevertheless, he is the puppet of his own ego and in some ways a different kind of social outcast.

"Insolence" was replaced in the third printing of *The Puppet Show* in 1967 with a poem called "Ah-e Ensan" [The Sigh of Mankind]. It is possible that the direct allegorical references in "Insolence" to the ruling monarch in Iran at the time instigated the censors to prevent its being reprinted. But while in "Insolence" Chubak uses satire to criticize the autocratic ruler, in "The Sigh of Mankind" his tone is quite serious and directed not against the ruler in his own country but against all those who rule the world and who Chubak feels are responsible for the misery and suffering of mankind.

"The Sigh of Mankind" is perhaps important for an understanding of the writer's psyche and his psychological state of mind vis-à-vis the world around him at the time, as well as his general perception of human history.[31] At the same time, under the guise of its title, the poem often makes specific references to Iran and Iranian society and history that would lead the reader to view the title not as the sigh of mankind in general but the sigh of an archetypal Iranian being. What also makes the poem different and therefore interesting is that, although like the other pieces in the volume it concentrates on a picture of human sorrow and suffering, and essentially the seamier side of human life, a positive, hopeful tone rings through the poem. The refrain of the speaker that begins the poem is, "I am not dead." He tells those who have gathered around him that despite his appearance, there is still life in him and he will be revived once again and start life anew. In the beginning of the poem, he asks those who have gathered around him to send the hearse back to the cemetery because he is not dead, and at the end he reports:

> The black dirty hearse
> Empty
> Returned to the graveyard.[32]

"The Sigh of Mankind," which was probably written sometime later or at least revised at a later date than the other stories of *The Puppet Show*, is a summation of Chubak's outlook and ideas at the time, and at the same time it differs from Chubak's other works in that it does not merely show a dark and negative picture of the society but allows a ray of hope for the future.[33] This attempt by Chubak at presenting a more hopeful outlook reaches its fruition of sorts in Chubak's two novels. But before reaching that point, Chubak continues with his extermination with Iranian social, political, and cultural history.

CHAPTER 3

The Fate of the Victims

I

Chubak's second volume of short stories, *Antari keh Lutiyash Mordeh Bud* [The Baboon Whose Buffoon Was Dead], was published in 1949 and includes three short stories and a play.[1] Similar to the stories in *The Puppet Show* the three stories and the play in this collection also revolve around the problems of concern in the society to Chubak and many other Iranian writers at the time. In terms of scope, however, in addition to addressing such social problems as poverty and prostitution, the second collection also deals with such abstract and philosophical concepts as freedom and fatalism.

The stories and the play in *The Baboon Whose Buffoon Was Dead*, particularly the short stories, can be characterized as more far reaching in conceptual terms than the first collection. They deal with broader concepts, such as freedom and fatalism, while the first collection deals with more culture-specific social ills and individual misfortunes, such as prostitution and poverty.

By and large, the favorite subjects of the writers in the 1940s revolved around political topics and often the effects of the changes on the lives of Iranians. Nevertheless, non-political topics, particularly those dealing with the effects of religious beliefs and superstitions, were not altogether neglected by these writers. "Chera Darya Tufani Shodeh Bud" [Why Was the Sea Stormy], the first story in Chubak's second collection of short stories, is essentially an exercise in combining several very descriptive character sketches and scenes from the seamier side of Iranian life.[2] The story opens with three truck drivers whose trucks are stuck on a country road near a swamp. The level of water and muck is rising rapidly and they have no other recourse but to sit on the bails of cotton they are transporting, drinking, chewing tobacco, and smoking opium. The fourth driver, Kahzad, has left on foot for Bushehr, a port town by the Persian Gulf, and he is the topic of conversation of the other three truck drivers.[3] Abbas who is smoking opium continuously wants to be left alone with his opium pipe. His first words in the story not only show his general outlook on life, but in a sense set the mood of the story as well: "I will smoke this chunk of opium to see what this misbehaving world demands of our lives. Why doesn't it take our lives and set us free?"[4]

The other two truck drivers are no less cynical about life in general. Nearly half of the story serves as an introduction to the main plot with picturesque descriptions of the truck drivers, their conversations about the absent driver, and their private thoughts. In the second part of the story we see Kahzad who has arrived in Bushehr under a torrential rain, anxious to find out whether or not Zivar, a prostitute who is pregnant with his child, has given birth. His mind is preoccupied with the thought of the child he has fathered:

> It is my own kid. Zivar herself said that she hasn't been with anyone else for a year; she's been only with me. I dropped the kid like a walnut in her belly. Zivar wouldn't lie to me. I would die for her. When I put my hand on her belly I feel the baby moving.[5]

He also plans to take the child and the mother to another city, Shiraz, along with Marjan who has been acting as Zivar's pimp:

> I'll take Marjan to Shiraz, too; it won't be fun without her. She's got to come to Shiraz with me so I can get rid of her there. I'll get rid of her somehow; she won't even have the time to figure out what happened to her. It's just about time to do it. Zivar doesn't need a pimp anymore. It'll be so easy. I can kill her like a dog, like drinking a glass of water. I can't be straight with this woman.[6]

Before long Kahzad arrives at Zivar's house. Zivar is in bed and sickly, and Kahzad is anxious to see the baby, to make love to Zivar, and begin his new life with his new family. A long scene in the story is devoted to the amorous conversation between the couple. Chubak's mastery of capturing the dialect, the thought process of the couple, and the conversation of these two characters is perhaps the reason that "Why Was the Sea Stormy" is regarded by many Iranian readers as his best short story. Chubak uses a popular folk song in dialect form to follow the simplicity and sincerity of the couple's feelings for each other. The man asks the woman to sing his favorite song. He tells her that it would not be enough even if he hears her singing the song a thousand times. She sings:

> If your key be made of silver, my lock is made of gold,
> If you want to trade it, it'll cost you double.[7]

He slides his hand on her belly and further down caressing the cloth between her legs, which arouses him sexually. She continues singing:

> Tell me the price of kisses and I'll pay for them.
> What's the use of putting the price on kisses?
> You can't taste the pomegranate if you don't crack it open.[8]

But the song is interrupted by the sound of thunder and lightning and the waves of the sea that rise and pound against the streets and buildings.

Chubak brings his story to an end with Kahzad's expression of fear of the storm and urging Zivar to leave Bushehr with him and go to Shiraz. Zivar's response to Kahzad who had asked her whether or not she is afraid of the storm in the sea and the thunder informs the reader of what has happened to the baby and also the couple's future:

> No, why be afraid? Be afraid of what? Nothing to be scared of wind and storm. The sea isn't always crazy like this. Sometimes when they throw the Koran or an illegitimate child in it, it goes crazy.
> They both became silent.
>
> Heavy tar-colored waves pounded the shore and returned to the sea, spraying the shore with their puffy moisture. The sound of the collapse of waves was deafening, the sea was drunk, the weather was sick to its stomach. The stomach of the sea churned,

> the sky was vomiting, and the sound of thunder boxed the ears of people, making stars fly out of their eyes, and the waves piled up, one on the top of another.[9]

The subtlety of the ending of "Why Was the Sea Stormy" was rather rare in the Persian prose fiction of Chubak's contemporary writers at the time the story was published. His use of simple dialogue and detailed descriptions presented to readers realistic, almost cinematic, life-like, vibrant and tangible characters with whom and their emotions and lives readers could empathize.

Similarly, in "Qafas" [Cage], with a simple short sketch Chubak portrays the life of a group of chickens and roosters living in squalor and filth in a cage of a vendor at the side of the street.[10] The story, in fact, represents the Iranian society and people, and illustrates the writer's pessimistic outlook regarding the society and its future. The way out of these dreadful circumstances for the animals is only possible when every once in a while "death" appears in the form of a hand that snatches one of them to meet its destiny.

"The Cage," which is a mere five-and-a-half pages long, is a short sketch, a favorite style for Chubak, which he also used in stories such as "Adl" [Justice]. This sketch of "The Cage" is simple: a cage packed with hens and roosters of different assortments, colors, and sizes, which is placed on the sidewalk next to a street gutter filled with debris and ice. Chubak's masterful naturalistic description of the misery and the stench make the story more vivid than many readers would like to experience.[11] But more haunting about this story are the observations of the third-person narrator that intensify this picture of misery:

> The floor of the cage was soaking wet. It was covered with chicken droppings. Dirt, straw, and millet shells were mixed in with the droppings. The legs and the feathers of the hens and roosters were soaking wet. They were soaking wet with droppings. It was cramped. They were crammed together. They were stuck together like corn on a cob. There was no room for them to roost. There was no room for them to stand. There was no room for them to sleep. They constantly pecked each other on the head and pulled on each other's crests. They were all victims. It was

> too cramped for all of them. They were all cold. They were all hungry. They were all strangers to one another. It was all stench. They were all waiting. Everyone was like everyone else, and no one's lot was better than anyone else's.[12]

The narrative of "The Cage" is almost obsessive. The writer seems obsessed with the idea of conveying a singular picture of misery to his readers. Chubak's use of language in this story also seems obsessive. He writes short sentences of no more than a few words, which are rather reminiscent of the choppy, angry prose style for which Al-e Ahmad is known. There is a great deal of repetition in the story, with the same picture presented again and again, as if to convey a sense of fatalism, the idea that nothing is going to change:

> As they were dozing off, they were all waiting, in expectation. They were bewildered. They didn't know what to do. There was no relief. There was no room to live, and there was no escape. There was no escape from that cesspool. Collectively condemned, they scraped through in the cold, alienation, loneliness, bewilderment, and expectation.[13]

Freedom from oppression for these creatures is only possible with death. Occasionally, a hand comes in from outside the cage, grabs one of the chickens and removes it from this oppressive environment. It is only the sharp knife outside the cage that can provide this freedom.

The theme of the next story of this collection, the title story, is social and philosophical determinism and freedom, which the writer presents from the perspective of a domesticated primate. In "The Baboon Whose Buffoon Was Dead," the link between freedom and oppression and the writer's pessimistic outlook are presented even more directly.[14] The story begins with the freedom of Makhmal, the baboon, who wakes one day to find his master has died. Makhmal, who has lived all of his life in captivity, eventually manages to free the end of the chain that his master has secured to the ground. But soon the momentary joy of having gained freedom turns to despair, because he realizes that even though he has pulled the chain out of the ground, it is still tied around his neck. This chain has been so much a part of his life that it has become a part of his very being, and he can never be free of it.

The relationship between Makhmal and his master, at least initially from the perspective of the animal, is the relationship between the oppressor and the oppressed. But as we continue reading this story, it becomes clear that it is also an interdependent relationship. It is true that the buffoon has subjugated the animal for the purpose of making a living. But Makhmal also needs his master to survive, because without him he is incapable of facing the world. Another symbolic chain that ties Makhmal to his master is his addiction to opium smoke, which his master used to blow in his direction whenever he smoked his opium pipe. Hence, even though Makhmal remembers all the punishments that he has suffered at the hands of his master, and he also knows that everything he has done in his life he has been forced to do, after having experienced a few hours of "freedom," he returns to the corpse of his dead master and seeks his protection.

Many phrases similar to those in "The Cage," such as "There was no escape" or "Everything was unfamiliar and threatening," also appear in "The Baboon Whose Buffoon Was Dead." While he sees oppression as an inevitable part of human life, Chubak also seems to suggest that freedom for those who have never experienced it is futile.[15]

Chubak's pessimistic and fatalistic outlook is not necessarily rooted in the political and social environment of the 1940s, when these stories were written. After over two decades of what many intellectuals and writers in Iran often characterized as the era of despotism and oppressive rule of Reza Shah, the interval between the shah's abdication and the overthrow of the government of Dr. Mohammad Mosaddeq was regarded as a short period of relative freedom in Iran. Many of the restrictions on human liberties which had been imposed, perhaps more intensely during the first part of the Pahlavi rule, were no longer enforced, which, as mentioned earlier, resulted in the appearance of many political parties and the publication of numerous books, journals, magazines, and newspapers. This environment of relative freedom, which provided Iranians with some hope, should have been conducive to a more optimistic and hopeful outlook than we see in Chubak's work during this period. Was Chubak as a young writer so clairvoyant that he could clearly see what was to come in the ensuing decades? Or is it that, as his stories suggest, those who live and are nurtured in an environment of pessimism and fatalism cannot look at the world and the future otherwise?

The concluding piece in this collection of short stories is a one-act play, "Tup-e Lastiki" [The Rubber Ball], which has never been staged.[16] This play, unlike the three stories in the collection, is a satire of sorts. Dalaki, a high-ranking official becomes extremely suspicious when he sees a policeman on watch near his home. Although he is sure that he has committed no violation, he agonizes in a state of fear, but also hopes that all will be fine. When he confesses his fear, anxiety, and suspicions with his friends and family, they all abandon him. His ego collapses because of his cynicism about what will happen to him. Finally he finds out that the policeman's son had thrown his rubber ball into the courtyard of his house and had not had the courage to knock on his door to retrieve his ball.[17] Dalaki then realizes that that is why the policeman had been hanging around outside his house. Upon learning this, he cries out in horror and faints. His son, a clear-headed young man, says: "Is the life you live worth this? Is there anyone in this dump who feels secure? Nobody can utter a word. You're all like cardboard puppets, paper tigers, eh."[18] He continued:

> Don't fool yourself, Sir! You're all as scared as dogs of each other. Wives fear their husbands, children fear their parents, sisters fear their brothers. Nothing but fear, fear, fear! Can this be called life? It's death. It's filthy.[19]

Commenting on this play in the introduction to *Sadeq Chubak: An Anthology*, F. R. C. Bagley observes that Chubak in this play "depicts the then prevailing mood of suspicion and fear in official circles and resentment in intellectual circles."[20] This prevailing mood of suspicion and fear, of course, characteristic of autocratic societies was not true exclusively of the time that Chubak wrote this play but has continued to the present and in some ways makes Chubak's play relevant to many societies, regardless of time.

II

Chubak, who had been known as a masterful short story writer, published his first novel, *Tangsir*, in 1963.[21] Based on an actual event that took place during the author's childhood in Bushehr, this novel tells the story of a rural worker who has been swindled out of his hard-earned savings by four prominent individuals in the city. Failing to gain legal redress, the protagonist decides to take the law into his own hands, and after killing the four involved in the swindle he flees the country with his wife and child. Even though initially, *Tangsir* received negative reviews in terms of its subject matter, which the engagé critics did not consider to be a true representation of the realities of the life of the oppressed classes in the society, ten years later when it was made into a popular movie by the well-known filmmaker Amir Naderi, it gained widespread praise, since the story was interpreted as a symbolic representation of the plight of ordinary people in their struggle against the Pahlavi regime. At the time of the publication of *Tangsir*, the critics' displeasure was because they thought that Chubak had deviated from his much-praised realistic portrayals of the poor and the downtrodden. The protagonist's successful revenge at the end of the story displeased the literary public and the intelligentsia, as it did not, they thought, depict "reality," the destruction of the oppressed individual.[22] For Chubak himself, though, *Tangsir* was not a deviation from his is earlier stories. In a rare published interview in which he discusses his work, Chubak says of the novel:

> To better understand *Tangsir*, you should know that what you read as a story is the merciless and the naked reality to which I myself have been witness. To comprehend this reality, you must belong to the sand deserts of the south, to the sea, to the people who eat date pits.[23]

Stories based on actual events often disappoint readers unfamiliar with the nature and function of fiction. Unlike journalistic accounts and historical recordings of events, the function of fiction is not to present an accurate record of what has occurred, but to create a fictional world in which some sort of order is created to make such events meaningful in an orderly, albeit imaginary and fictional context.[24] The story of *Tangsir* is a case in point. Many devoted readers of modern Persian literature and the intelligentsia who were accustomed to reading stories that showed oppression by the regime at the time, the dire conditions of the lower classes, and the helplessness and inevitable failure of the people in their struggle for justice, naturally did not find *Tangsir* a reflection of these concerns. Perhaps what Chubak intended to convey and even teach his readers was to abandon their defeatist outlook. By creating a folk hero of an ordinary laborer, he created a heroic character as a model for the people to emulate. Early in this novel, when the bull belonging to a widow has gone wild, injuring several people and escaping into a palm grove, the people of the village ask Zayer Mohammad, the protagonist, for help. Zayer Mohammad heroically is able to tame and bring back the bull to its owner. In the meantime, he is quite preoccupied in his thoughts with rectifying the injustice that he has suffered and is determined to right the wrong that embezzlers of his hard earned money have done to him. Similar to heroes in legends and myths, Zayer Mohammad, after telling his wife that he will be going on a long journey, sets out on a quest. He arms himself with a rifle, marches through the city, and after killing the embezzlers, escapes by diving into the sea. Certain scenes in *Tangsir*, such as the scene mentioned above in which Zayer Mohammad fights and tames the bull with his extraordinary physical strength, or the scene when he escapes the government forces that are pursuing his capture by diving into the sea and successfully fighting a ferocious shark that bites his leg, create a heroic figure of Zayer Mohammad. As scholar and critic Mohammad Mehdi Khorrami observes, in *Tangsir*, "One can see indications of an effort—consciously or subconsciously—to create a mythological identity for an ordinary individual, an identity that based on its nature goes beyond the narrow and limited specific political and social ideas."[25] *Tangsir* was published in 1963 during the riots and uprisings in Tehran and many major cities, particularly, in Qom, the seat of Shiite religious learning and seminaries, incited by Ayatollah Khomeyni who opposed certain aspects of the so-called White Revolution and reforms initiated by Shah Mohammad Reza Pahlavi, including women's right to vote and land reforms. The heroic success of the victim of embezzlement and injustice in *Tangsir* did not seem to reflect and mirror these events that resulted in the killing of thousands of rioters, mostly from the lower classes and religious seminary students.

Some critics see the characters in *Tangsir* as stereotypical in the tradition of Hollywood Western movies and do not regard either the character of Zayer Mohammad or the embezzlers and others as round, developed characters.[26] This may be true to some extent, since Amir Naderi's movie adaptation of *Tangsir*, which initially Chubak disapproved of but later praised, was a major box office success appealing to all classes. In the light of Chubak's expectations for Hollywood adaptation of *The Patient Stone* discussed in the concluding chapter of this book, it is quite possible that Chubak was writing both novels with an eye on and hoping for and expecting a movie adaptation of his stories to reach a wider audience.

III

Two years after the publication of *Tangsir*, in 1965, Chubak published another collection of short stories, *Ruz-e Avval-e Qabr* [The First Day in the Grave]. This collection contains nine short stories and a play.[27]

The stories in *The First Day in the Grave* once again generally focus on the seamier side of life and the depiction of characters from the unfortunate classes; however, in some of the longer pieces of this collection, such as the title story, Chubak delves into the psyches of socially successful and affluent individuals who are haunted by the voice of their conscience because of their past actions.

The first short story in the collection, "Gurkanha" [Grave Diggers], happens in a small village the people of which, we are told, are extremely superstitious and fanatical.[28] The protagonist, Khadijeh, is a young girl who has become pregnant with an illegitimate child. For this reason, the children gather around her, throw stones at her, and sing obscene songs referring to her condition. Bewildered, Khadijeh tries to get away and hide from them, going from one alleyway to another, but the people, not hesitating to use any violent measures, intend to have her baby aborted. Everyone is involved. For example, "She was not yet two months pregnant when Mash Gholam, the owner of Siyah

Kolah, took her, tied her to a plow to plow his land ... but no matter what she did, she did not miscarry, as if she had seven lives, like a cat."[29]

Out of desperation, the poor girl takes refuge in a stable whose owner thinks she'll bring bad luck but whose wife welcomes and tries to protect her. Finally she delivers, but knowing that the stable owner will kick her out, she leaves and goes to a nearby forest, kills her child, and buries it. The story ends when the gendarmes who have seen her go into the forest and became suspicious arrive on the scene. The final paragraph of the story is a grim description of the fate of the young girl and the attitude of the populace represented by the official police:

> The gendarmes removed the loose, moist soil. The baby appeared in view. The officer stood erect, swallowed his saliva, and said: "Take her to the station!" The gendarmes pushed the little girl toward the guard station, one of them carrying the baby, while the officer was looking for a cigarette in his pocket, gazing at the edge of the hole. Then he undid the buttons on his trousers and pissed in the hole, turning on his flashlight to watch himself pissing.[30]

The next story in the collection, "Cheshm-e Shisheh'i" [The Glass Eye], is a psychological examination of a young boy who has lost one eye, returning home from the doctor's office with his parents.[31] His parents try to console him and pretend that his glass eye looks real. But once the boy is standing in front of the mirror looking at himself and his glass eye, his parents' consolation does not seem to have changed the reality of the boy's dilemma:

> The little boy had placed the mirror on the table, had taken out his glass eye from its socket, placed it on the mirror, and was gazing at its white ball with its dead pupil standing on the mirror. He was gazing in amazement at his other eye bending over the mirror. The empty hollow socket seemed to be making faces at his glass eye.[32]

The next story in the collection is "Dasteh Gol" [The Flower Bouquet].[33] The protagonist of the story is a small beardless man, limping and dragging one leg, reminiscent of characters in the stories of Victor Hugo and Dostoyevsky, among others. He decides to take revenge on his cruel oppressive boss. In contrast to the stories by Victor Hugo and Dostoyevsky, we are not provided with a detailed account of the lives of this individual and his emotions. Instead, Chubak, using the art of showing instead of telling his story, presents the character of his protagonist through long detailed letters that he writes to his boss. For example, he writes:

> Don't you realize how you torment those who were working under you? How you bully them? Don't you know how I despise you, your appearance, your attitude, the way you look at others, and your merciless eyes? I can gaze into the eyes of a leopard for hours and find a sense of empathy and humanity in them. But your gruesome eyes that have no humanity at all burn the core of my existence.[34]

The obsessed protagonist also threatens his boss:

> I know very well how you will suffer when you receive this letter. You probably want to know who I am. Of course you will, but not now. I promise you that just before you die, I will introduce myself to you. You will see me. But when? When standing over your head with a revolver, and you, you're rolling in your own blood. This is a part of my plan, but it is a dangerous wish. I might give my life for this wish for no reason. But I do not want to break your heart and annihilate you if you do not know who has done it. After all, I am an honorable killer, and you must know exactly what will happen to you.[35]

The boss, tormented and frightened by the letters he receives and the threat to kill him, cannot rest or sleep. He goes to the police department and complains. The police arrest some people, but it does not improve his condition. Life has turned into a hell for him. He resigns from his position and on his last day, when he goes to collect his belongings, as he arrives at the office, frightened, he looks around. Suddenly, a vagrant boy of 12 years of age appears before him and explodes a fireworks. The sound of the explosion shocks and stuns the boss, who collapses on the ground. He is taken to the hospital, but before he arrives he dies. During his burial ceremony, the writer of the letters shows up. He is a small beardless man who is carrying a withered bouquet of flowers trying to join the others who have gathered around the grave. When he reaches the grave, he bends down and places the bouquet of flowers on the grave.[36]

Similar to *Tangsir*, with this story Chubak is perhaps trying to wake up government administrators and those who control the lives of ordinary citizens, thereby complying with the dictates of engagé literature. Also similar to *Tangsir*, the poor and socially powerless protagonist's victory and revenge is meant to satisfy and meet the aspirations of common people oppressed by the agents of the autocratic regime.

"Yek Chiz-e Khakestari" [A Grey Thing] is the next story in the collection.[37] A young boy with his mother and a man reading a magazine along with two other men are in a dentist's office. Each is busy doing something or talking. From their conversation, the reader learns about their anxieties and concerns: the man throws the magazine on the table, puts his hand over his mouth, wiggles in his chair and talking to himself, says: "They are grinding something grey." He asks himself, "Why grey?" Then, answering his own question, he says: "To hell with whys. Let them go to hell." When the machine stops grinding, laughter is heard and someone says: "When I was a kid my mother was an adult and now that I have become an adult my mother has turned into a kid."[38]

"A Grey Thing" uses the same seemingly pictorial representation of life as "Justice," discussed in the previous chapter. In this case, if there is a theme, it is the isolation of individuals in the modern world, in their own small world, with their own private concerns and thoughts, the theme that is central to Chubak's last novel, *The Patient Stone*, discussed in the following chapter.

"A Grey Thing" is followed in the collection by "Pachehkhizak" [Fireworks].[39] In this story which some critics consider the best in the collection, we see Chubak at work with his biting satire. The story begins with the description of a remote village and its people who are enslaved to their superstitious beliefs and futile pastimes:

> The little market of the village was swept and clean, and cool air waved under the big poplar tree that spread like an umbrella over the water storage tank. Small hunched dwarfish stores were arranged around the village square.[40]

Further on the descriptive narrative continues with:

> Spot by spot next to the lazy and sickly stream, sat farmers and workers who had their bread bundles spread before them and were eating their lunch, and the teahouse owner's business was thriving. The lukewarm spring breeze drove sleep into the veins.[41]

Mash Heydar, the grocer, suddenly emerges from his shop with a mousetrap and displays the mouse to other shopkeepers on the square. Everyone has an opinion about how to kill the mouse. A gasoline tanker arrives and the driver's assistant suggests that they pour kerosene on the mouse and set it on fire. They do so, and the mouse escapes, running like a fireworks under the gasoline tanker, which of course explodes, showering on the people and the shops, setting everything in the village on fire.

Like "The Flower Bouquet," "Fireworks" is also a story with a lesson. Similar to the old employee in "The Flower Bouquet," the mouse also represents a victim of injustice, and the fire that destroys the village is the victim's revenge, albeit unintentionally and instinctively in this case.[42]

The next story, "Ruz-e Avval-e Qabr" [The First day in the Grave], which is also the title story of the collection, is a play on "the first night in the grave," important to Moslems because it is believed to be the beginning of reward or punishment during the purgatorial phase before the Day of Judgment.[43] Moslems believe that angels visit the deceased person on his or her first night in the grave, when the deceased learns about his or her fate. Reminiscent of Sadeq Hedayat's novel, *Haji Aqa*,[44] this story is about Haj Mo'tamed, a rich man in his old age who, relaxing in his courtyard garden, reviews his past, remembering how he accumulated his wealth by embezzlement and fraudulent transactions as well as his sexual escapades and other criminal acts. He also plans for his life in the next world. Having built a tomb in his own courtyard garden, he philosophizes: "You're happy that you're alive as always and are free to mistreat others, but you do know that your being always alive is worse than your death." Further on, still a target himself, he goes on: "Everyone who comes and associates with you tastes your mistreatment and then dies. This is like spitting and a curse on you forever. If you really want to know, everyone hates you. And if they pretend to respect and flatter you, it is because they're afraid."[45] For the first time in his life, he decides to talk to God: "Before today, I did not know how to talk you. Even though I talk to you in my daily prayers several times a day, I cannot talk to you the way I want, because I speak in Arabic and don't understand the words I repeat in my prayers in Arabic."[46]

There is nothing innovative either in terms of themes and concepts or narrative style in this story. Its inclusion in the collection and using it as the title story may be Chubak's way of paying tribute to his mentor, Sadeq Hedayat.

"Hamrah" [Companion], the next story, is an experiment in presenting the same story in two different styles.[47] The first version is written in a poetic style while the second is presented in a simple, almost commonplace, language. The story which is included later in the collection is about two hungry wolves that in a severe cold winter are descending the mountain for prey. There is heavy snow and the wolves cannot find anything to eat. One of them collapses and dies and the other devours its companion.[48] Using animals to symbolize humans and their instinct for survival may have been inspired by the work of Jack London, and even the Donner Party. In addition, the presentation of this story in two language registers is perhaps Chubak's experimenting with language, an art that he perfects in *The Patient Stone*.

The next story, "Arusak-e Forushi" [A Doll for Sale], is the story of a young boy wandering in the streets on a cold winter day.[49] He begs people for help but they ignore him. He is hungry, but no matter how much he begs of restaurant and food store owners, they give him nothing. Finally he sneaks into a big house and steals a large doll to sell in order to use the money to buy some food. But no one buys it from him. Tired and hungry, the boy goes to sleep in some corner in the street and freezes to death.[50] Similar to many short stories by Chubak, "A Doll for Sale" shows the author's obsessive preoccupation with characters abandoned and forgotten by society. With this preoccupation and writing about the lives of the downtrodden, Chubak seems to be launching a campaign, as it were, to help improve the condition of the poor, and perhaps rid himself of a sense of guilt for living an affluent life. This sense of guilt is not specific to Chubak, most literary artists at the time came from affluent families, and in fact a great part of the ideological bend of the so-called committed literature inspired by socialism and communism inculcated a sense of guilt in the practitioners of this predominant school.

"Yek Shab-e Bikhabi" [A Sleepless Night] describes a fifty-year-old bachelor's anxieties about his life and mortality after having seen a dog that day run over and killed by a car.[51] He tries to rid himself of sleeplessness by reading the poetry of Rumi and pontificates:

> I am sure that Rumi worked at night. Otherwise how could he have accomplished so much in the sixty or seventy years that he lived. *The Divan of Shams* alone is the work of a lifetime. How could he write all the really good stuff that he wrote and talked about among all those fanatical pseudo-religious people? I guess he wouldn't show some of this stuff to others.[52]

In contrast to earlier collections of short stories that display a thematic unity, stories in *The First Day in the Grave* lack thematic unity. Most of these stories, "A Sleepless Night" included, seem to be mere experiments in language.

The concluding piece in the collection is "Hafkhat" [Sly].[53] As in much of his work, in "Sly," Chubak's characters are taken from among the poor. The play is an ironic treatment of a villager who has come to the big city, Tehran, to earn a living as a construction worker, and he falls in love with a city girl. The protagonist, Mohammad, who is a physically strong man asks Goli, the object of his love, for her hand in marriage, but he is rejected. His friend advises him that he should have his whole body tattooed, telling him that like a charm, it will make the girl fall in love with him. One night Mohammad climbs the wall of the house without his shirt and sneaks into Goli's room. Goli wakes up frightened and yells for help. The police and the owner of the house come, and when the police try to put handcuffs on

Mohammad, the charm seems to have worked, Goli is gradually mesmerized by Mohammad's athletic beautiful body. Taking his side results in her arrest and they are both charged with robbery.[54] This play that has never been staged, as a psychological study of an uneducated migrant laborer, deserves critical attention as an investigation into the problems of young villagers who migrate to the large cities in search of a better life in the latter decades of the Pahlavi rule.[55] In this play, Chubak juxtaposes traditional and new values concerning relations between men and women.

By and large, *The First Day in the Grave* should not be included among Chubak's best work. While earlier collections attracted critical attention because of their form of presentation, language, and thematic content, the early negative reaction of critics to *Tangsir* who regarded Chubak a successful short-story writer and not an accomplished novelist, in reaction to and perhaps encouraged by critics, Chubak seems to have been trying to make an attempt to publish another collection of short stories. Perhaps for the same reason, in the same year that he published his last and final work, *The Patient Stone*, he also published his last collection of short stories, *Cheragh-e Aker* [The Last Alms or The Last Light], a title that seems to foretell Chubak's final effort or even desire to write more short stories.[56]

IV

The title story, "The Last Alms," is also the longest story in the collection. Javad, an intellectual young man takes a journey on a ship to Calcutta to continue his education. On the ship, he witnesses the performance of a traditionally popular performer and storyteller who tells stories of sacred religious figures and martyrs. The performer has succeeded in gathering a large audience on the deck of the ship with his fast-talking salesman-like oratory. Javad believes that the people are smart enough not to be deceived by the performer who uses religion, religious beliefs, and religious stories to pocket their money and is disappointed even when many people actually generously give money to the performer and even feed him. After the performance, Javad who is standing in some corner watching the performer gobbling up his supper, realizes that the performer has a bottle of booze in his sack from which he drinks, concealed from the eyes of other people, even though drinking is prohibited in Islam. Feeling that he must expose him and protect the people, in the middle of the night when the performer and all the passengers are sleeping, Javad steals the performer's equipment and canvas screen and tosses them into the sea, symbolically destroying the symbols of superstition.[57]

Similar to *Tangsir* and "The Flower Bouquet," in "The Last Alms" Chubak seems to suggest that in order to get rid of superstition in the society, it is the duty of the intellectuals to destroy its symbols. Although Javad may have gained a degree of satisfaction from his action, because he fights the outward manifestations of superstitious beliefs, in the long run he fails to achieve his goal, since the people gathering around the performer at the end of the story are as angry as he is, and they blame the loss of the performer's canvas screen and other equipment on "infidels."

Quite resembling stories such as "Justice" and "The Cage," "The Hubcap Thief" is the story of a young boy who is caught while stealing a hubcap.[58] The people on the street, the shopkeepers, and others who catch him start beating him and everyone blames every hubcap ever stolen and even the recent robberies in the neighborhood on the little boy:

> "I'm sure it was you who stole the ewer from our house just the day before yesterday."
> "Just tell me, who let you know about this neighborhood?"
> "A few days ago a pot was stolen from my house."
> "Nobody can remember so many petty thefts in this neighborhood."[59]

The rest of the story consists of comments by the people surrounding the boy, and everybody contributing to beating and kicking him. The story concludes with: "The little boy was crouched up on the ground, white form oozing out from the corner of his mouth, and the asphalt of the street was soaked with his urine and turned red."[60]

A similar sketch is the story, "Kaftarbaz" [Pigeon Flyer], which in some ways is reminiscent of Sadeq Hedayat's "Dash Akol."[61] While flying his pigeons, a street smart pigeon fancier sees his neighbor and falls in love with her. The narrator describes the girl poetically: "Those two black indigo-lined eyes branded his heart. The flock of pigeons looked homeless flying over his head. He forgot about his mother, the pigeons, Shiraz, and himself.[62] This story is also perhaps Chubak's tribute to Sadeq Hedayat. In classical Persian literature, similar to other national literatures, particularly in romance novels, love and falling in love are generally exclusive to princes and notables. Complying with Jamalzadeh's pioneering ideas that modern literature should deal with the lives of ordinary people, "Pigeon Flyer" is an exercise or a contribution to what was thought to be humanizing the common people.

"Omarkoshun" [Omar Killing], which has been omitted from the latest addition of *The Last Alms* published in the United States in 1990, is a story in which Chubak seems to draw on his recollections of early childhood experiences in Bushehr during the public ritual of the burning of the effigy of Omar, the second caliph, regarded by the Shi'ites as the usurper of the leadership of Moslems. Its omission from this edition may indicate awareness of the sensitivity of Sunni Moslems regarding the second caliph and awareness of the author and his publisher of the story not being "politically correct" outside Iran.[63]

"Bacheh Gorbeh'i keh Chesmanash Baz Nashodeh Bud" [The Kitten Whose Eyes Had Not Opened] is once again a mere exercise in sketch-like description of an ordinary scene.[64] A little kitten has crawled into a deep hole on the street. She is meowing as if in pain, and a little boy concerned about it is trying to bring her out and take her home and raise her. He pleads with a village man standing nearby to help him bring the cat out, but he refuses saying that the hole is too deep, and that the boy should leave the kitten alone to die of hunger, because he could not sleep the night before and his sleep was disrupted with the constant meowing of the kitten. As usual, others gather to see what is going on, each making some suggestion. The picture is completed with:

> At this time, a scrawny black cat with tired shy eyes, the skin of her belly sagging between her arms and legs, appeared on the pavement among the feet of the people who were standing there watching the fighting between two of the onlookers. It was as if the cat

> had emerged from the ground. She first walked to the chicken [that one of the fighters had put on the ground] and sniffed its head. She then jumped up into the hole of the light pole and the meowing of the kitten stopped.[65]

"Asb-e Chubi" [The Wooden Horse], in my opinion, is the best short story in the collection.[66] It is told from the perspective of a young French woman who married an Iranian from a traditional family while he was a student in Paris. After six years of marriage and the experience of living in Iran for three years with her husband, Jalal, the woman is spending her final hours in Iran in a bare room alone with her young son on a cold Christmas night. Reviewing her past, she remembers and presents a depressing picture of Iranians and their society. She remembers how she fell in love and married Jalal, and then when their son was born, they came to Iran. Upon their arrival, Jalal's family forced them to remarry in accordance with Islamic law. Her impressions and memories of Iran are most unpleasant. She remembers the days when she arrived in Iran for the first time, the nauseating smell of the outhouse that seemed to be in the air everywhere, the brothers and sisters of Jalal who seemed to be suffering from some sickness and starvation, the death of her husband's young sister who was afflicted with typhoid, and her own serious affliction with the same disease that brought her to the verge of death. On top of all that, her husband begins to change and subsequently marries a fat ugly-looking cousin and abandons his foreign wife and her son. In contrast to her experiences in the early days when they were in France and were living happily, her experiences in Iran make the French woman decide to leave, determined to keep her son from ever knowing the identity of his father, and to rid herself of the horrible nightmare of her years in Iran. The symbolic throwing of a wooden horse, a gift to the little boy from his father, into the fireplace symbolizes for her the elimination of any sign and indication of her nightmarish experience.[67]

As a vehicle to show the Iranian leaders who and what they are, Chubak in this story engages in social criticism more in keeping with much of his own and other writers' work in the latter half of the 20th century. Perhaps conscious of the xenophobic climate dominating the post-Mosaddeq and pre-Islamic revolution decades, in this case, the story is an attempt to place the blame on the Iranians rather than the common practice of blaming Westerners for all that goes wrong in Iran. The French woman is indeed the victim of injustice and gains the empathy of Chubak's readers.[68]

In "Atma, Sag-e Man" [Atma, My Dog], which is an unusual blend of reality and fantasy, a dog is the symbolic representation of the conscience of a retired lonely man who has committed many crimes and is responsible for many atrocities during his life.[69] The man is trying to live a life away from others. One day his German neighbor comes to this house and asks for his permission to allow the man's servant to feed his dog while he is away on a trip. Reluctantly, the man agrees, but time passes and the German neighbor does not return. Later news arrives that his neighbor has died and will no longer return. The German ambassador convinces the man that he should take care of the dog, and he agrees. To him, it appears that the dog is both a companion and a nuisance. There is something about the dog he has named Atma that fills his mind with the thought of killing the dog. After a long time agonizing about how to kill the dog, he finally determines to poison the dog's food, but later he is afraid to check to see whether or not the dog is dead. Finally, he gathers up courage and checks on the dog. To his surprise he finds that the dog is alive and has not touched the food. He is happy that the dog is not dead, but realizes that the dog is even incapable of protecting him against thieves, because his house was burglarized one night without the dog even making any sound. The reader is never sure whether actually the dog is dead or the man imagines that he is alive. The dog continues to linger outside his room, sometimes even coming in and licking his feet. But still even he is not sure whether this is real. Suddenly, one day the man hears a voice, assuming that it is the dog's:

> The bedroom of the giant
> Is filled with fear.
> Rest a while
> If you can
> If you had not come into this world
> Or had died in childhood
> You would never have committed so many crimes

And you would not have approved so many executions of the people
You're the cesspool of life
All cesspools
Are in you.[70]

For a long time the man hears the voice uttering similar statements. Finally he asks the voice whether or not he will die soon and hears:

You are already dead
But not buried
Now a secret pain
Is clawing your insides
And soon you shall perish
But
There is neither another world
Nor any torture
More than what you have experienced and will experience
In this world
Your hell is here.[71]

In response, the man takes his revolver, shoots at the dog, and passes out. When he regains consciousness, he feels an excruciating pain in his shoulder and sees the dog leaning over him, with two eyes that burn him inside, licking his wound.

The psychological sense of guilt of oppressors is, of course, a main theme of this story. The dog becomes a symbol of the monster within that gnaws at his conscience. But as in many of his stories, Chubak tries his hand at an inventive modern poetic language.

"Rahavard" [Souvenir] is a story written in modern verse, similar to the style of "Sigh of Mankind" which was discussed in the introduction to this book.[72] An old adventurous warrior returns home after many victories and conquests. He is welcomed by the poor hungry people, who have no other choice, victorious and bragging, and goes through the city to his beloved, anticipating the fulfillment of his sexual desires. The beloved asks him what he has brought her as a souvenir. The warrior says that he has brought her a magic carpet which represents all seasons adorned with precious jewels, gold and silver, with designs of winter in spring and autumn in winter, and tells her that when she sits on it, rain will caress her body and when she sleeps on it in summer, starlight will cover her naked body, and in winter when she sits on it, her body will be covered with blood-colored autumn leaves. He orders the carpet to be brought in, but when they unfold the carpet, they find the body of a dead child. The beloved spits on the face of the warrior and flees.[73]

Again in this long narrative poem, Chubak is experimenting with poetic language in the tradition of many classical poets such as Nezami-Ganjavi.

"Parizad va Pariman" [Parizad and Pariman] is an exercise in the language of mythology.[74] Parizad and Pariman are a brother and sister whose mother has died and are the children of a man who decides to take a beautiful wife from a family of monsters (*div*s in Persian mythology). In time, the beautiful wife turns into an ugly monster and demands of her husband to kill the children and feed their flesh to her, which would make her beautiful again. The man takes his children outside the town and tells them what he has been told, asking them to leave for another land. The children do so and in their journey they reach a mythical tree under which they rest and become husband and wife.[75] Parizad becomes pregnant and gives birth to a colt. Pariman is shocked and wishes to abandon their offspring while the mother, Parizad, cannot do so and wants to take care of and raise their child. When the child grows up into a horse, the father suggests that they should ride the horse, but the mother is reluctant. The horse signals them that they should get on its back, and once they are mounted on it, he flies into the sky and lands in the country of Ahriman (the force of darkness, evil, and lies, akin to Satan). In the land of darkness rule wild boars who kill and feed on the flesh of their subjects. The arrival of Mehrak, the horse, representing light, truth, and goodness, turns darkness into light. Worried about the fate of the land of darkness, Ahriman the king of the land of darkness uses every monster and form of magic to destroy Mehrak, but he fails. Mehrak, who has brought light to the land of darkness, tells the people that darkness is over, that their land will be filled with pleasing scents and refreshing, sights, deafness and blindness will be cured, and suffering and misfortune will be eliminated. The people are hesitant, because they are accustomed to life as it is. They tell Mehrak:

You are a stranger,
Because something burning emits from your body
That
Burns our eyes.
Get away from us
And take this eternal damnation
That rises from your body
From this land.
Our eyes
Burn from your light
Go away
And take away
All this misfortune and suffering
We are accustomed to our lives
And
We want the same thing
Not you.
The suffering
That lands on our eyes
From your body
Is deadly.[76]

Ahriman who is concerned about the fate of the Land of Darkness uses his last trick turning a monster into a beautiful woman, and tells Mehrak that if he wants to bring the rule of Ahura Mazda (the force of good, truth, and light) into the land of darkness and be one of its denizens, he must take a mate from among the denizens, in other words, the monster that he has turned into a beautiful woman. Mehrak consents, upon which the *farr* of kinship is taken away from him, because he agrees to his mother becoming the wife of Ahriman and he marries a she-monster. Darkness takes over light, the wild boars return to the city, and eternal darkness gains victory over light.[77]

This mythological story is perhaps an allegory of such events as the rise and fall of the popular government of Mosaddeq in the early 1950s in Iran. The forced departure of the shah from Iran and the promises of a democracy, and then the return of the shah instigated by foreign governments and the willingness of the people to continue their lives as before, are analogous to what happens to the people of the Land of Darkness.

"Dust" [Friend], the final story in the collection, is in a sense the reverse side of "The Wooden Horse."[78] The narrator is going through mandatory military training with a group of educated Iranians with higher educational degrees, some of whom have studied abroad and have married foreign wives. The narrator on the first day meets Fereydun, a young agricultural engineer who has married a French woman, Lucy, while studying in Paris. He has volunteered to serve in the military for a while because it provides him with better pay while his wife is also working as a secretary. Financially, according to the narrator, they are not doing well. Fereydun is so preoccupied with the thought of spending more time with his wife that the narrator feels that he must help him in any way can. Fereydun also has another friend whom the narrator meets when he visits his house, described as a mansion with expensive furnishings. Karim, Fereydun's friend, comes from a rich family and often helps them financially without any expectation, it seems. On Christmas Eve, the recruits with foreign wives are usually given leave to spend Christmas with their families. After some effort, Fereydun succeeds in getting a leave and goes to spend Christmas with Lucy. The narrator is very happy about this. But later in the evening, Fereydun comes back to the barracks, drunk and depressed. Eventually the narrator learns that when his friend went home, he found his wife in bed with Karim.[79]

With the exception of "The Wooden Horse," the stories in *The Last Alms* seem almost forced, an obligation for Chubak to write short stories for which he was known. This is also true of many of the stories in *The First Day in the Grave*. The reason for this is perhaps that Chubak during these years and actually since the publication of his first collection of short stories was working on completing *The Patient Stone*, which will be discussed in the next chapter.

CHAPTER 4

On *The Patient Stone*

I

Some regard literature as a reflection of society, therefore, a study of a national literature, of even one particular work of art, is a natural outcome of a desire to better understand the society from which that literature or work has sprung. Others view literature, more specifically a single literary work, as representing merely a fleeting insight or individual worldview. About the novel, Stendhal remarks, "It's a mirror one carries down a road."[1] And Henry James espouses the belief: "The only reason for the existence of a novel is that it does attempt to represent life."[2] In truth, the novel is perhaps the most problematic of literary forms in this respect, in that it creates the illusion and appearance of reality, but at the same time calling attention to its own fictionality.[3] The novel dwells in a liminal state between existing as a record and representation of the life and reality of society and as an individual vision of the world. From this perspective, Sadeq Chubak's *The Patient Stone*, as an important work of Persian fiction, not only reflects something of the society in which it was conceived, but also brings into focus an individual point of view in its attempt to "represent life." Aside from its merits as a literary work of art, The importance of *The Patient Stone* lies also in its function as a "mirror and conscience" of Iranian society, considering both the novel's contemporary social issues and its historical aspects. Even though the events of the story are given to have taken place about 1934, many of the social issues depicted in the novel, including religion, politics, nationalism, and the rights of women, are still pertinent.

But the image reflected in *The Patient Stone*, the mirror that Chubak holds to his society, is not a pleasant one; it is a picture of poverty, murder, disease, oppression, and social injustice. Alarmed by such a picture, the Iranian audience of *The Patient Stone* has often reacted disapprovingly to the novel, some condemning it on moral grounds, while others on nationalistic and others still on political grounds. These reactions can best be seen in the written "criticism" of Chubak's novel, often appearing in the guise of literary criticism but remaining almost always both "sensationalistic" and "journalistic" in nature. In effect, *The Patient Stone* has provided the opportunity for various self-serving critics either to expound their ideologies or to justify and preach their personal biases and prejudices to their own reading publics. Other critics have also expended much effort to show that Chubak's novel is unsuccessful since it does not conform to their own preconceived notion of what a novel should be. The entire body of commentary written on *The Patient Stone*, even taking into account various mentions of and short comments on the book in survey articles, consisted of approximately one hundred pages of a book by the late 1970s. However, in recent years, particularly since Chubak's death in 1998, a volume of essays, many of which were previously published, appear in *Yad-e Sadeq Chubak* [In Memory of Sadeq Chubak]. The art magazine, *Honar*, and the important literary journal, *Iranshenasi*, both published in Persian in the United States, each devote one issue to Sadeq Chubak. Another important Persian-language literary journal published in the United States, *Iran Nameh*, also contains articles on this author in one of its issues. Even so, considering the generally limited amount of fictional criticism written in Iran, this amount of commentary in itself asserts the significance of Chubak's contribution to modern Persian literature. However, of those who have concerned themselves with commentary on *The Patient Stone*, only a handful of critics are worthy of mention in any review of the literature on this novel. One of the earliest written remarks on *The Patient Stone* expresses the critic's conviction that this novel can neither be completely accepted nor rejected. Hushang Golshiri, novelist, short story writer, and critic who was considered to be one of the most important literary voices in the 1970s through the 1990s, does give Chubak credit for "occasional success" in telling the story through the viewpoints of the five characters, but he goes on to list the author's numerous "failings" as due to his "taking sides, giving lessons in psychology, issuing anti-religious proclamations, and his inability to use 'interior dialogue.'"[4] Another critic, Abdolali Dastgheyb, considers the novel from a different viewpoint, primarily sociological. He criticizes Chubak for having abandoned the "realism" of his earlier short stories, and in doing so only looking at the ugliness of society, which is neither an accurate reflection of nor of any benefit to that society.[5] A third critic, Mahmud Kiyanush, finds the work a boring compendium of imitations of Western writers, with unrealistic, puppet-like characters, in essence, a short story which "the writer, through loquacity and repetition, stretches ... to four hundred pages."[6] Hasan Nekuruh, on the other hand, in an article in which he surveys the works of Chubak, finds in *The Patient Stone* the full maturation of the author, as he has achieved a balance between the representation of reality and the expression of ideas. However, this critic finds a flaw of the novel in the inclusion of the myth of creation play at the end of the novel. He feels that in this novel, the writer has taken refuge into a world of dreams and has consequently lost touch with reality.[7] Finally, the prominent literary critic, Reza Baraheni, in a most detailed study of *The Patient Stone*, praises it as a masterpiece, and provides insight into the work from stylistic, thematic, and technical viewpoints.[8] In terms of Chubak's use of language, as it reflects the personality and individual world of each character, Baraheni finds *The Patient Stone* unsurpassed in its accurate reflection of an era of terror, through the novel's basic theme, loneliness. No other Persian work of fiction, he believes, has been able to show the loneliness of people as has *The Patient Stone*. Perhaps this critic's most significant observations about the novel concern its technique. In his view, the story consists of three sets of events, with Gowhar, Ahmad Aqa, and Seyf ol-Qalam respectively the centers of the three sets. In all three sets of events, Gowhar is seen as a victim. His analysis, however, seems to break down with his rather obscure diagram consisting of four concentric circles, the first three of which represent the three sets of events and the fourth the myth of creation episode that ends the novel. In expounding on his analysis, he explains that Gowhar is the central "axis" around whom all the characters revolve and who, in turn, revolves around each of the characters, all this in addition to his claim that Gowhar, Ahmad Aqa, and Seyf ol-Qalam are the centers of the three sets of events. His assessment also reveals a shortcoming in that in his consideration of the structure of the novel as a whole, he accounts for neither the drama episodes of the book nor the epic poem, which he suggests could, along with the myth of creation, be omitted without in any way damaging the story. In fact, he attributes Chubak's insertion of the epic poem to the writer's "patriotism," and the inclusion of the myth of creation play to Chubak's desire to see knowledge triumph over religious superstition. Nevertheless, on the whole, Baraheni's observations on the novel concerning its characters, language, and themes are quite useful for an understanding of *The Patient Stone*.

The reception of *The Patient Stone* in Iran, on the whole, has been unfavorable. Among the handful of critics who have praise for the novel in the early years after its publication, there is general disagreement as to its specific merits and shortcomings. One critic, for example, feels that in its use of dialogue and monologue *The Patient Stone* is a masterpiece, the best Persian novel ever written; however, this same critic suggests that the novel would have been an even better work without the excerpt from Ferdowsi's *Shahnameh* [Book of Kings] and the drama episodes of the book. Another critic says of *The Patient Stone*:

> At times it is so enrapturing, being unmatched in the fiction writing of the last thirty years. And at times it is so weak that he [Chubak] makes the writer of weekly magazines look good by comparison.[9]

The Patient Stone, then, seems to have challenged the values of and sparked varied reactions from different individuals. One condemns it for its lack of political "commitment," another for its ridicule of religion; another is offended by its language, while another objects to its satirical treatment of Iranian history. Yet even for those who do not utilize extra-literary judgments in critiquing *The Patient Stone*, the novel's break with established literary conventions in Persian fiction becomes a disturbing factor.

With the exception of Reza Baraheni, for the most part early commentators on *The Patient Stone* addressed their criticism to finding fault with the novel (a seemingly prevalent Iranian approach to literary criticism). For this reason, little attention has been paid to a critical treatment of the novel as it is, not as it should have been. In fact, some critics actually seem to be carrying on a quarrel with the text rather than attempting either to understand or explain it.[10]

What seems to have been generally overlooked in critical appraisals of *The Patient Stone* is the consideration of this work in light of the fact that a novel must, by definition, be "novel." Indeed, this concern for novelty is a preoccupation of Ahmad Aqa, the schoolteacher and would-be writer in *The Patient Stone*, in the opening pages of the book, as he ponders over what he should write about, considering that everything he would like to concern himself with has already been written. He muses: "The world isn't lacking anything anymore. You won't find anything new in it. Everything's either old or at least second hand."[11] Assuming that Ahmad Aqa verbalizes a concern of all novelists, including his creator, what then can a writer offer to such a world? Perhaps Chubak with *The Patient Stone* offers a new way to look at old issues, a new way of looking at the reality of life.

Even though by no means exhaustive in scope, in the following analysis I will focus on an examination of *The Patient Stone* primarily from a literary viewpoint, but also take into consideration the literary and social atmosphere influencing its creation as well as its reception in Iran. Hence, in the first part, I will examine the novel from a technical viewpoint in the light of the stream of consciousness novel, comparing Chubak's use of various techniques to that in a number of other works of this genre. This is followed by an interpretive look at *The Patient Stone* considering the novel's symbolism and themes, with an examination of the main characters of the work.

II

No one in the last quarter-century has challenged E. M. Forster's view that the common denominator of all novels is that they tell a story, even given the experimental fiction of Samuel Beckett, Alain Robbe-Grillet, and Italo Calvino, among others.[12] Sadeq Chubak's *The Patient Stone* is no exception, although opinions might very well differ on exactly what its story is. In fact, if one were to ask the question at random of persons having read Chubak's novel, at least three obvious responses might be rendered: *The Patient Stone* tells the story of a series of murders in the city of Shiraz; it depicts the miserable life of a young girl driven to prostitution, then murdered, and the effects of her disappearance on the lives of several people around; and, *The Patient Stone* is the psychological study of a young schoolteacher with dreams of becoming a writer. To choose any of these or similar statements as an accurate summation of the story of *The Patient Stone* would prove incomplete and unsatisfactory. One would even be hesitant to conclude that a combination of the various statements about the story could accurately describe the novel. However, the question of what story the novel recounts is only one of many that can be asked. A second, equally vital question, one that concerns the novel's ontological nature, the "novelness" of the novel, is: How is the story told? While the common denominator of all novels may be their storytelling function, by far the most distinguishing feature of every novel is its technique. Let us look at *The Patient Stone* from this perspective.

The story of *The Patient Stone* is told as the mental impressions, reactions, and reflections of five characters, four of whom are tenants in the same house: Ahmad Aqa, a poor, young schoolteacher, the only educated member of the household; Belqeys, the ugly wife of an impotent opium addict; Kakolzari, the young child of a woman, Gowhar, who has recently disappeared; Jahansoltan, an old, bedridden, dying servant-woman; and Seyf ol-Qalam (who does not live with the other four), a psychopath who has set upon himself the task of ridding the world of venereal disease by killing off prostitutes. The story revolves around the disappearance of Gowhar and its effects on the lives of the five characters. However, *The Patient Stone* is not a novel of external action, but rather an account of the internal workings of the minds of those five characters in the course of a few days. For this reason, Iranian critics of the work have often mentioned such novels as William Faulkner's *As I Lay Dying* and *The Sound and the Fury* and James Joyce's *Ulysses* and pointed out that Chubak's novel shares certain characteristics with them, in particular the "technique" of stream of consciousness. Unfortunately, however, adequate attention has been paid neither to a clear definition of the term "stream of consciousness" as it applies to this novel, nor to a comparison of *The Patient Stone* with other similar novels from a technical viewpoint.[13] In the following part, therefore, I will examine *The Patient Stone* in light of: the general characteristics of the stream of consciousness novel, the general techniques it employs to represent the flow of consciousness, the conventions used to represent the individual consciousnesses of the various characters, and the conventions which provide the novel with its overall design and unity of structure.

III

When William James first used the term stream of thought, or consciousness, he was, of course, concerned with explaining the actual flow of the thought process.[14] But stream of consciousness in terms of literature concerns itself with the production of the "effect" of the actual workings of the mind. As Austin Warren explains:

> If one examines "stream of consciousness" novels, one soon discovers that there is no "real" reproduction of the actual mental processes of the subject, that the stream of consciousness is rather a device of dramatizing the mind.... But there is little that seems scientific or even "realistic" about the device.[15]

What, then, is a stream of consciousness novel? Robert Humphrey believes that a novel in this genre can be identified first of all by its subject matter:

> The novels that are said to use the stream-of-consciousness technique to a considerable degree prove, upon analysis, to be novels which have as their essential subject matter the consciousness of one or more characters.[16]

In effect, rather than having a narrator inform the reader directly about what happens in the consciousness of a character, the text is given the appearance that it is a record of the natural flow of the character's consciousness. In *The Patient Stone* this effect is achieved both through the absence of a narrator and through the use of twenty-six monologues distributed among five characters. Each character's consciousness is presented in separate sections, and the story must be pieced together by readers as they contemplate the reflections of these characters.

Not only does the stream of consciousness novel have as its subject matter the consciousness of its characters, but it has other characteristics as well. For example, Erich Auerbach, considering stream of consciousness and similar techniques as modern approaches to the representation of reality, describes its features:

> These are the characteristic and distinctively new features of the technique: a chance occasion releasing processes of consciousness; a natural and even, if you will, a naturalistic rendering of those processes in their peculiar freedom, which is neither restrained by a purpose nor directed by a specific subject of thought; elaboration of the contrast between "exterior" and "interior" time.[17]

In terms of Auerbach's explanation, general though it may be, does *The Patient Stone* adhere to the features suggested? Auerbach's first feature, "a chance occasion releasing processes of consciousness," is evidenced frequently throughout *The Patient Stone*. In the first monologue by Belqeys, for example, the character's mind wanders from subject to subject: her husband, Gowhar, a holiday excursion, her desire to sleep with Ahmad Aqa. Suddenly, she happens to look outside:

> Day of Resurrection! What a rain, like a horse's tail. If Ahmad Aqa'd just touch me, I'd plop me down like a chicken in heat and spread out. I wish all that water pouring out of the sky'd find the way into my belly. See! See how he's leanin' over into the pool to catch them fish? Brat. I hope to God I see you laid out in a patch of ground. He's about to fall in the pool and there ain't nobody in the house to pull him out neither. The world will be rid of him. None of my business. I hope to God he falls in the pool.[18]

Her chance glance outside brings the rain into focus and shifts her train of thought to her sexual desires, the rain symbolically linked to the "water" she would like to fill her belly. And once again a shift of thought occurs upon the chance stimulus of seeing the child Kakolzari playing beside the pool. Her thoughts are re-channeled from her sexual desires to her contempt for the child. This excerpt from the novel serves also to illustrate Auerbach's second feature marking a stream of consciousness work, "a natural ... rendering of those processes [of consciousness] in their peculiar freedom, which is neither restrained by a purpose nor directed by a specific subject of thought." On the surface, there is no apparent coherence of subject matter; that is, there are no apparent connections between the rain, Belqeys' sexual desires, and her hatred for the child, although both thematically and symbolically the reader will find relationships on a deeper level in the context of the story as a whole.

The third feature in Auerbach's explanation, "elaboration of the contrast between 'exterior' and 'interior' time," is also found throughout the novel, but particularly in the sections devoted to Ahmad Aqa. As an illustration, in Ahmad Aqa's second monologue, he recalls having seen Seyf ol-Qalam, who was preoccupied with urging Ahmad Aqa to read "the book of Rasputin." Ahmad Aqa reflects on the Indian's neat appearance, which leads him to contrast his own shabby appearance, then to wander outside the boundaries of time to a timeless state, interior time, in which he pictures Stone Age society, social behavior, and feelings, in a sense the common fate of mankind. But once again he returns to the exterior time of the novel and continues his thoughts on Seyf ol-Qalam and his chance meeting with the man that day. Parenthetically, it is noteworthy that a direct shift of tenses occurs as Ahmad Aqa considers human history and Stone Age man. Whereas his first reflections on Seyf ol-Qalam occur in the past tense, his thoughts on caveman society suddenly jump into the present tense. And when he begins again the thoughts on Seyf ol-Qalam, there is a noticeable shift of tenses, from past to present, from present to past.[19]

The Patient Stone seems thus to belong to the genre of the stream of consciousness novel. But in that genre there are novels employing entirely different methods or techniques that are often quite dissimilar. Each, in a sense, generates its own techniques, as does *The Patient Stone*. The different techniques used in the stream of consciousness novel have been analyzed by various critics, among them Robert Humphrey in *Stream of Consciousness in the Modern Novel*, Leon Edel in *The Modern Psychological Novel*, and Melvin Friedman in his *Stream of Consciousness: A Study in Literary Method*.[20] Although Friedman and Edel describe and identify various aspects of technique and devices used by stream of consciousness novelists, Robert Humphrey's basic classification and general identification of these methods and devices are most clearly delineated, and will, therefore, serve as the basis of this discussion.

Humphrey sees four basic techniques: direct interior monologue, indirect interior monologue, omniscient description, and soliloquy. In general, he defines interior monologue as "the technique used in fiction for representing the psychic content and processes of character, partly or entirely unuttered, just as these processes exist at various levels of conscious control before they are formulated for deliberate speech."[21]

He then sets up a distinction between "direct" and "indirect" interior monologue. The former presents consciousness rendered "directly to the reader with negligible author interference,"[22] and with no listener in mind, the purpose being to reveal psychic identity. The latter uses an omniscient narrator who presents the consciousness of another as though it came directly from the mind of the character, but with guiding commentary and descriptions. "It differs from direct interior monologue," Humphrey says, "basically in that the author intervenes between the character's psyche and the reader."[23] Another technique, omniscient description, he explains, is a conventional mode, and when used in stream of consciousness novels it involves representing "psychic content and processes of a character" through the descriptive narration of an omniscient author.[24] The last method he describes of those used in representing consciousness, soliloquy, assumes the presence of an audience (the reader), thus this method exhibits a greater coherence than interior monologue. Its function appears to be the communication of emotions and thoughts related to the action and plot of the story to the reader. Consequently it is less candid than interior monologue. Soliloquy is not literally spoken, but could be. It is organized, coherent, an interiorized discussion or debate. It uses complete sentences rather than phrases or isolated clauses.[25]

In light of Humphrey's classification, two of these techniques, indirect interior monologue and omniscient description, can be disregarded as concerns *The Patient Stone* since both presuppose the presence of the author in the form of a narrator in the text. The other two techniques, however, do apply to Chubak's novel, and often alternate within any given section of the book. *The Patient Stone* may be described as a collection of the soliloquies of five characters. Because of the general coherence of the consciousnesses portrayed, the reader is able to follow the external events, that is, the plot and action of the story. Thus the classification of soliloquy, which is considered the more coherent of the two techniques, is most applicable to the greatest part of the novel. However, lapses into direct interior monologue, which are less revealing of action, thoughts, or emotions, but which reveal, rather, the psychic nature of the characters, do occur within the soliloquies of each of the characters, to greater or lesser degrees. A few examples below illustrate the use of the two techniques in *The Patient Stone*.

Perhaps the clearest examples of soliloquy are found in the sections devoted to Ahmad Aqa, who generally philosophizes about history, social problems, existential questions, his desire to write, and the girl, Gowhar, who has disappeared:

> At one time I thought about becoming a writer. I thought about writing some things about Gowhar's life and about these few tenants who live with me in this house. I wanted to write about the life of Gowhar. She's like the ewer of New Mosque's outhouse. Whoever needs to go badly grabs it, fills it up with water, takes it to the outhouse, and when he finishes his job, abandons it in the corner of the outhouse. In the end, I'll write it. But for now, just let the quakes finish. Eventually I'll do something. Now, I don't feel like working. Now, I want to escape the earthquakes.[26]

The marked coherence of this passage suggests that Ahmad Aqa could just as easily have been speaking to someone else, to the reader, to another character, rather than to himself, so to speak. The passage provides the reader with insight into the external events of the story, some information about Ahmad Aqa's aspirations and attitudes, about Gowhar's situation, even about the location of the story. The level of consciousness represented is that close to the surface, a feature that, according to Humphrey, characterizes the technique of soliloquy.[27] In its use of soliloquy, *The Patient Stone* shows some similarity with William Faulkner's *As I Lay Dying* in that in Faulkner's novel the plot unfolds through the soliloquies of fifteen characters. In other words, each soliloquy contributes to the development of the action of the story. If one were to consider the monologues of all the characters in *The Patient Stone*, with the exception of those of Ahmad Aqa, a striking technical similarity would exist between the two novels, since in *The Patient Stone*, too, the plot unfolds through the soliloquies of its characters. However, with the addition of Ahmad Aqa and his concerns that extend far beyond the time and space of the external events of the novel, the similarity ends.

A second technique utilized by Chubak for the representation of consciousness in the novel is that of direct interior monologue. Although employed throughout the novel, the technique is perhaps best illustrated in the sections devoted to Jahansoltan, especially as she approaches death. In the passage below, she imagines having seen the angels Nakir and Monkar who appear to question the newly dead, and much of her life flashes before her as her mind weaves in and out of dreams, fantasies, and flashes of "reality":

> I'm a Moslem. The maggots took it out. Ow, ow, it's so heavy. Long and skinny and dark, with a ton of dirt on my chest. Come take me, I'm alive. I ain't dead, I can hear your voices. Soon as I lifted up my head to come out of the grave, my head hit the headstone in the grave and I got knocked out and fell down from upstairs and seen the maggots putting on all kind of makeup going to the bridal chamber, to Haji; and Akbar Aqa's waiting for me in the bridal chamber, so the maggots brings me in the bridal chamber. Blood spouting out of his nose like out of the ewer spout. Hey, run off, get away, they brung a bastard in the shrine. The maggots run. Ow, I'm gonna say it now, it's on the tip of my tongue.[28]

The main purpose of this passage, as its incoherence suggests, is not to communicate an idea by the character, who is alone just seconds before her death, but rather to provide insight into the workings of the dying woman's mind, to suggest the fear and urgency that possess her thoughts in the grip of death. Ideas interrupt, cut across one another, depicting a consciousness flowing from subject to subject. There is no attempt to adhere to the reader's expectations, no clear explanation of what many of the images that come to Jahansoltan's mind signify, although in the context of the entire novel the reader is prepared to speculate. In addition, lack of communicative purpose is suggested by the constant changes of tense, from present to past and back again, as her thoughts dictate. And finally, the private nature of the disordered consciousness of Jahansoltan does not contribute directly to the external events, the action, of the novel. All this is notably different from the ordered flow and purpose of the contrasting passage quoted from Ahmad Aqa.

The disordered nature of Jahansoltan's consciousness, as seen in the passage just cited, has an evident similarity to that of Quentin, preoccupied with disturbing thoughts of suicide and incest, in Faulkner's *The Sound and the Fury*, and to the wandering thoughts of Molly Bloom as she falls asleep at the end of Joyce's *Ulysses*. As in Jahansoltan's case, the thoughts of Quentin and Molly Bloom in these passages do not affect the external events of their respective stories.

The identification of passages thus cited from *The Patient Stone* should not suggest that the entire novel is clearly delineated as sections of soliloquy and those of direct interior monologue. Rather, in general, snatches of direct interior monologue suddenly intervene in the coherent flow of soliloquy with no ample warning to the reader, as occurs, for example, in the passage below from Ahmad Aqa, who has been called to Seyf ol-Qalam's house to identify the body of Gowhar. He is reminded that he had not been sincere and truthful about his feelings for the dead woman, and, in a sense, begins to justify himself:

> I grew up with lies. I was conceived in lies. My dad always lied to my mom, and some of his lies were so childish that even I, as a kid, knew it. Do you still say we've got to be truthful? Kahzad and Qamartaj. Doctor Vakil of Lab-e Ab District. Robab sold the furnishings to Miyur the Jew. With her husband and the Indian Doctor, they went to Sa'di. Sheykh Mahmud finally found a way to make a living for both himself and her. Oh, what those corpses looked like! Full of pus and blood, stink and shit, welded together, shrivelled skin. Robab. On Straw-mat Weaver's Hill, Gholam-Hoseyn's secondhand shop. Miyur the Jew. The price of the clothes all together, eleven tomans and four hezars. Seyyed Mohammad Ali, twenty-six-year-old son of Haji Seyyed Abd ol-Mottaleb, born in India. Zangi water. Doctor Vakil Saheb Seyf ol-Qalam.[29]

The passage is a continuation of an ordered flow of rational thought when it is suddenly broken by a distorted series of names and references, direct interior monologue, which seem to rush forth from the recesses of Ahmad Aqa's mind, disturbing the coherence of his soliloquy. In general, direct interior monologue seems to be brought on in *The Patient Stone* by the character's inability to cope with a particularly gripping experience. In Ahmad Aqa's case here, for instance, he is horrified by the decomposed bodies he has seen, especially that of Gowhar. And in the passage cited from Jahansoltan, death is the overpowering experience she faces.

The use of direct interior monologue in *The Patient Stone* to signify a character's confrontation with an overpowering experience is in sharp contrast to Joyce's use of the technique in the Molly Bloom passage referred to earlier, since she is merely falling asleep. On the other hand, there exists a degree of similarity in the use of the technique in *The Patient Stone* and its use in Quentin's passage in *The Sound and the Fury* as he is faced with overpowering thoughts.

Basically, then, following Humphrey's classification, two major techniques, soliloquy and direct interior monologue are used to present the consciousnesses of the characters in *The Patient Stone*. And although the passages quoted above were selected to illustrate most clearly the use of these techniques in the novel, there is often no clear-cut distinction between the two as they are used in the book. Indeed, one could say that they at times seem to be blended together. And although these techniques may share certain similarities as they are used in *The Patient Stone* and other stream of consciousness novels, the different uses to which those techniques are put definitely separates the novels.

IV

The consciousness of one person is, because of its private nature, understandably alien to someone else. One cannot assume that the consciousness of another would be clearly understood, even if it could be recorded. In stream of consciousness fiction, when novelists intend to give the appearance of having recorded a character's consciousness, they must retain the aspect of strangeness, alienness, foreignness, of that character's consciousness if it is to be at all believable. However, if this aspect were to be completely and accurately presented, the reader would find it all but impossible to decipher a story. If it is true that every novel tells a story, it must be possible for the reader to decode it, to comprehend it. Given this situation, a conflict seems to exist between two tasks facing the writer of a stream of consciousness novel: to depict consciousness as uniquely individual and hence potentially indecipherable and to present a story that will be understood by the reader. Seemingly, the only way in which this conflict can be resolved is through a set of consistent techniques or conventions to which the writer adheres and which the reader can identify. In other words, there must be a "contract" between the two.[30] In the stream of consciousness novel, these consistent conventions are particularly important given the fact that this genre does not follow traditional narrative techniques in storytelling.

In *The Patient Stone*, these conventions serve chiefly two purposes. Those in the first category are employed to represent the consciousnesses of individual characters. They include: free association, typographical devices, dramatic form, the use of allusions, and speech styles. These conventions, it must be stressed, are used to render individual consciousnesses, not to make those consciousnesses necessarily comprehensible to the reader. This goal is accomplished by the conventions, not by consistent employment of various conventions, not by their mere use, so that the particular qualities of each character's psyche emerge through a kind of repetition. The second category of conventions unifies the story and includes: Gowhar as a symbol, external and internal plots, and themes. These conventions have no function related to the representation of consciousness, but rather serve to bring together various elements of the novel to communicate a story.

The most important convention in fiction for controlling the movement of stream of consciousness is the use of the principles of free association.[31] Free association suggests the movement from one thought to another, one word, thought, or image triggering another subsequent word, thought, or image. An example of this convention can be drawn from the consciousness of Kakolzari, the child, whose relative innocence allows for a less complex psyche, one less influenced by abstract thought than those of the other characters:

> I'm the wandering nightingale, wandering over hill and dale; my cruel papa slayed me, my mean stepmama ate me, and my kind sister washed my bones seven times wif rose cologne, and buried them under the roses. And I turned into a nightingale and flied up in the tree. But I don't got no sister. Don't got no brother neither. I'm alone. All alone. Oh, boy! So many fishes in the pool. One, two, free, four, five, six, seven, eight, nine, ten, eleven, twenty, firty-ten, hundred of them, fousand of them.[32]

The opening lines of the monologue (I'm ... under the roses) consist of the lines of a well-known nursery rhyme that the child has apparently committed to memory. These lines trigger his imagination, which carries him into the fantasy in which he has become a nightingale. But he instantly returns, though still under the influence of the nursery rhyme, to the "reality" that he has no sister in contrast to the character in the rhyme, possibly the word sister initiating the thought also of his having no brother. This reality is summed up in his reflection that he is alone, which reminds him, by contrast, of all the fish near him in the pool, and he almost perfunctorily begins to count them. The simple nature of Kakolzari's mind facilitates the reader's understanding of its free association quite clearly. His mind travels in the realm of the concrete; even the fairy tale world seems real to him. However, the more complex the characters become, the more abstract their thoughts are; thus their free associations become more complex to reflect the multilateral nature of their thoughts. And, understandably, the more difficult the task becomes of explaining the connections among their free associations. Although a somewhat more complex character than Kakolzari, Seyf ol-Qalam displays a pattern of free association that is also rather simple. But this simplicity is the result of Seyf ol-Qalam's totally obsessed mind. His every thought and every move seem calculated, channeled toward the completion of his "mission" to rid the world of all the poor and all the prostitutes. Any passage taken randomly from Seyf ol-Qalam's only monologue would serve to illustrate his total preoccupation with this "mission." Whether he recounts or plans the day's events,[33] talks with a constable on the street,[34] or "speaks" with God,[35] his thoughts are directly linked with his obsession. His "mission" seems to be his sole purpose in life.

Similar to Seyf ol-Qalam in her obsessed mind, although her obsession is nowhere as complete as Seyf ol-Qalam's, is Belqeys, who has primarily one preoccupation, her sexual desires. Although she does reflect on different people around her and on various events, almost all her thoughts are tinted with her sexual obsession. In the passage from Belqeys quoted earlier,[36] for example, even the rain brings forth sexual thoughts, which, when they are explicit, generally include Ahmad Aqa as the object of focus. She confesses that she would "plop down" and "spread out" readily if Ahmad Aqa would merely touch her. As a sexual image, the rain then becomes the symbolic "water" she wishes would enter her body. Jahansoltan is a more complex character than either Belqeys or Seyf ol-Qalam in that she has concerns which extend beyond her own immediate wants and needs, in addition to the anxiety she displays in response to the knowledge that she is rapidly deteriorating, mentally and physically, yet powerless to control her own destiny. While her body lies motionless in the corner of the stable, her mind constantly jumps from one subject to another. In the following passage, for instance, after recollections about the birth of Kakolzari, Jahansoltan curses Haji Esma'il, the father who has cast off his wife and child:

> I hope to God your tongue gets writhing with maggots, what you gonna answer to God tomorrow? God help me. Gowhar deserved better. I told Sheykh Mahmud, "now that I'm lame and can't do bending and bowing, what about my prayers?" He says, "Just as you're laying down,

> do the bending and bowing gestures with your eyes and eyebrows." Girl, what are you staying out of the house at night so folks start talking about you, and your child's chirping all around like a motherless chick? Makes your heart ache for him. Don't you ask yourself, What's happening to poor Kakolzari and Jahansoltan in this dump of a house? As for that soldier's slut, Belqeys, she wouldn't even piss to save a cut hand.[37]

With her thoughts about Haji Esma'il, who has caused the misfortunes of Gowhar, Kakolzari, and herself, she begins to think of her own infirmity, because of which she is unable to do her prayers. And once again thoughts of Gowhar and Kakolzari come to her mind. Finally, she is reminded of Belqeys, who, in contrast to Gowhar, refuses to help her. Jahansoltan's stream of consciousness consists primarily of the repetition of her thoughts on a rather limited number of subjects. For the most part, she is preoccupied with her physical condition, her concern for Gowhar and Kakolzari, reveries of the past, religion, and her impending death. As she approaches death, these thoughts rush through her mind at a seemingly increased speed, till finally the flow of her thought with its rapid change of subjects becomes almost incoherent.

With Ahmad Aqa, whose mind for the most part follows a logical train of thought, the task of explaining the connections among and patterns of his free associations might, at first glance, appear rather simple. Ultimately, however, this task proves more problematic with Ahmad Aqa than it does with all the other characters. In the passage quoted above from Ahmad Aqa illustrating the blending of soliloquy and direct interior monologue,[38] for example, the character recollects certain aspects of the scene he has witnessed. Various names, events, and details, all seemingly related in some way, come to his mind. But at the same time many are unknown to the reader. Certain facts about Seyf ol-Qalam may be identified, but a series of names and references to events that do not yield positive identification by the reader are interspersed throughout the passage. Identification of the connections between thoughts, therefore, becomes more elusive. In addition, with Ahmad Aqa, although his monologues are often more coherent than those of the others (he seems to rationalize more than do most of the other characters), the many abstract forces which play a role in his thoughts, perhaps because of his education, require of the reader knowledge and understanding outside the boundaries of the story. The passage below, for example, records part of Ahmad Aqa's train of thought during the act of sexual intercourse with Belqeys:

> Don't you know, this is the act that, in addition to making offspring, has created all kinds of art, music, poetry, and literature? This is the very act that every bastard who's come along has, right off, set up rules for, to the extent that it's become like going to the outhouse, it's got to be done secretly, brushed under the carpet, with fear and anxiety. And here you are, one who's got heaven between your legs, and you don't even know it. You poor thing, if you'd been born in Arabia, they'd have buried you alive because a woman wasn't even worth a mangy camel. But, don't you ever forget that in that same day and age the monarchs of this country were Purandokht and Azarmidokht, and no one ever buried their daughters alive.[39]

Not even during this physical act do Ahmad Aqa's thoughts remain in the realm of the concrete. His mind begins to wander into the realm of abstraction. He does not relate to the act of sex he is engaged in; the sexual act represents for him, rather, an artistic catalyst and a social phenomenon. Even the woman with whom he shares this physical moment evokes an abstraction, as she calls to his mind the place of women in social and historical contexts.

The patterns of free association of the five characters in *The Patient Stone* are generated, in every case, by the individual concerns of each character. It is the repetition of those particular concerns that distinguishes one character from another, making it relatively easy for the reader to identify a given passage from the novel as belonging, for example, to either Belqeys or Kakolzari.

The use of typographical devices is of particular interest in *The Patient Stone*. Indeed, a glance at the novel reveals that the reader can expect to be influenced by more than mere words. Perhaps the most immediately noticeable typographical device is the use of italics interspersed in the various passages.[40] But these devices also include the absence of punctuation and the use of parentheses. Italics appear in the monologues of all the characters in *The Patient Stone* with the exception of those of Kakolzari, and are most prevalent in the sections devoted to Ahmad Aqa. In general, they serve to warn the reader that another narrative voice has been introduced. These voices generally share the speech styles of the various characters and thus might well be thought of as "second selves." Italics have also been used in the stage directions of the dramatic segments of the novel; but since the plays are not meant for stage production, it would be reasonable to regard the directions in italics as the "voice" of the playwright, Ahmad Aqa, which is different from that of the personae of the dramas. For Ahmad Aqa, the "voices" might be said to be for the most part, those of his "other self" or double or of A-Seyyed Maluch the spider, although in one instance the "voice" apparently belongs to Gowhar.[41] These additional voices serve to contradict the character's train of thought at the time, either adding a new dimension to the ideas being contemplated, or else signifying a degree of self-consciousness in the character, thus setting up what might be termed an "internal dialogue" between the "self" and the "other."[42] Early in the novel, for instance, after several pages of internal argument, the "double" suggests that since Ahmad Aqa is so unhappy, he might as well commit suicide. Whereupon, Ahmad Aqa finds reasons to live:

> For me, life is still well worth seeing. I'm just twenty-five. I should at least live to come to know the people. It's not right for me to enter like a jackass and exit like a cow. I should stay to find out what's at the bottom of all this.[43]

The response of the voice reflects the opposite point of view: "*The bottom of all this can never be found. It's all suffering and torture, migration and separation. And there's no end to human sorrow.*"[44] And further on, when Ahmad Aqa reveals a sense of nihilism, the voice strikes a positive, optimistic note: "*Why are you always singing despair? You are only twenty-five years old and have a long time yet before you die.*"[45] Even though the voices in Ahmad Aqa generally appear antagonistic throughout the novel, virtually all the voices presented in italics, with the exception of one or two instances, seem to redirect the character's thoughts.[46] A similar conclusion may be drawn concerning the voices that occur in the monologues of other characters. In the only instance of italics occurring in Belqeys' monologues, for example, Belqeys has expressed her fear that Jahansoltan might come back to life and choke her. Whereupon the voice reassures her: "*She couldn't walk even when she was alive, how's she gonna get up and walk now that she's dead.*"[47]

Italics frequently occur in the monologues of both Jahansoltan and Seyf ol-Qalam. At times Jahansoltan's "voice" functions to correct an error she has made in remembering,[48] to divert her thoughts away from death,[49] or to warn her that she must say her testaments.[50] The inner voice of Seyf ol-Qalam, on the other hand, seems for the most part either to redirect his thoughts,[51] encourage him in his mission,[52] or advise him.[53] However, toward the end of his monologue, the voice appears in the middle of his dialogue with the prostitute he is preparing to poison, and here it becomes almost one with his own voice, seeming to function as silent "speech" that he does not wish his companion to hear. A similar phenomenon occurs once in a monologue of Ahmad Aqa's, when in his dramatic recreation of his argument with Sheykh Mahmud, the voice represented in italics appears to be Ahmad Aqa's own rather than that of his double or of A-Seyyed Maluch. In a "silent speech," he reprimands Gowhar for having become the concubine of Seyf ol-Qalam.[54]

Other writers of stream of consciousness novels have used italics in their fiction, most notably Faulkner in *The*

Sound and the Fury.[55] In Faulkner, italics are also used as a kind of signal to the reader; however, in *The Sound and the Fury* the change of print usually indicates either a change of time from that of the event being reported or a shift to direct interior monologue.[56] The clearest examples are found in the monologues of Benjy and Quentin.

A second typographical device used in *The Patient Stone* is the absence of punctuation in several passages of the novel. Although the introduction of punctuation marks is relatively new in Persian script, Chubak employs them rather consistently throughout *The Patient Stone*. This consistent and careful use of punctuation in the novel calls to attention four instances in which there is a marked absence of punctuation. In all four instances, the passages parody a particular style of writing or speech and are not intended as carriers of meaning as much as they are representations of mere verbiage. In two instances, the passages reflect a religious justification for the institution of temporary marriage;[57] in one, an explanation of a Shi'ite practice;[58] and in another, the passage imitates the pompous style of older writers of "modest prose."[59] The absence of punctuation in the works of Faulkner and Joyce, in contrast, usually marks the writer's attempt to illustrate the unbroken flow of the character's thoughts, or as Melvin Friedman suggests, it may indicate "a level of awareness considerably removed from consciousness."[60] And as it is an unusual phenomenon in English script, the English reader's attention is immediately drawn to such passages as representing something uncommon. Chubak's use of this device in Persian print, however, is much in keeping with the conventions of older forms of Persian writing. Therefore, the absence of punctuation for a Persian reader carries quite different connotations, and suggests an archaic quality not only in form but also in content.

In several instances in the monologues of Ahmad Aqa, Chubak employs another typographical device, parentheses, generally when the character appears to be practicing the art of writing. The parenthetical remarks tend to show a shift in narrative voice, containing satirical remarks that seem to serve a purpose similar to the so-called dramatic "comic relief."[61] Parentheses are also used by another stream of consciousness writer, Virginia Woolf, but for quite a different purpose. Woolf generally uses parentheses to indicate a subtle shift of the level of consciousness represented, as Robert Humphrey suggests.[62]

Another convention used in the presentation of the consciousness of one character, Ahmad Aqa, in *The Patient Stone* is the representation of thought in terms of a dramatic dialogue. In several instances, Ahmad Aqa's thoughts are externalized in the form of personified entities: historical or mythological figures, people he knows, even animate and inanimate objects.

Persian commentators on the novel have often criticized *The Patient Stone* for these dramatic presentations and have generally treated these segments without considering that these so-called dramas occur within the monologues of Ahmad Aqa, a would-be writer, and are not separate entities in the book.[63] When considered in the context of Ahmad Aqa's monologues, these dramas provide the reader with a means to better understand his character.

The use of dramatic form in the stream of consciousness novel is rare, a notable instance of it occurring in the fifteenth chapter of Joyce's *Ulysses*, where, as Humphrey observes, the mind of Stephen and Bloom are represented in an objectified fashion.[64] On the surface, there are similarities between some of the dramatic presentations in *The Patient Stone* and that of Joyce's novel (e.g., the personification of inanimate objects and stage directions), but on the whole, both the context and the purpose of this technique as employed in the two novels differ. One immediately recognizable difference between the episode from Joyce and the dramas in Chubak's novel is that the latter dramas are the representations of the externalized consciousness of only one character, Ahmad Aqa, rather than the interaction between the represented consciousnesses of two characters. Furthermore, in contrast to the rather chaotic, confusing, and hallucinatory nature of Joyce's episode, the dramas that appear in *The Patient Stone* are, for the most part, coherent, intelligible units which either provide the reader with a clearer understanding of actual events or give insight into the mind of

Ahmad Aqa in regard to his views on various historical, cultural, religious, and theological matters.

Allusion is another device used in *The Patient Stone*. Informed readers will find the book rich in its use of allusions of many varieties, among them cultural, historical, religious, mythological, and literary. The most recognizable of them are probably the references to the stories of Imam Reza and the Deer;[65] Anushirvan and the Chain of Justice;[66] and Ya'qub Leys and the Bread, Onions, and Sword.[67] There are also many lines quoted from famous poets, found mainly in the monologues of Ahmad Aqa, and there is an entire chapter which contains a segment of Ferdowsi's *Book of Kings*.[68] But there are also more obscure allusions which only a careful reader could identify. An example of such an allusion is found in Ahmad Aqa's recollection of how he pleaded with Gowhar to spend the night with him:

> I'd like you to quietly open the door of my room one night and come in; and I'd be asleep and wake up to the sound of your breath telling me, "I've come"; and you'd slip into my bed.[69]

Ahmad Aqa's frequent mention of the poet Hafez and quotations from his poetry justify the reader's recognizing in his plea an allusion to Hafez's famous lines:

> Yesternight she came, sat by my bedside,
> Bringing her face close to my ear with a sad singing voice,
> She murmured, "Oh, long time lover mine, are you asleep?"[70]

In effect, Ahmad Aqa seems to identify Gowhar as the ideal beloved of Hafez's poem. The use of allusion has a significant function in *The Patient Stone* not only in that the allusions contained in the story signal that the work is the product of the Iranian experience, but also, and perhaps more importantly, in that they provide greater insight into the consciousnesses of the characters in the novel. In Ahmad Aqa, for example, allusions reveal particularly the character's knowledge of and concern about history and literature. In Jahansoltan, whose mind may be considered an encyclopedia of Iranian folk and religious lore, and Belqeys, who recounts popular vulgar rhymes, on the other hand, they indicate something of their social class and individual psyches.

Still another convention that gives insight into the particular characters in *The Patient Stone* is that of speech styles varied according to the character portrayed. In other words, the use of language in the representation of the consciousness of each character distinguishes the individuality of each. Four of the five characters, Belqeys, Jahansoltan, Kakolzari, and Seyf ol-Qalam, have singularly distinct language patterns, each with his or her own idiolect: individual idioms, expressions, syntax, and pronunciation. The fifth character, Ahmad Aqa, however, is capable of reproducing a variety of individual speech patterns. This ability, in a sense, reflects the multifaceted aspect, the complexity, of his character.[71]

The various conventions discussed thus far have basically one common function, that is, they serve to represent the consciousnesses of the various characters in *The Patient Stone*. But the question arises: Could the representation of the consciousnesses of five characters adequately tell a story, which, as was noted earlier, is the common denominator of all novels? If the answer is to be in the affirmative, the novel must employ certain conventions that will impose some degree of order on the apparently disordered flow of consciousness.[72] In other words, the novel must contain certain unifying features in order that a story be adequately revealed. In any novel these unifying features are many and varied, often all but inseparable from one another. In *The Patient Stone* as well, they are at times indistinguishable threads that weave the portions of the story together. However, for purposes of the analysis of their function in the novel, they will be more or less arbitrarily, and by no means exhaustively, classified as follows: Gowhar as a symbol, external and internal plots, and themes.

The central female figure of *The Patient Stone*, a symbol around whom the story revolves, is encountered by the reader only in the reflections of other characters in the book, primarily through Ahmad Aqa, but also through Kakolzari, Belqeys, Jahansoltan, and Seyf ol-Qalam. Gowhar, then, is the embodiment of these others' conceptions of her. To Kakolzari she is not only a mother, but also a potential means of gaining a father. "How come all the kids got a daddy and I don't? Come on, go buy me a daddy and come home," he reports having told her.[73] But she is more. She is tied together at times in the child's mind with fairytale elements, with a fantastic white horse, his white horse.[74] To Jahansoltan she is the daughter the old woman could have had and loved but never did have. In addition, she is the realization for Jahansoltan of a poor girl's dream of marrying well, as Gowhar had done with Haji Esma'il, the rich merchant. To Belqeys she is a rival for Ahmad Aqa's attention, her disappearance having provided Belqeys with the opportunity to gain sexual favors from him. But Gowhar is also a living reminder of the beauty that pockmarked Belqeys has never had. To Seyf ol-Qalam, Gowhar is merely one prostitute among many through whose deaths he intends to cleanse the world of poverty and venereal disease. To Ahmad Aqa she is both beggarly prostitute and, in contrast, the personification of the ideal beloved of Hafez's poetry. In fact, she is an embodiment of all womankind—as mother and daughter, wife and mistress, prostitute and beloved—and Ahmad Aqa sets out on a quest to realize this embodiment. He finds her in reality among the corpses, a rotten piece of flesh. But he cannot cope with this reality and so he escapes to the world of imagination, to art, mentally transfiguring Gowhar first into the image of the Virgin Mary (in a Raphael painting), then into the mythological character of Eve/Mashyaneh, the primal woman. Placing Gowhar in the domain of art, Ahmad Aqa can be assured that she will never be corrupted, never decay, never be destroyed.

Gowhar serves not only as a unifying symbol which preoccupies most of the characters in the novel, but also as the most important element in the novel's external plot. There are basically two plots in The Patient Stone, one external and one internal, and the disappearance of Gowhar sets the external plot in motion. The external plot concerns itself primarily with the events relating to the disappearance of

Gowhar, the deaths of Jahansoltan and Kakolzari, and, possibly, the arrest of Gowhar's murderer, Seyf ol-Qalam, by the police. In this plot there is a unity of time and place: the events take place in the course of a few days in the year 1934 in the city of Shiraz. In essence, the external plot concerns itself with the concrete, with individuals and events. On the other hand, the internal plot, revealing the workings of Ahmad Aqa's consciousness, consists of more expansive symbolic concerns and deals with ideas and abstractions with universal implications. Although if taken out of context, this plot appears limited neither by time nor place—historical events are called forth, imagination reaches back to the time of creation, "scenes" take place in Ctesiphon, the Seventh Heaven, all dependent only on what Ahmad Aqa's fancy dictates, when considered in the context of the novel as a unified whole, the picture changes considerably. Boundaries do exist; briefly they are the limitations of the time of the external plot and the inherent limitations of Ahmad Aqa's consciousness. The "clock time" boundaries of the external plot, in the course of a few days, are also the boundaries of the internal plot. In other words, the internal plot consists of the record of Ahmad Aqa's consciousness within the "clock time" of the external plot of the novel. On a technical level, the presence of the epic poem and the several drama episodes in *The Patient Stone* can only be accounted for when they are viewed in the context of the book as a whole, as part of what occupies Ahmad Aqa's thoughts during this time period. If they are not considered as such, the poem and dramas tend to be seen as isolated fragments that have been added with no apparent relationship to the work. In a sense, the shared temporal boundaries between the external and internal plots establish a structural unity. But boundaries and unity of structure alone cannot justify the presence of the poem and the dramas. It is on the level of meaning that the relationships between the various parts of the story are established. In *The Patient Stone* it is primarily the themes that give the story its overall structure and ultimate meaning.

Among the most important themes in *The Patient Stone* are those of loneliness, death, sexuality, and religion. These themes form a network of threads tying together the internal and external plots of the novel. Perhaps the most pervasive of the themes is that of loneliness, as the two couplets that preface the novel and indeed the title itself suggest.[75] Not only is this loneliness shared by all the major characters, many of whom appear in the dramas, and even by the protagonist of the epic poem, but it is reflected in the format of the book as well. The isolated monologues suggest the isolation, loneliness, of every character, as if each were "boxed in" within the “walls" of each section. Another thematic thread running through the novel is the theme of death. Ahmad Aqa, Belqeys, and Seyf ol-Qalam contemplate death at various moments, and Jahansoltan, Kakolzari, and Gowhar, among others, are taken by it. In fact, the question of mortality and death is a major theme in the "myth of creation" episode at the end of the novel, where even the supposedly immortal creator, Zervan, is destroyed. Likewise, sexuality as a theme runs through both the external and internal plots. Ahmad Aqa desires Gowhar sexually and has relations with Belqeys, while Belqeys is preoccupied with her sexual deprivation. Jahansoltan reminisces about sexuality in her youth, Kakolzari is sexually abused by the landlord's children, and Seyf ol-Qalam is obsessed with ridding the world of prostitutes. There are also Gowhar's religiously sanctioned prostitution and the relationships of Mashya, Mashyaneh, Ahriman, and Zervan in the play that ends the novel. Similarly, one can follow other themes in the story, including religious superstition, fatalism, justice, and oppression, among others. Together with the other unifying features, they give the novel its structural design, a design which may be symbolized by the complex, precisely constructed spider web A-Seyyed Maluch describes in detail in the first section of the book.[76]

To sum up, *The Patient Stone* adheres to the general characteristics of the stream of consciousness novel. It is the fictional record of the consciousnesses of five characters. Like all stream of consciousness novelists, Chubak uses certain methods or techniques in order to create the impression that the reader is actually witnessing the flow of a character's thoughts. The primary techniques used in *The Patient Stone* include what have been termed soliloquy and direct interior monologue. In addition, a number of conventions have also been employed in the novel to represent the individual consciousness of each character, including free association, typography, the dramatic extensions of a character's mind, individual speech styles, and allusions. These conventions, in a sense, give an identity to the individual consciousnesses portrayed. But a collection of the recorded consciousnesses of five individuals, even if they were rendered comprehensible by repeated and hence "characteristic" devices, would not necessarily combine to tell a story. The writer, then, has to employ other conventions, unifying conventions, to weave these consciousnesses together in such a way that the reader can glean a story from them. These conventions in *The Patient Stone* include Gowhar as a symbol, the enclosure of the internal plot of the story within the space and time of the external plot, and the interweaving of themes throughout the novel. Novelistic techniques and fictional conventions alone, however, do not make a novel. A novel, as E. M. Forster points out, tells a story. What, then, is the story *The Patient Stone* tells? Ultimately, of course, that question is left to each individual reader to answer. As Leon Edel observes in contrasting the old-time reader with the reader of modern novels:

> The old-time reader of novels sat down with his book and made a simple demand upon the author: "Beguile me, offer me comedy and tears, tell me about droll people and lovers, and a story that will keep me rooted to the spot and my eyes glued to the page." The case is reversed when we come to the subjective novel. It is the author who says to the reader: "Here is the artistic record of a mind, at the very moment that it is thinking. Try to penetrate within it. It is you, not I, who will piece together any 'story' there may be. Of course I have arranged this illusion for you. But it is you who must experience it."[77]

As one "experience" of the story of *The Patient Stone*, what follows is my reading of *The Patient Stone* in view of some of the themes and symbols of the novel as an inquiry into its "meaning."

V

Sadeq Chubak's *The Patient Stone* represents a chaotic world, a world turned upside down. It is a world of appearance versus reality in which its doctor, Seyf ol-Qalam, kills his patients with cyanide instead of healing them; in which Ahmad Aqa, a beggarly, helpless schoolteacher, calls himself the Prophet Solomon; and in which Sheykh Mahmud, a representative of spiritual and religious life, is in actuality a pimp. It is a world in which people are not what their names signify, but often quite the contrary: Gowhar [Jewel or Essence] is in fact a prostitute; Belqeys [the name of the Queen of Sheba] is an ugly, pockmarked washerwoman; Jahansoltan [the Sultan of the World] is a maggot-infested, rotting piece of flesh; Kakolzari [Goldenlock (a fairy tale name)] is the disowned son of a father who considers him a bastard. It is a world whose creator, Zervan, the God of Time and Fate, the ultimate Almighty, is represented as a foul, horned monster; and its Satan, Ahriman, the Lie, is a kindly, enchantingly beautiful, golden-haired fairy. It is a world in which a spider boasts of engineering and a jackass speaks of philosophy. It is a world whose destruction and end come at the beginning and whose creation and beginning at the end. But the world of *The Patient Stone* is not a "real" world; it is a fictional one. And as such, everything contained in that text is potentially meaningful, even chaos. *The Patient Stone*, in fact, is a multifaceted text, one open to many and varied interpretations, no one of which can be authoritatively declared the ultimate meaning, as it were. As a preliminary interpretation of Chubak's novel, therefore, in this segment I will discuss several significant aspects of this work, including: the earthquake as a symbol; the epic versus the modern world as concerns *The Patient Stone*; the characters, in light of the themes of loneliness and the impossibility of communication; the legend of "The Patient Stone" as it applies to Chubak's novel; and Ahmad Aqa's myth of creation at the end of the story as a reflection of the chaos and decay of the modern world.

One of the possible approaches to an interpretation of *The Patient Stone* might be found in Chubak's own remarks about his novel:

> *The Patient Stone*, ...like a poem, has an opening key. The symbols must be recognized; one must be aware of the past. The past, time, place, and atmosphere must be taken into account. There is a knot lying in every page. The opening key lies in the turns of these symbols, these knots.[78]

Perhaps an "opening key" can be found in the opening line of the novel: "Now, of all things, we've got earthquakes."[79] Ahmad Aqa's attention is first drawn to the immediate effects of the earthquakes around him, to the shaking of doors, walls, ceilings, and the water in the pool. But soon his vision expands and he pictures the whole earth, alluding to the myth that a Bull supports the earth on its horns: "It's like the Bull's gotten tired, so it tosses the earth from one horn to the other."[80] Facts and fiction become confused and Ahmad Aqa begins to theorize about the beginning of the world:

> Since the world began, there've been earthquakes.... Once in place of all these mountains and hills that stretch up to the sky there were valleys and seas. Earthquakes scrambled up the heart and guts of the earth so much that the bottom went up to the top and the top down to the bottom.[81]

At the beginning of the novel, the reader assumes that earthquakes have actually occurred, convinced by Ahmad Aqa's apparent recalling, among other things, a radio broadcast concerning the disaster the quakes have caused in the city. However, as the novel progresses and Ahmad Aqa is evidently preoccupied with the quakes, using them as excuses even for his inability to write, one begins to question his credibility concerning them. Then, when one realizes that no other character in the novel is concerned with earthquakes (almost all merely mention rain, if they refer to natural phenomena at all), one begins to suspect that Ahmad Aqa's earthquakes exist only on a metaphoric level. What, then, are these earthquakes? They can be regarded as Ahmad Aqa's symbol for the destructive and disruptive forces that have created a sense of instability in his world. Directly aware of the chaos and instability of the world in which he lives, Ahmad Aqa, the principal character of the novel, sees this world as beset by constant earthquakes from which he seeks desperately to escape. But his inner voice, his "double," reminds him that escape is impossible. He contemplates escaping from his ruined house to the sanctuary of the tomb of Sa'di, to the mountains, to the desert, but the inner voice reminds him that such attempts are futile, for earthquakes have struck everywhere and will strike anywhere. Ahmad Aqa feels he has been cut from his roots and thrown into space; he has lost all sense of security and wanders aimlessly, one suspended entity among others. His roots in history, art, and tradition have been cut. Thus, Ahmad Aqa rhetorically questions:

> I ask you, didn't this country have anything? Did the Achaemenians, the Parthians, and the Sassanians come from under the bush? No books, no art, no economy, no religion, no army, no stories, no poetry, no buildings, nothing?[82]

And he answers for himself that all has been destroyed by various invasions (earthquakes) and other disasters.[83] For this reason, Ahmad Aqa feels that it is futile to write, as his writings might also be buried under the rubble, as other writings have been. He seems to see the writing of the past as a source of continuity, of established roots, which have been destroyed. When his inner voice urges him to write, to leave something which is a part of himself to posterity, in a sense to continue the chain which would have existed had it not been demolished, Ahmad Aqa senses the loss of the destroyed writings of the past and the inevitability that his own efforts will come to naught. But he does write, and in doing so he rewrites history, a continuous history to help establish his own roots in the world. Ahmad Aqa's awareness of a sense of discontinuity and disconnectedness in himself and those around him sets him on an intellectual but at the same time imaginary quest to discover "What's at the bottom of all this?"[84] Thus, he searches for the source of his disconnectedness in history. He wonders:

> What's happened to human history anyway? What do we know about ourselves? The world and

> mankind so ancient and just six or ten thousand years of bits and pieces of history. How I'd really like to know what Stone Age man was like and how he lived.[85]

In his imagination he recreates Stone Age society, and finds a group of lonely, frightened people. Unsure of the accuracy of the picture he has imagined, he sighs: "Alas, we know nothing of ourselves."[86] Hence, perhaps because he distrusts the accuracy of his own imagination, or perhaps as an escape from the disorder around him, Ahmad Aqa takes refuge for a short time in the ordered world of the epic Book of Kings. This epic world is a stable one. There is no room for unanswered questions. Everyone and everything is at home in that world.[87] Right and wrong are clearly distinguishable. In the epic world of the *Book of Kings*, the good belong to the camp of Ahura Mazda and the bad to that of Ahriman. In the epic world, man has a place in the universe, things are balanced, through the stars the course of future events is calculable. It is for this reason that Rostam Farrokhzad, a commander of the Persian army, reporting on the Arab-Islamic invasion in the seventh century laments "the calamitous day ahead."[88] His lamentation is not simply a mourning for his own death and that of those around him, he is not simply lamenting the defeat of his army; through the stars he foresees the breakdown of the ordered and properly structured universe of which he is a part. He predicts the day when the reign of Ahura Mazda will come to an end and that of Ahriman will begin, when:

> Honor and truth shall be rejected;
> Lies and baseness shall be respected.
> True warriors shall they dismount,
> And the boastful and vain will surmount.
> The fighting gentry shall be cut from the root;
> The artful race will bring forth no fruit.
> This one shall rob that, the other this;
> 'Tween curse and praise they will judge amiss.
> That within will be worse than that shown;
> The heart of their king will be hard as stone.
> The son shall wish his father undone,
> The father shall plot against his son.

A worthless slave as king will be brought;
True greatness and lineage will count for naught.[89]

In effect, he laments the day when the orderly world will be turned upside down. Ahmad Aqa recollects this particular piece of the poem because it points to his world. But although Ahmad Aqa and Rostam Farrokhzad belong to opposite worlds, one orderly and the other chaotic, Ahmad Aqa's sad chanting of the poem echoes the lamentation of the epic hero. There are basic differences between the hero of the *Book of Kings* and Ahmad Aqa, for Rostam Farrokhzad belongs to an age "when the starry sky is the map of all possible paths," as Georg Lukacs observes of the age of the epic. For the epic hero, he explains:

> The world is wide and yet it is like a home, for the fire that burns in the soul is of the same essential nature as the stars; the world and the self, the light and the fire, are sharply distinct, yet they never become permanent strangers to one another.[90]

For Ahmad Aqa, a modern man, on the other hand, the starry sky is not at all "the map of all possible paths"; in fact, there is no map at all. He belongs to an age of uncertainty and doubt. Not only is he unsure of what tomorrow will bring, "I don't know what my own fate will be,"[91] but he is even unsure of who he is: "Perhaps I'm not Ahmad Aqa after all, and I'm someone else."[92] Taking his sense of the decay of the epic world into the past, Ahmad Aqa undercuts Ferdowsi's glorification of the Sassanian king in the *Book of Kings* and portrays the court of Anushirvan in his next monologue skeptically. For Ahmad Aqa, the ordered epic world crumbles: the heroic wars of the king are seen as massacres, and his justice only a facade, as the celebrated legendary Bell of Justice falls upon the ground and proves to be nothing more than a hollow animal hide.

There remains another difference between the world of the epic to which Rostam Farrokhzad belongs and the modern world of Ahmad Aqa. In the epic world, communication is possible. In spite of his seemingly hopeless and desperate situation, Farrokhzad is still able to communicate. He can write both to his brother about his sorrows and to his enemy about his military stand, assured that he will be understood in both cases.[93] He can speak to others of what he reads in the stars, of the imminent disaster he foresees. But Ahmad Aqa, on the other hand, cannot tell others of the earthquakes that have shaken and are shaking his world. In his world, communication is impossible. Neither Ahmad Aqa nor the other characters can speak to one another of their individual fears and sorrows. If and when they do, they are misunderstood. Thus, Ahmad Aqa explains his inability to write: "Writing is such an imperfect art. You can never put the truth down on paper,"[94] because no one would believe it. It is perhaps as an expression of the impossibility of communication that the book is written as a collection of monologues. Instead of speaking to each other, the characters seem only to speak to themselves, as discussed earlier. And it is perhaps to suggest the impossibility of communication that the novel is prefaced with the couplet from Orfi Shirazi:

> Whenever my eyes and those of a kindred soul met,
> We gazed at one another, wept, and passed.

The impossibility of communication creates a world of isolated, lonely individuals. And this loneliness, as the two prefatory couplets suggest, is certainly a major theme of the novel. The book is crowded with people of various kinds. But the characters whom the reader comes to know remain lonely beings, not only when they are by themselves, but also when they are with others. The couplet by Rudaki that prefaces the novel seems to epitomize the theme of loneliness in the novel:

> Lonely with a hundred thousand people,
> Lonely without a hundred thousand people.

The reader has entered into a fictional world in which earthquakes symbolically establish the first premise of the story, that the world—it bears repeating—is turned upside down, shaken from its roots. It is an unstable world with lonely characters who all appear to suffer from a sense of disconnectedness. They are suspended entities, like trees uprooted in an earthquake and tossed into a void. For them, relationships are all but impossible to establish. Each appears to live in the isolation of his or her own self. But each character has insight into why he or she is rejected by others, and each attempts to escape into something which helps alleviate his or her sense of loneliness. Each character also strives to escape the isolation of the self by trying to establish relationships with others, although all their efforts are doomed to failure.[95] Belqeys, for example, remains a solitary figure whether she is by herself in her room or on a holiday excursion she makes on the thirteenth day of the Persian New Year, a day when crowds of people join in feasting and celebration in the open fields, outside the confines of the walls of their houses. On this day, she complains, she had to stand by herself outside a teahouse while her husband spent the day smoking his opium. She longed to participate in the celebrations around her, or at least to join her husband in the teahouse, but she was reprimanded for her wish to come inside as her husband told her it was no place for a woman. She belonged neither to the world of the feasting people around her nor to the world of the men in the teahouse. From almost as far back as she can remember, she has not belonged:

> From the start God hit me on the head and I was born with no luck. I don't even know my right hand from my left yet when my ma drops dead and I catch the pox. Then I always get beat up by my pa's wife, work like a servant, like a jackass, till I get myself stuck with you, pimp, that can't even do nothing.[96]

After having lost her mother, she had been treated as a servant, an outsider, in her father's household. And she has not fared much better in gaining a husband, to whom she has remained a stranger, always separated from him, both symbolically and physically, by the opium brazier. It is as an outsider that Belqeys enviously views the world around her. She is either "on the roof checking out what's going on,"[97] as Jahansoltan observes, or spying on others from her room, as she admits herself. And when she sees others together, and wishes to be part of what she sees, her loneliness becomes more evident to her. When she spies on

Ahmad Aqa sneaking into Gowhar's room one night, for example, she enjoys listening to them for a long time, and wishes she could have seen them together. But in her envy, she admits, "I was feeling sorry for myself."[98] Belqeys is almost totally obsessed with sexual thoughts, for in her lonely and miserable life, these thoughts seem to be the only outlet for her frustration. Sexuality appears to Belqeys to be the one solution to all her problems—as if this desperate woman, who blames her pock-marked face for her being rejected by everyone, could belong to and be united with the rest of humanity through sex alone! Her jealousy of Gowhar lies not merely in the knowledge that Gowhar has Ahmad Aqa's affection and attention while he will not give Belqeys a second look, but also in the awareness that Gowhar constantly has men available to her. She contrasts herself with Gowhar:

> Gowhar keeps bringing them young fellas left and right to ride her, and she sucks the juice out of them like a ripe, juicy pomegranate, and her face getting more like the color of pomegranate blossoms every day; but goddam me, spending my life shoving your piles back in.[99]

She condemns Gowhar for being a prostitute, but admits that she wouldn't mind being one herself. What she seems to fear most is that she will die before being able to enjoy sexual union with a man:

> I'm gonna die in the end and not even one man ain't gonna sleep with me; but that slut Gowhar's got one every night, one every day. I sure would like to be a whore and go to Mordessun District; that's where them drunk soldiers come. It's dark at night so they won't know. Their eyes can't see nothing. Just keep riding me over and over. One goes out, one comes in.[100]

After Jahansoltan's death, out of fear of the dead and fear of being alone, she goes to Ahmad Aqa's room. As he makes sexual advances towards her, she appears to forget, at least momentarily, all her fear and anxiety. But soon after her sexual encounter with Ahmad Aqa, the fear of loneliness returns. She tells him,

"I'm scared to stay in the house alone."[101] But when he pays no attention, she is at a loss to understand why her sexual relationship with the young schoolteacher has not provided the refuge from loneliness she expected. Surprised, she reflects: "Seemed like he didn't know me at all. Like he hadn't done that kind of thing with me at all."[102] Symbolically, the loss of her virginity is the loss of innocence for Belqeys. In her innocence, she expected sexual union to establish for her a bond with others. But the loss of her innocence, symbolized by the loss of her virginity, brings with it awareness that she still has not established a bond with those around her.

Similarly, Kakolzari realizes that he is alone, all alone. Renounced and cast away by his father and abandoned by his mother, he feels he is like the "wandering nightingale, wandering over hill and dale."[103] An unprotected target of Belqeys' hatred, ridiculed and rejected by other children on the street, he is another of the suspended entities of the novel. Like Belqeys, Kakolzari does not "belong." His short life has consisted of a series of rejections beginning with that of the crowd in the Shrine who angrily threw him out when his nose began to bleed, a supposed sign that he is a bastard. Then his father expelled him and his mother from his home in reaction to the "proof" that he is a bastard. Then he was repeatedly sent away from his mother's room, or out of her bed, when "the monsters" came to visit her. After his mother disappeared, he was sexually abused by the children of the landlord, removed from their house, and brought back to the hatred and physical abuse of Belqeys. Finally, he is convinced that no one likes him, not even the fish in the pool, previously his only friends. Belqeys blames her own rejection on her pockmarked face, and although Kakolzari may not fully realize why he is rejected by others, he understands that he is separate from other children and he interprets this separation as the result of his not having a father. In a sense, like Belqeys, Kakolzari is also obsessed, but with the idea of getting a father. He reports having asked his mother to go and buy him a father and has specified: "I don't want no daddy like them that keeps coming and going away all the time. I want a daddy that stays with me."[104] Unlike Belqeys who seeks to escape her loneliness through transitory moments of sexual gratification, Kakolzari, even in his innocence, seeks a more permanent bond, through a family unit consisting of both father and mother. With the family unit comes a kind of stability and order, or so it appears to Kakolzarl. He naturally understands that there is a difference between adult and child, but he can also explain, for example, differences between himself and other children in terms of privileges and how they are related to the family unit:

> I ain't a growed up man yet so my shirts got pockets. Ahmad Aqa's clothes got pockets. Ali Aqa got a lil pocket too. Well, he gots a daddy and a mama, so he gots a pocket.[105]

Throughout the novel, Kakolzari expresses the wish that Ahmad Aqa would be his father. In reality his wish is not fulfilled, but in his final monologue his imagination takes flight (like the wandering nightingale) and he sees himself as the teacher's child:

> Now I'm Ahmad Aqa's kid. I go to sleep in his room at night. I'm gonna wear new pants at New Year like Mirza Asadollah's kid. I'm gonna put shoes on. They gonna dye my hair with henna and I'm gonna put a hat on. They gonna buy me a pretty, pretty sparrow too. And I'm gonna dye its fuzz with henna. I'm gonna chew roasted chick-peas and put it in his mouf.[106]

Jahansoltan's loneliness is evident, if in no other way, in her physical isolation. Confined to her bed in the ruined stable, apart from the rest of the household, the old woman is a prisoner of her own body, its stench like prison bars that keep her from others and others from her. When Ahmad Aqa comes to visit, for example, he is forced to stay so far away that she cannot hear him.[107] Belqeys even refuses to help her, complaining that her smell reaches all the way down the street.[108] Even Kakolzari, who tries to remove the bedpan of excrement from beneath her, is forced to run into the courtyard to escape the smell.[109] Ironically, it is Jahansoltan of all the characters who would be most likely to get up and help others if she had the physical capability; but she does not, and she suffers without much aid. Almost instinctively, Jahansoltan is capable of overcoming the isolation of the self, for despite her condition, she is mentally preoccupied with others more than with her own self. It is through her caring for and kindness toward others that she tries to establish a bond between herself and those around her. But her misfortunes, ironically, again, have come about as the result of this very kindness, since she was kicked down the stairs while trying to protect Gowhar.[110] In the world of *The Patient Stone*, dominated by self-centered characters such as Belqeys and Seyf ol-Qalam, Jahansoltan is out of place, she does not belong. It is perhaps to counteract this feeling of not belonging to this present world that her thoughts travel back to her past, to a better life, when she was capable of caring for Gowhar and her child, when she was part of Haji Esma'il's household. Imagination for Jahansoltan, as for Belqeys and Kakolzari, is a refuge from the harsh reality of her lonely cell. Although her wishes have not been fulfilled in actuality, her imagination provides the opportunity for fulfillment. Through it, she wings her way up to heaven, sits with God smoking a water pipe, and becomes the future bride of one of the angels;[111] and she is able to witness Kakolzari's circumcision under the Golden Rainpipe in the holy city of Karbala.

Perhaps even more marked than all the other characters as an outsider and stranger is Seyf ol-Qalam, who himself realizes that he does not belong:

> I am a stranger here. I know Persian better than they do; but this stinking Indian accent makes me an object of ridicule for them. I am short in stature. I am ugly. Scrofula has made my face resemble the dead. I am moneyless, and no one pays any attention to me. I am all alone.[112]

Conscious of his peculiar accent and appearance, he constantly seeks by various means to be like others, to be accepted as one of them. He takes pains to assure most everyone that he is, like them, a Twelver Shi'ite. He tries harder than any of the other characters to socialize, whether it is with a policeman on the street or with Ahmad Aqa, whom he invites home with him. Even his "great mission" in life—to kill off all prostitutes and rid the world of poverty and syphilis—can be seen as an attempt to gain the acceptance of the society to which he strives so hard to belong. His mission can also be seen as his way of escaping from loneliness. His name, Doctor Seyyed Vakil Saheb Seyf ol-Qalam, is a mixture of Arabic and Persian with colonial European titles, and it alone suggests that he can never wholly belong to any one society.[113]

More than any other character, Ahmad Aqa is aware of his loneliness. As though contemplating Rudaki's couplet, which prefaces the novel, he has given up the society of others and chosen solitude. If one is lonely with or without others, he has chosen to be without them. He explains in his first monologue:

> I ran away from everywhere and everyone, came to the corner of this house and took refuge under a blanket not to have to see anybody or talk to anybody. But you don't let me be for a moment.... What is it you want from my life anyway? ...Let me rot in my own solitude.[114]

But, by his inner voice, he is reminded of the terrors of loneliness: "Without me you'd be terrified from loneliness... You don't have anyone else in the world."[115] He realizes that he shares his loneliness with all humanity, but the knowledge brings him little satisfaction. To escape his loneliness, he seems to want to establish a bond between himself and others, but is unable to do so. He says that he loves Gowhar and wants to marry her, but he cannot commit himself to her, perhaps inhibited by the very social values he professes to scorn. He identifies with the child Kakolzari and expresses concern for his well-being, but is unable, again, to commit himself to the boy's care. He also expresses concern for the crippled, dying Jahansoltan, but all he can do is watch her die. He sympathizes with Belqeys' frustration, but he remains confined to the lonely prison of the self even during his sexual encounter with her. At times he escapes his loneliness and his unstable, shaky environment through flights of imagination, through creativity, through his intellect. Here he seems to have followed the advice he indirectly gives to the fly: "If the fly had any wits or intelligence it would never sit on ground that shakes all over from quakes. It would always fly. Because there are never earthquakes in the air."[116]

The world of *The Patient Stone*, then, is composed of lonely entities who try to establish bonds with others; but in their failure to do so, it appears that their common bond is, as Ahmad Aqa realizes, their very loneliness, fear, and anxiety. And it is to a patient stone, which symbolizes a person's suffering and loneliness, that they all must turn.

But what is that patient stone? According to an old legend, there once was a young girl who lost the handsome young man she was promised in a prophecy because of a trick played on her by her maidservant. As a result, the young girl was forced to toil miserably for seven years as a servant to her own maid in the young man's house. When the young man set out on a journey one day and offered to bring her back a souvenir from town, her only request was for a patient stone, which the man was, with some difficulty, finally able to find. He was instructed that the stone was to be given to one who had a grieving heart. That person was to tell the stone all his or her sorrows. If they were true, the stone would grow to the point of bursting. At that moment, the girl was to tell the stone that either it had to burst or she would burst; whereupon, the young man was directed that he should jump into the room, embrace the girl, and demand that the stone burst in order to save the girl. He returned with the stone, listened behind the door to the girl's story, and when she told the stone to burst or she would burst, he rushed into the room, embraced her, and told the stone to burst, which it did. The truth was revealed, the girl and the young man were finally united, married, and they lived happily ever after.[117] It is from this legend that the patient stone gets its folkloric meaning. The stone becomes a friend to the lonely and friendless, who can reveal their sorrows only to this listener. The characters of Chubak's story, too, have their sorrows, and they seek their patient stones as well. One tries to find a patient stone in a spider or in the grave of a young brother; another in the fish in a pool; one talks to the maggots which have infested her body; and another still tries to escape loneliness by speaking to the cold corpses of women he has killed. Hence, *The Patient Stone* is a record of the sorrows and sufferings of these individuals. In this record,

Belqeys relates her anguish over her ugly face, her impotent husband, and her resultant sexual frustration; Kakolzari reveals his fear of the "monsters" and his discontent at not having a father; Jahansoltan laments her physical infirmity, but also the misfortunes of Gowhar and her child; Seyf ol-Qalam complains of being an outsider, and of being ignored; and Ahmad Aqa tells of the loneliness, grief, and sorrow of not only himself and those around him, but also of all mankind, as on the wings of his imagination he travels back through history. In trying to comprehend the problems of mankind, his most reliable guide seems to be his own self as a model:

> I know from my own self that sorrow and happiness then was just like it is today. Man suffered from the beginning from sickness, tyranny, hunger, and loneliness; and man was happy with comfort, a full belly, companionship, and freedom. I imagine man has always wanted to be free and full, to have a beloved and a mate. I imagine man was always frightened of loneliness from the very beginning. I'm lonely too.[118]

And in the myth of creation that ends the novel, the problems seem not to differ, as Ahriman sees the source of Mashya's discontent in his loneliness, aimlessness, misery, and fear.[119] In the myth of creation episode, Ahmad Aqa reaches the end of his quest, finding the answer to his question, "What's at the bottom of all this?" In other words, what has started it all? The story of creation he tells is for Ahmad Aqa the answer to his question; it is a modern man's answer, a modern man's myth of creation: Once there was a god, Zervan, Time and Fate, who created a world, populating it with many creatures created for mere sport. To one of these, Mashya, he gave the power of thought, which became a source of the creature's discontent, his feeling of loneliness. As part of a plot against Zervan, Ahirman, the Lie, Zervan's assistant, made use of Mashya's discontent, created for him a mate, and together they destroyed the monster god. Ever since, the world has been ruled by Ahriman, the Lie.

Ahmad Aqa's myth of creation includes Judeo-Christian, Islamic, and, for the most part, Zoroastrian elements. The Garden of Eden, the angel Michael, and the Tree of Knowledge are, for example, Judeo-Christian and Islamic; Zervan, Ahriman, Mashya, and Mashyaneh, on the other hand, are taken from various Zoroastrian myths. In some cases a deliberate mixture of certain characteristics of these myths occurs (e.g., Mashya and Mashyaneh are replaced with Adam and Eve in some instances.[120] But many of the elements of these various myths have also been turned upside down. According to Zoroastrianism there exists a clear dichotomy between good and evil and the entities that represent these forces: "God [Ahura Mazda] is all goodness and light, Ahriman all wickedness and death, darkness and deceit."[121] However, in *The Patient Stone* there is an obvious deviation from this principle; there is no clear distinction between good and evil. Zervan, the God of Time in the heretical, monotheistic sect of Zervanism, is portrayed in the novel as the ultimate creator, but also as wicked and ugly.[122] And Ahriman is not portrayed as all evil, a horrible fiend, but rather as an enchanting fairy, a friend to Mashya. In addition, in Zoroastrianism the universe and man are created by God to help fight Ahriman: "God is forced to create the universe as a weapon with which to defeat Ahriman. Creation is for him a necessary weapon in his fight with the Fiend, and man is in the forefront of the fray."[123] But in *The Patient Stone*, it is Ahriman who uses Mashya to destroy Zervan. In Zoroastrianism, then, creation serves a well-defined purpose, nothing is mysterious:

> For the Zoroastrians neither evil nor creation is a mystery. There is no problem of evil because it is a separate principle and substance standing over against the good God and threatening to destroy him. There is, then, nothing mysterious about creation, for God needs Man's help in his battle with the "Lie."[124]

But in *The Patient Stone* there is no "good God" separate from and fighting against an opposing "bad Demon"; the dichotomy breaks down, resulting in creation becoming a purposeless act, as Zervan himself admits having created the world merely for his own amusement.[125] And while in the Judeo-Christian and Islamic myths, Adam and Eve are expelled from the Garden of Eden against their wishes, in *The Patient Stone*, by contrast, Mashya and Mashyaneh constantly strive to escape from the Garden to freedom. Early in the novel Ahmad Aqa describes a monster that resides inside Gowhar:

> A monster who tortures tyrannically and fries man's flesh to a crisp in the sticky fires of hell. If he feels like it, he forgives and grants salvation. But to forgive, he demands payment. His payment is weeping, moaning and groaning, self-flagellation on the chest and on the back with chains, banners, passion plays, and self-laceration.[126]

Since this passage specifically suggests common practices of the Twelver Shi'ite Moslems in Iran, the monster may be identified as the Islamic God; but this monster has many of the characteristics of Zervan, who has a hell waiting to be filled, of which he complains:

> I keep thinking about this Hell of mine that I've built; it's been a while now since I made it; I keep fueling it regularly, but it's all empty. It keeps blazing up all the time and saying, "Fill me up." But I don't have anything to throw in it. If that's the way it's going to be, what is it good for? It's just an added expense.[127]

And Zervan also enjoys being worshipped: "You have no idea," he confesses, "how much I like it when they fall on the ground prostrating before me."[128]

Does the book's end, with the destruction of Zervan, then, mean that the monster inside Gowhar has been killed? Is this an optimistic conclusion? Perhaps, but the end of the novel also represents the mythical beginning of the history of the world. Was Zervan an external god who was destroyed, but now exists as a "double" inside man? Does the novel, in that case, tell us that man has killed the external monster, but that the internal one lives on? And what of the final scene, after Zervan's life bottle is broken, when thunderous storms result? What does this scene tell us?

> *The earth quakes, the stars break to pieces and fall to the ground. MASHYA and MASHYANEH are in each other's arms. Low and high lands are leveled, and as far as the eye can see, the earth is flat. Only the TREE OF KNOWLEDGE remains green and fresh, in place; and from behind it, the sun boils out of the ground, its warm and bloody flames shining on MASHYA and MASHYANEH.*[129]

Several critics have interpreted the final scene of the myth of creation as the novel's glance into a hopeful future.[130] This view is plausible to some extent when one interprets the last scene of the novel in terms of its seemingly optimistic symbols: the destruction of the monster-god, the prominence of the Tree of Knowledge, and the shining of the sun. But the ambiguous language of the final passage, which avoids yielding a single, clear-cut meaning, challenges the view that the novel definitely ends on an optimistic note. It is true that the monster-god has been destroyed, but his destruction has also brought with it a devastating earthquake, flattening the earth as far as the eye can see. And the stars, which have been established in the epic section of the novel as signs in foretelling the future, have shattered and fallen. It is true that Mashya and Mashyaneh seem to have escaped loneliness, as they are left in each other's arms, and the Tree of Knowledge remains, with the sun shining from behind it on the two; but there seems an unavoidable ominousness in that very sun "boiling" up from the earth with "bloody flames" that shine from behind the Tree of Knowledge on Mashya and Mashyaneh. The fact is that the conclusion of the novel remains ambiguous. And this ambiguity reflects a sense of uncertainty. The future is by no means unequivocally hopeful, it is only uncertain. Hence, the reader cannot expect to be provided with a clearly decisive conclusion, especially given that the conclusion of the book, a fanciful myth of creation, is incorporated in the last monologue of Ahmad Aqa, the character who is even unsure of his own identity. Indeed, this last "dream" of Ahmad Aqa's seems to parallel the uncertainty of his world.

The Patient Stone is a reflection of modern man's uncertainty about his life and the world in which he lives. It is the story of human sorrows and suffering. It depicts the lives of a small group of people in the early decades of twentieth century Iran. It speaks of the loneliness and fear of these people. It speaks of the isolation of individuals who cannot communicate with one another. It speaks of ill-treated women, abandoned children, rootless strangers, and frustrated intellectuals. It speaks of a chaotic world in which joy seems conspicuously absent. It speaks of injustice, political oppression, and religious superstition. It depicts a particular people, a particular era, a particular country, but in doing so, it also speaks of human history. It presents a decaying society, one symbolized by the old woman, Jahansoltan, whose flesh is infested with maggots her own body has nourished, which slowly eat away at it. Like the maggots, this society's institutions continue to eat away at its aged body, the society depicted in *The Patient Stone* representing a microcosm of the world as a whole, decaying and chaotic.

CHAPTER 5

Conclusion and Reassessment

With an overview of major novelists and short story writers in the past one hundred years, in this chapter I will discuss the overall contribution of Sadeq Chubak to the art of fiction in Iran. Also, with a look to the future, I will try to reflect on whether or not Chubak will be remembered and his work will be read a century after his death. In other words, I will address questions pertaining to how lasting his work will be and whether *The Patient Stone* (1966), his magnum opus, and his entire body of work, will become a part of the canon of modern Persian fiction, similar to the works of literary artists of classical Persian literature or world literature. Finally, in this "reading" of Chubak, I will examine Chubak as a writer of fiction and as a person, and try to find the links between Chubak as a product of the cultural, political, and social events and climate of his lifetime. What was, what is, and what will be the status of Chubak as a major twentieth-century Iranian writer is also a question that I will address.

I

The history of modern Persian fiction has been a process, one might say a tradition, of experimentation and innovation since its inception. Beginning with Mohammad Ali Jamalzadeh's *Yeki Bud Yeki Nabud* [Once Upon a Time] in 1921,[1] in which he experimented with the genre of the short story and also introduced social and political themes as well as advocated "literary democracy" and making use of colloquial language, and later Sadeq Hedayat's presentation of his haunting and terrible vision and critique of Iranian culture in his surrealistic novel, *Buf-e Kur*

[The Blind Owl] (1937),[2] and other works, Persian fiction was set on a course of development within a relatively short period of time into a mature genre in Persian literature. While it can be argued that, similar to poetry, changes had begun in the content of Persian prose literature in the nineteenth century and continued at a greater speed in the twentieth-century from more or less elitist subject matters to more mundane social and political concerns in Persian fiction, similar and perhaps more daring changes also occurred and continued in regard to the form, structure, and language of Persian short stories and novels. A cursory survey of the works of Iranian writers of fiction reveals that the major figures among these writers can generally be divided into two groups in terms of their approach to the art of fiction, namely, storytellers and experimentalists. I should add, however, that both groups have been experimenters, in a sense. In other words, while the storytellers often experimented with and built on the tradition of storytelling, the second group has paid greater attention to form, structure, and narrative technique. I would like to suggest that the storytellers have essentially followed the path that was begun by Jamalzadeh, and the experimentalists that of Hedayat. More importantly, what I would like to suggest further is that such a survey also shows continuity in this tradition. In other words, in the same way that the works of these literary artists were not created in a social or political vacuum, they were also not written in a literary vacuum.

The metaphor of a staircase is what I would like to employ for the process and progress in the art of fiction writing in Iran since, I hope, it somewhat conveys the idea that each participant in this endeavor furthers the effort toward a goal from where the ones before him or her leave off. In fact, I am almost tempted to employ the metaphor of a relay sport, in which other players standing along the route help the advancement toward the finish line. In other words, each generation of writers or each writer contributes to the progress of the art of fiction (even though the notion of the finish line is obviously problematic for my purpose). What I am actually proposing is that each writer learns from those before him or her, and builds on the accomplishments of previous generations.

The history of modern Persian fiction in some sense begins with *Siyahatnameh-ye Ebrahim Beyg* [The Travel Memoirs of

Ebrahim Beyg] (1903-1909),[3] by Zeynol'abedin Maragheh'i in the early twentieth century, just before the Constitutional Revolution of 1905-1911. This work is a fictional version of the dominant literary genre of the *safarnameh* or travel accounts of the nineteenth century, usually written by or written for prominent figures. Maragheh'i uses the format of the popular genre in his novel to address social and political issues and especially social ailments and political corruption in late Qajar Iran. In some respects, particularly in terms of language and theme, *The Travel Memoirs of Ebrahim Beyg* as well as the writings of Ali Akbar Dehkhoda and others should be considered the first step on the staircase of modern Persian fiction that sets the tone for the well-known collection of short stories, *Once Upon a Time*, by Jamalzadeh. Linguistically and thematically, Jamalzadeh follows Maragheh'i's example, although he is more conscious of and advocates the use of the colloquial language of the ordinary people, and his approach in criticizing various social and political problems is seasoned with humor. The success of *Once Upon a Time* was obviously due to its novelty and its author's consciousness of advocating and attempting to implement a break with tradition, or rather a change in the focus of literature, and not necessarily innovation in terms of technique, structure, and other aspects of fiction writing. And perhaps in this collection as well as his other work in general, Jamalzadeh was not interested in imitating the Western genres, but rather in modernizing the art of storytelling by building on traditional Persian anecdotes and tales.

Even though there is a host of writers of fiction, including the writers of historical and romance novels, among the generation that followed Jamalzadeh's early phase, Sadeq Hedayat and Bozorg Alavi in that generation should be regarded as writers who helped Persian fiction reach the next step. Hedayat's contributions are multifaceted. He brought Persian narrative techniques to new heights, tapped folkloric elements and beliefs in his work, and perhaps most importantly, in his more reflective work, he introduced a modern philosophical outlook that influenced many Iranian writers in the ensuing generations. What is innovative in the character of the narrator of *The Blind Owl*, for instance, is that he is an archetypal representation of the modern Iranian male, or more specifically, the intellectual who struggles to come to terms with the burden of the tradition and history of his culture, on the one hand, and the challenges of the modern world, on the other. Even though seemingly more political in his outlook, Bozorg Alavi is also interested in exploring the character of the modern Iranian individual, but perhaps with a more psychological outlook. Alavi's short stories, such as those in the collection, *Chamadan* [The Suitcase] (1934), and his novel, *Cheshmhayash* [Her Eyes] (1952), undoubtedly represent a major step in the art of fiction in Iran.[4]

Among the writers of the following generation, Sadeq Chubak should be credited with advancing Persian fiction another step. An important aspect of Chubak's work from the very beginning of his literary career, with the publication of his short sketch-like stories, is his ability to "show" rather than to "tell" a story. This he does masterfully in stories such as "Adl" [Justice], in which with a minimum amount of description he vividly brings to life a picture or a scene. Chubak's second contribution to the art of Persian fiction is the recording and transcription of colloquial Persian as it is actually spoken. As mentioned in the introduction to this book, earlier attempts by Jamalzadeh and Hedayat, among others, were merely confined to the use of colloquial expressions and lexical items, paying little attention to the syntax of spoken Persian. Chubak, on the other hand, is conscious of all aspects and variations of spoken language, a feature that helps make each character in his work unique and memorable. And of course, Chubak's attention to form, structure, and narrative technique in all of his work, particularly in his last novel, *The Patient Stone*, distinguishes him as an important figure among writers of modern Persian fiction.

Chubak's reputation as a writer was established with his first volume of short stories, *The Puppet Show*, a number of which were published earlier in the important literary journals of the time. He was particularly praised for his sketch-like, almost photographic, short stories such as "Justice" and "Yahya," as well as other short stories such as "Fresh Flowers," "Under the Red Light," "A Man in a Cage," "The Maroon Dress," and in particular "An Afternoon in Autumn." The absence of narrators in many of these stories was also an innovative technique that Chubak introduced into Persian fiction. In some respect, they are reminiscent of the work of Alain Robbe-Grillet, the French writer. Short stories such as "The Cage" in his second collection,

The Baboon Whose Buffoon Was Dead, which were written in the vein of the sketch-like stories, as well as stories such as "Why was the Sea Stormy," and especially "The Baboon Whose Buffoon Was Dead," helped establish Chubak as a master short story writer. With the publication of *Tangsir* in 1963 and the negative reaction of the critics who had already decided that Chubak's talent was in writing short stories and not novels, Chubak's reputation suffered to some extent. As mentioned in the previous chapters, that may have been the reason why Chubak decided to publish two collections of short stories, *The First Day in the Grave* and *The Last Alms*, within a period of one year. With few exceptions, such as "The Wooden Horse," most of the stories of these two collections seem to be mere experiments that often seem uninspired and are not consistently successful. In these collections, one can easily detect Chubak's experimentation with language registers and the transcription of colloquial Persian, the local dialect of Shiraz and Bushehr, and various other formal and informal as well as poetic and inventive high register literary prose. These experiments may have been merely practices for Chubak's final work, his novel *The Patient Stone*. Although this work displays Chubak's talent in the use of language, his sophisticated use of novelistic techniques, his knowledge of classical Persian literature and history, and his power as a writer to incite empathy and emotion in readers, it became one of the most controversial works of fiction in the twentieth century. The majority of critics at the time and later on attacked *The Patient Stone* as an incoherent, structurally flawed, socially and politically irrelevant, and esthetically unpleasant literary failure. From an experimental and technical point of view, this novel was quite innovative at the time it was written and published. In terms of language and presentation, there are monologues in this work that make the story and its locale, characters, sights and sounds, and even smells so vivid and tangible that they emotionally and physically affect most readers.

Chubak's talent in the use of language is unquestionable. As discussed in the previous chapters, like a tape recorder, by sitting in some corner in a restaurant or public place and listening to ordinary people of various classes, Chubak accurately records in his mind the actual language used by various people of various classes and educational backgrounds, even totally illiterate people, and then transcribes it in the form of utterances so faithfully and accurately that most readers find it difficult to follow and understand. In some respect, Chubak's almost obsessive preoccupation with the actual and accurate recording of various language registers is reminiscent of Mark Twain's *Huckleberry Finn* and *Tom Sawyer*, which readers often find difficult to follow. It is perhaps for this reason that the writers in the following generations, learning from the readers' experiences in reading the work of Sadeq Chubak, modified their use of colloquial language in fiction in a way that it would not alienate readers. Efforts at transcribing and innovation in the use of colloquial language were not exclusive to Chubak and his predecessors. Ebrahim Golestan, the prominent fiction writer and filmmaker, for example, has experimented and one could even say perfected this particular use of colloquial Persian in a musically harmonious poetic style. Another prominent fiction writer, Jalal Al-e Ahmad, also experimented with language and developed a very effective conversational style of writing that he employed both in his stories and novels and in his polemical books and essays. This modified use of transcription of colloquial Persian has been employed and improved by the ensuing generations of writers such as Hushang Golshri, Mahmud Dowlatabadi, Simin Daneshvar, Goli Tarraqi, Mahshid Amirshahi, Moniru Ravanipur, Ghazaleh Alizadeh, and Shahrnush Parsipur, among others. Parenthetically, idiosyncratic use of colloquial language and its transcription by playwrights such as Akbar Radi, Esma'il Khalaj, and others followed a similar route. Readers in particular, and sometimes audiences, of the plays of such prominent playwrights as Akbar Radi have encountered similar difficulty.

The next step in Persian fiction writing was taken by writers such as Jalal Al-e Ahmad and Ebrahim Golestan, both of whom introduced new prose styles in fiction. In addition to the use of more reader-friendly transcription of colloquial language than that of Chubak, even though Al-e Ahmad often paid little attention to the formal aspects of short stories and novels, his emphatic focus on social and political issues in all his writing has been emulated by many younger writers. In contrast to Al-e Ahmad, Ebrahim Golestan distinguished himself by his penchant for structure and other technical aspects of the art of fiction, as well as a unique musical prose style, as mentioned above.

A special place in the development of Persian fiction should be reserved for Bahram Sadeqi, for whom, perhaps more than any other writer, the art of fiction, or as he called it, writing "pure stories," was important. He is the first writer who, as Hasan Mir-Abedini observes, by changing the relationship between the writer and the characters of his stories, confers a part of the authority of the writer on the characters in fiction in order to declare the birth of the reader and the possibility for various interpretations at the price of the death of the writer.[5] Even though few writers have been able to follow his footsteps, Sadeqi pushed the boundaries of story writing in Iran to new heights. For this reason, a talented writer such as Hushang Golshiri considers Sadeqi to be the best writer Iran has ever produced and the greatest influence on himself as a writer.[6]

Another major figure on the progressive continuum of Persian fiction writing is Gholamhoseyn Sa'edi, whose talent for writing dialogue and also his in-depth presentation of the psyche and psychology of his characters have contributed to the enhancement of the art of fiction in Iran. The influence of Sa'edi's prolific output, including novels, short stories, and of course plays can been seen in the work of prominent writers of the present generation, such as Moniru Ravanipur.

The art of storytelling in Persian has certainly been advanced with the work of Simin Daneshvar, particularly her major novel, *Savushun* (1969); Ali Mohammad Afghani, the author of one of the first long novels in Persian, *Showhar-e Ahu Khanom* [Ahu Khanom's Husband] (1961); the humorous social satirical stories of Mahshid Amirshahi; Goli Taraqqi's profoundly thought-provoking works; and the experimental work of Nader Ebrahimi, among others. With the work of two major writers, Hushang Golshiri and Mahmud Dowlatabadi, Persian fiction reaches newer heights and the level of a mature art in Iran. Golshiri's *Shazdeh Ehtejab* [Prince Ehtejab] (1969) is already considered a masterpiece in the canon of modern Persian fiction, and Mahmud Dowlatabadi's monumental five-volume novel with nearly 3,000 pages, *Kelidar*, the publication of which began in the late 1970s and continued for several years, is regarded as a modern epic and a significant experimentation in the Iranian storytelling tradition. And certainly the novels of Ahmad Mahmud (1931-2002), such as *Hamsayehha* [Neighbors] (1974), *Zamin-e Sukhteh* [Burnt

Land] (1971), and *Dastan-e Yek Shahr* [The Tale of One City] (1981), as well as his short story collections that focus for the most part on life in southern Iran, should not be overlooked in any survey of Persian fiction. Similarly, Esma'il Fasih (1935), with novels such as *Sharab-e Kham* [Raw Wine] (1968), *Khak-e Ashna* [Familiar Soil] (1970), *Del-e Kur* [Blind Heart] (1972), *Dard-e Siyavash* [The Pain of Siyavash] (1983), *Dastan-e Javid* [The Story of Javid] (1985), *Sorayya dar Eghma* [Sorayya in a Coma] (1986), and *Farar-e Foruhar* [Foruhar's Flight] (1993), has recorded the fictional saga of an Iranian family, but also the entire nation in the twentieth century. Both Mahmud and Fasih should be considered among the great storytellers of modern Persian fiction.

With the major social and political changes that occurred in Iran in the last two decades of the twentieth century, namely the Islamic Revolution and its aftermath, and of course the Iran-Iraq war, as well as the ongoing process of social and cultural changes and struggle for democracy, changes have also occurred in Persian fiction writing. Many of the older writers have continued not only to mirror the new conditions in the society in terms of their subject matter, but they have also provided us with new experiments in Persian fiction. Examples of such experiments are *Jazireh-ye Sargardani* [Island of Bewilderment] (1993) by Simin Daneshvar, *Ayenehha-ye Dardar* [Mirrors with Doors] (1992) and *Jennameh* [The Book of Jinns] (1998) by Hushang Golshiri, and *Khaterehha-ye Parakandeh* [Scattered Memories] (1994) by Goli Taraqqi. Nevertheless, younger writers such as Shahrnush Parsipur, Moniru Ravanipur, Ja'far Modarres-Sadeqi, and Ghazaleh Alizadeh should be credited with advancing the art of Persian fiction to another step. Modarres-Sadeqi's *Gavkhuni* [The Marsh] (1983) and *Kalleh-ye Asb* [Horse's Head] (1991) have already gained this writer a reputation and have in fact been translated into English.[7] Significant works of fiction such as *Zanan Beduneh Mardan* [Women Without Men] (1989) by Shahrnush Parsipur and *Ahl-e Gharq* [The Drowned] (1989) by Moniru Ravanipur have established these two writers as among the major figures in modern Persian literature. And the works of Alizadeh, such as her novel *Khaneh-ye Edrisiha* [The House of the Edrisis] (1998, 1999), have opened new horizons to Persian fiction. The relatively rapid success of Parsipur and Ravanipur may have also paved the way for the emergence of an increasing number of women writers with noteworthy collections of short stories and novels.

Even a passing glance at the list of new works of fiction published every month and the very useful reviews and surveys by Hasan Mir-Abedini show the emergence of many new writers of promise. Works such as *Sumanat* (1998) by Abutorab Khosravi, *Noskheh-ye Avval* [First Copy] (1998) by Shiva Arastu'i, *Safar beh Samti Digar* [Journey in Another Direction] (1998) by Reza Zangabadi, *Nimeh-ye Ghayeb* [The Absent Half] (1999) by Hoseyn Sanapur, *Sa'at-e Gorg-o Mish* [The Twilight Hour] (1999) by Mohammad Reza Purja'fari, *Ziyafat-e Shabaneh* [Party at Night] (1999) by Farzaneh Karampur, and *Zan dar Piyadehro Rah Miravad* [Woman Walks on the Sidewalk] (1998) by Qasem Kashkuli are a small sample of recent contributions to the evolution of Persian fiction.

With a great deal of omission, I have outlined a more or less chronological list of the major Iranian fiction writers and their contributions to the development and advancement of Persian fiction. What is meant to be implied by this outline and chronological list, which I would like to state more explicitly at this point, is that, like all human endeavors and accomplishments, the art of Persian fiction writing has undergone constant changes, not only from the work of one writer or one generation of writers to another, but even in the course of the literary careers of individual writers. However, these changes constitute a continuum in the history of this literature. Inevitably, the content and the subject matter of the short stories and novels in each generation and at various times have been subject to many factors, including the social and political events and developments and the general environment, as well as the individual circumstances of each writer. Under certain conditions, like other artists everywhere, Iranian fiction writers have had to resort to different styles and approaches, for example, the use of symbolism and enigmatic writing as a subterfuge to escape the scrutinizing eyes of the censors. Such writing may be viewed as belonging to one or another particular literary movement, and each writer may or may not consider himself or herself as belonging to that movement. It is, of course, the task of literary critics and literary historians to group and categorize, or to assign different writers and their works to different movements, periods, and in a sense, pigeonholes, a task that is necessary and even desirable for a general understanding and overview of literary history. Nevertheless, in the same way that no creative work is produced and can be understood in a vacuum, separate from its social, political, economic, and cultural environment, the work of Persian fiction writers is not produced and cannot be appreciated thoroughly in a historical vacuum, that is, isolated from the continuous process of development to which each writer and each generation of writers have contributed and continue to contribute.

It is in the context of this brief historical survey of Persian fiction writing and Iranian novelists and fiction writers that I would like to assess and reassess the impact of the work of Sadeq Chubak, using his last novel as a touchstone. In contrast to Sadeq Hedayat's *The Blind Owl*, which, for example, has survived more than half a century after the suicide of its author and, despite the negative climate that was, and continues to be, perpetuated by many middle-class educated families, even psychologists and psychiatrists, and of course many traditional literati, among others, remains popular in Iran and is perhaps the only modern Persian literary work that has acquired some degree of acceptability and popularity internationally, Sadeq Chubak's *The Patient Stone*, on the other hand, which did not become popular even among intellectuals in Iran, despite having been translated into several languages, remains relatively unknown and obscure both in Iran and internationally. Similarly, in contrast to Hushang Golshiri's *Prince Ehtejab*, a novel in which the author uses a very complex narrative with multiple narrative voices, a novel that immediately established Hushang Golshiri as an important literary figure in Iran; in contrast to the monumental novel *Kelidar* by Mahmud Dowlatabadi, which is a modern epic about the Kurdish people in Khorasan and in the tradition of such masterpieces as the eleventh-century *Shahnameh* [Book of Kings] by Ferdowsi, which became a record bestseller at the time of its publication with millions of copies sold; and in contrast to some of the commercially popular romances in the past century, especially since the Islamic Revolution, such as *Bamdad-e Khomar* [The Morning of Hangover], which has become the best selling novel of all times in Iran, Chubak's work in general and his masterpiece *The Patient Stone* have not been read by more than a relatively small number of people. Likewise, as mentioned earlier, critics were not kind in their reviews of *The Patient Stone* and other works to some extent because of Chubak's friendship and association with his schoolmate, Abbas Hoveyda, the Shah's Prime Minister in the 1960s and 1970s. It is possible that a century from now Chubak's work will be rediscovered and will find its place in the canon of modern Persian literature; otherwise, Chubak and his work will most likely remain a footnote in the annals of Persian literary history. For now, at the time of writing these lines, even though Chubak is not as popular as many other writers, his importance in the history of modern fiction of Iran is undeniable. Even fundamentalist supporters of the Islamic Republic seem to be unable to ignore him. A major Islamic encyclopedia in Iran asked me to write an article on Chubak, which I agreed to do. However, the chief editor, a well-known conservative scholar and an influential figure in the Islamic Republic, Gholam'ali Haddad-Adel, who is now the speaker of the Iranian parliament, was offended by Chubak's rather uninhibited use of what Haddad-Adel called "obscene language" and stories; he asked me to mention that Chubak's writing was religiously and culturally offensive to the Iranian people, a request that I declined immediately and without any hesitation. Hence, it can be argued that the impact of Chubak and his work, and his reputation, are undeniable, even on individuals on ideologically opposing sides.

In terms of his philosophical outlook and his respect and awe of Sadeq Hedayat, whom Chubak regarded as his mentor, Chubak tried to emulate Hedayat in various ways. Many short stories written by Chubak, as pointed out by critics, seem to be a rewriting of Hedayat's stories, perhaps as a tribute to his mentor, or perhaps with a sense of competition and an effort to liberate himself as a writer and emerge from the haunting and dominating shadow of Sadeq Hedayat. This is even evident in *The Patient Stone*. As mentioned above, in *The Blind Owl* Hedayat presents his narrator as an archetypal representation of the modern Iranian man, or more specifically, the intellectual, who struggles to come to terms with the burden of the tradition and history of his culture, on the one hand, and the challenges of the modern world, on the other. The character of Ahmad Aqa in *The Patient Stone* is also in some ways reminiscent of the narrator of

The Blind Owl in terms of his outlook on life, his abhorrence of anything religious, his powerlessness to change the world, and his impotence and dependence on others. Was Chubak able to free himself from the shadow of Sadeq Hedayat? After the publication of *The Patient Stone*, Chubak virtually abandoned writing, with the exception of the translation of a purported Indian tale that turned out to be a hoax and his often-referred-to memoirs that mostly focused on Hedayat.[8]

II

As champions of defending and writing about the lives and suffering of the poor, the downtrodden, and the outcasts of society, the first and second generations of Iranian writers contributed to gradually turning the attention of the authorities to the plight of these classes. With the socialist and communist movements and the coming to power of socialist and communist governments in various parts of the world, especially in Russia, Iran's neighbor with which there has been a great deal of interaction not only in the territorial wars of the nineteenth century but also culturally, many Iranian writers, particularly of the second generation who began their careers in the wake of World War II when the Allies occupied Iran and provided some degree of political freedom and freedom of expression that had been denied to them, particularly during the dictatorial reign of Reza Shah, found socialist and communist ideologies compatible with their idealistic fight in defending the forgotten classes, and many of them joined the newly established socialist and communist parties. This was perhaps natural and inevitable, since after all the members of every society, especially the intellectuals, are affected by the *Zeitgeist*. But in addition to socialism and communism and the international conflicts that brought about World War II, a truly worldwide destructive phenomenon, the *Zeitgeist* also gave rise to certain objectionable ideas in the years prior to the war, namely nationalism and anti-Semitism. The Iranian government, the Iranian intellectuals, and the Iranian nomadic tribes, which were taken advantage of and used as ensnared instruments of the policies of the remnants of foreign colonialist powers, were also affected, perhaps blindly, by Hitler's Nazi propaganda and ideology of nationalism and anti-Semitism, given the anti-British sentiments that had begun to develop in the early years of the twentieth century, especially the British occupation of Bushehr, the birthplace of Sadeq Chubak. One could surmise that stories such as "Monsieur Elyas," discussed in Chapter Three, in which Chubak uses Jewish characters with negative stereotype characteristics of stinginess, worshiping gold, and being dirty is the result of the impact of this *Zeitgeist*.[9] I wonder if this attitude could also be the result of the prevalent anti-Jewish attitude and the treatment of Jews in the city of Shiraz, where Chubak's family moved during his school years.[10] Similarly, not only in the work of Chubak, but in the work of Sadeq Hedayat and many other prominent writers, at times one sees overt and sometimes covert traces of anti-Jewish sentiment in addition to strong resentment of non-Iranian Arabs and their culture.[11] Let me add parenthetically that such sentiments toward Jews and Arabs have existed in the past, the latter especially due to the mistreatment of Iranians at the hands of the Arabs after the Islamic invasion of Iran in the seventh century, and even in modern times with the strong anti-Iranian content of elementary and high-school textbooks in many Arab countries.[12] The impact of these unpleasant effects of the *Zeitgeist*, however, seems to go much deeper and be more lasting. In the case of Sadeq Chubak, in my frequent telephone conversations and the occasional meetings with him in the 1980s, I became certain that these sentiments were deeply rooted and ingrained in the psyche and character of Chubak, and indeed many intellectuals who claim to be champions of defending the poor, the downtrodden, and the religious and ethnic minorities in Iran.

In the late 1970s, when I was translating *The Patient Stone* and writing about the novel, and contemplating the publication of the translated text, I attempted to locate and contact Sadeq Chubak. Through friends, acquaintances, and colleagues, I learned that the person who knew Chubak's whereabouts was the British scholar, F. R. C. Bagley, who was a lecturer in Persian Studies at the University of Durham in the School of Oriental Studies. Given that Iran was not a signatory to the international copyright laws, and many books were translated, pirated, and published in Iran without the permission of the copyright holder, I was cognizant of the fact that legally neither the publisher of the work nor I was obliged to obtain permission from the author who held the copyright in Iran. Nevertheless, for ethical reasons and also in order to obtain answers to some of the questions that I had regarding the local idiomatic expressions and the like in the Persian text of *The Patient Stone,* I felt obliged to contact Mr. Chubak. Hence, I wrote a letter to Mr. Bagley,[13] while at the same time I had contacted Ehsan Yarshater, the Chaired Professor of Iranian Studies at Columbia University and the founder and editor of the Modern Persian Literature Series, which is devoted to the publication and promotion of original and secondary books and sources of modern Persian fiction and poetry. In response to my letter of inquiry regarding the publication of the novel, I received a correspondence from Mr. Bagley dated November 2, 1979. [14] He informed me that an anthology of Chubak's work, including his first novel *Tangsir*, was being prepared by Marziya Sami'i and Bagley himself, in addition to translations of some of the short stories and a play by other translators. Mr. Bagley made a series of suggestions, including his making my translation more "idiomatic" and adding explanatory footnotes, which were already included extensively with my translation, suggestions that were totally unacceptable to me, since my translation had been described as "brilliant" by a colleague and former friend and as "a unique accomplishment and the best translation made of a Persian literature work" by Ehsan Yarshater.[15] Mr. Bagley had also included a copy of his letter to Mr. Eng, who, as I understood at the time, was in charge of the Modern Persian Literature Series.[16] Subsequently, I wrote a letter to Mr. Chubak introducing myself and asking for his permission to publish the translation.[17] In a letter dated 23 Khordad 1359 [12 June 1980], Chubak acknowledged my hard work and effort in translating *The Patient Stone*, and he said that for certain reasons he did not want to have the translation published at that time. He also acknowledged my "efforts that are evident in every line" of the translation, telling me that "some day when we meet we might pursue" the publication of the novel.[18] In the meantime, in a telephone conversation later on while he was still in London, where he had moved after his retirement in 1974, having told him about the reluctance of several publishers to publish the translated novel, perhaps to a great extent because of the anti-Western Iranian Islamic Revolution and the hostage crisis, I suggested that no other publisher would be better or more prestigious than the Modern Persian Literature Series. He consented to the publication of the translation in that series, and then warned me to make sure that I would not be "duped" by Dr. Yarshater. I responded that in the course of the years that I had known Dr. Yarshater, and even before that, given his reputation as a dedicated scholar who had devoted his life to the teaching and promotion of Persian literature and Iranian culture, I had never had the impression that he was out to "dupe" anyone. In any case, I had the consent of Chubak, and subsequently I informed Dr. Yarshater about my conversation with Mr. Chubak. It appeared that all was in order, and having received no definite answers from other publishers, as documented in my correspondence with them,[19] I proceeded with the decision to publish the translation in the Modern Persian Literature Series. Dr. Yarshater asked me in a telephone conversation to make some revisions, which I completed and sent to him along with a letter.[20] In early 1980, Mr. Chubak moved to northern California near Berkeley, to El Cerrito. My wife and I decided to spend our Christmas-New Year break that year visiting Mr. Chubak and his wife. I called Mr. Chubak and he was excited about our visit. I told him that I intended to bring the manuscript of the translation to ask him some questions, and he said that he would be happy to answer my questions. We set out by car and after several days of traveling reached California. We enjoyed a couple of days in the company of Mr. Chubak, spending some time on my questions. He said that he would send me in writing his comments and answers. During this time, Mr. Chubak informed me that he was writing his memoirs, a great deal of which dealt with his mentor, Sadeq Hedayat. He showed me some handwritten pages and said that he did not want to publish his memoirs until twenty-five years after his death, and that he had decided to give all of his papers to the British Museum for safekeeping.[21] Among other things, I learned that he had become extremely interested in American soap operas and was spending a great deal of time watching such shows. We returned to Charlottesville, quite excited about and enthralled with our visit. In another telephone conversation with Mr. Chubak, I asked him to send me a brief biography of himself, although I had already gathered information from various sources.[22] Because of the reservations Mr. Chubak had expressed early on, once again I sent him a letter, in

June 1980, explaining that publishing the translation with Bibliotheca Persica in their Modern Persian Literature Series, in my opinion, was the best choice.[23]

The preparations for the publication of the translation of *The Patient Stone* were under way; a contract was signed from which I would receive a fee for the retyping of the manuscript after revisions. The fee mentioned in the contract was equivalent to that which would have been paid to a professional typist. Also, as instructed by Mr. Chubak, all the rights to the work, including the Hollywood movie rights, were given to Mr. Chubak. Interestingly, Mr. Chubak's view of his work was that it was flawless and that it would be the perfect novel for a Hollywood producer and director to make into a successful box office movie. Parenthetically, later on when the translation was eventually published by another publisher, Chubak had asked the publisher to send copies to the Nobel Prize Committee.

In early August 1982, I received a shocking letter from London from Mr. Chubak, where he was visiting at the time,[24] in which he informed me that he did not know anything about my efforts to publish the translation of the novel, conveyed to me that he had found over fifty mistakes in my translation,[25] and that he had told me about them during our visit to his home in 1980 in El Cerrito, that I was disregarding his rights and those of his heirs, that I should have known how the writer of *The Patient Stone* hated bullies, injustice, deception, and so on, and that I was selling him out and deceiving him for a fistful of dollars. Furthermore, he threatened that if I proceeded with the publication of the translation, the establishment of Mr. Yarshater and I would receive the next letter from his attorney.

Shocked and dismayed by this letter, which was apparently the result of the efforts of someone who was egging Mr. Chubak on, or his complete loss of memory for some reason, I responded to the letter, indicating that I was abandoning the project and anything else that I was doing related to his work.[26] The insulting letter revealed to me certain other unpleasant aspects of the author, and I was depressed and dismayed for having spent several years of my life on his work. What I did not know was that during the interval, Mr. Bagley's project and the contract with Bibliotheca Persica had been a bone of contention between Mr. Chubak and Dr. Yarshater, for reasons that I discovered later.

Even though *Sadeq Chubak: An Anthology* had been printed and was ready for distribution, it was never distributed. This discord had obviously influenced Mr. Chubak's decision to write the shocking letter to me. In a telephone conversation around this time, when Mr. Chubak had returned to California, after having received my letter, he revealed another unpleasantly shocking aspect of his thinking and character. He told me that he did not have any problem with publishing the translation, which he described as a very good translation, but he said that he did not want to have anything to do with Yarshater, "the Jew turned Baha'i," revealing his prejudice and simultaneously insulting two religious minorities in Iran.[27] Once again, I was totally stunned and dismayed, and now regret that I did not respond appropriately, perhaps because of my reluctance to hurt the feelings of an aging Iranian intellectual and writer.

Years passed, and I received messages through friends and colleagues from Mr. Chubak, expressing his concerns and apologies, and encouraging me to make another effort to find a publisher other than the Modern Persian Literature Series. On the encouragement of a colleague and friend, I visited Mr. Chubak once again in California, discussing possible publishers for the translation, and asking him to give me a list of the mistakes that he had indicated that I had made in the infamous letter he sent me in July 1982. I also told Mr. Chubak that I would be willing to consent to the publication of the translation without any changes, since I held the copyrights of the translation in the United States, and that I would not expect any compensation and that all royalties, if any, would belong to Mr. Chubak. Upon my suggestion, he decided that Mazda Publishers should publish the translation and asked me to facilitate contact and recommend the book to the publisher that had published a number of works by me. Some time after my second short visit with Chubak, I wrote a letter to him asking him for the notes regarding *The Patient Stone* that he was supposed to send me.[28] He did so some time later following a letter from Mazda Publishers regarding his final decision in late May 1988.[29] After a long conversation, I informed him that I had decided to give all the rights of the translation to him and I had informed the publisher of my decision that the rights to the original book as well as the translation would belong to Mr. Chubak. He said that the number of published copies in the first printing should be specified in the contract. Mr. Chubak said that arrangements should be made so that after the printing and the sale of the translation, Mazda Publishers would receive its share of the sales for its expenditures of the publication of the translation and the rest would go to Mr. Chubak. I said that I would convey what he had said to Mazda Publishers.[30] He said that he wanted the money because there was the question of prestige, a notion that I did not completely comprehend at the time, and regarding which I was reluctant to ask for an explanation.

My main intention in writing the chronicle of my interaction and experience with Sadeq Chubak and the episode related to the translation and publication of *The Patient Stone*, in addition to providing an example of certain aspects of Chubak's own personality, his self-view, his view of others, and his manner of interaction with others, in the context of which ideally his work should be examined and analyzed from a postmodernist perspective, rather than the perspective of New Criticism which I have used more or less in examining and analyzing his work, particularly *The Patient Stone*, has been to make available certain facts to the present and future generations of young scholars to produce more insightful interpretation and reading of Chubak's work, not only in the context of the social, political, and cultural climate in which he wrote, but in the context of Chubak's character, outlook, progressive ideas, and prejudices. This is the most important thing that I hope to have accomplished, even if partially, in this book.

Chubak had almost totally lost his sight to macular degeneration in the final years of his life. Throughout his retirement, the only work that he published was *Mahpareh* in 1991, the Persian translation from English of *A Digit of the* Moon, a supposed English translation of a Sanskrit fable by Francis William Bain (1863-1940).[31] Even though Bain later admitted that the book was not a translation at all but his own fabricated imitation of the *Kathasaritasagara*, a fact of which Chubak was unaware, Chubak received unanimous praise for his masterful use of language and prose style in *Mahpareh*.[32] This work was completed when Chubak was unable to read on his own because of his loss of vision. Hence, someone else had read the English version to him line by line and he had dictated the translation.

In May 2002, at the Fourth Biennial Conference of Iranian Studies in Washington, a young scholar from Israel approached me shyly, alerting me about and at the same time apologizing for the paper she was going to present on the works of Sadeq Chubak, basically challenging my previous writing on this author, especially *The Patient Stone*.[33] I told her that I was most interested in hearing her paper and would discuss her ideas after her presentation. She presented a very insightful and well researched scholarly paper, the main thrust of which challenged my views of the novel. Afterwards, I told her that I liked her paper, and that I basically agreed with her, since I had changed my views to some extent, like any other scholar, over the course of more than 20 years. I mention this encounter as an indication of, or perhaps as a wish for, further studies of Chubak's work, especially from different perspectives, as the literary record of several generations on which also greatly depend the survival and popularity of this important figure in twentieth-century Persian literature.

CHAPTER NOTES

Chapter 1: Introduction

[1] *Nakhostin Kongereh-ye Nevisandegan-e Iran* [First Congress of Iranian Writers] (Tehran: Anjoman-e Ravabet-e Farhangi-ye Iran va Etehad-e Jamahir-e Showravi-ye Sosiyalisti, 1947), p. 131. All translations from Persian in this and the following chapters are my own, unless otherwise indicated. A summary of parts of this chapter was published as an introduction to the translation of *The Patient Stone* by M. R. Ghanoonparvar (Costa Mesa, California: Mazda Publishers, 1989).
[2] Reza Baraheni, *Qessehnevisi* (Tehran: Ashrafi, 1969), p. 77.
[3] Mohammad Ali Jazayery, "Recent Persian Literature: Observations on Themes and Tendencies," *Review of National Literatures* 2, No. 1 (Spring 1971):11.
[4] Hassan Kamshad, *Modern Persian Prose Literature* (Cambridge: The University Press, 1966), p. 31.
[5] For detailed discussions on the Iranian political events of the twentieth century, see: Fred Halliday, *Iran: Dictatorship and Development* (New York: Penguin, 1979); Amin Banani, *The Modernization of Iran (1921-1941)* (Stanford, California: Stanford University Press, 1961); and Donald N. Wilbur, *Iran: Past and Present*, 8th ed. (Princeton, New Jersey: Princeton University Press, 1976).
[6] Mohammad Ali Jamalzadeh, *Yeki Bud Yeki Nabud*, 4th ed. (Tehran: Ebn-e Sina, 1954).
[7] Jamalzadeh, "Dibacheh," *Yeki Bud Yeki Nabud*, pp. 5-21. For an English translation of this preface, see: Haideh Dargahi, "The Shaping of the Modern Persian Short Story: Jamalzadih's 'Preface' to *Yiki Bud, Yiki Nabud*," *The Literary Review* 18 (1974):18-24. Copies of Jamalzadeh's book were actually burned when they reached Iran. See Mohammad Ali Jamalzadeh, "Dibache-ye Mo'allef," *Amu Hoseyn Ali: Shahkar* 2nd ed. (Tehran: Ma'refat, 1957); and Vera Kubičková, "Persian Literature of the 20th Century," in *History of Iranian Literature* by Jan Rypka, ed. Karl Jahn (Dordrecht, Holland: Reidel, 1968), p. 389.
[8] For a brief discussion of this revolutionary era and its effect on and reflection in Persian literature, see: Kubičková in Rypka's

History of Iranian Literature, particularly pp. 355-358; and Kamshad, pp. 31-40.

[9] Zeynolabedin Maragheh'i, *Siyahatnameh-ye Ebrahim Beyg*, 3rd ed. (Tehran: Andisheh, 1975). This work consists of three volumes, the first of which is generally regarded as important in the development of modern Persian fiction.

[10] The translation of this book by Mirza Habib Esfahani, entitled *Sargozasht-e Haji Baba-ye Esfahani*, is available in a reprint in the United States (Costa Mesa, California: Mazda Publishers, 1996).

[11] Kamshad regards the Persian translation of this work a "very loose rendering of the original" (p. 24) that exaggerates to an even greater degree Morier's critical view of the country.

[12] These articles were published later in a collection: Ali Akbar Dehkhoda, *Charand Parand* (Tehran: Sazman-e Ketabha-ye Jibi, 1962).

[13] See Munibar Rahman, "Social Satire in Modern Persian Literature," *Bulletin of the Institute of Islamic Studies*, Nos. 2 and 3 (1958 and 1959):68-69; and Kamshad, pp. 37-40.

[14] Jamalzadeh, *Yeki Bud Yeki Nabud*, p. 11.

[15] These interventions included the rivalry between British and Russian powers before the Russian Revolution of 1917 and, later, Britain's attempt to make Iran "a mandated territory under British tutelage" (Kamshad, p. 34).

[16] Ehsan Yarshater, "The Modern Literary Idiom," *Iran Faces the Seventies*, ed. Ehsan Yarshater (New York: Praeger, 1971), p. 304.

[17] The first English version was translated by D. P. Costello (London: Calder, 1957; New York: Grove Press, 1957), a new edition of which has been reprinted frequently (New York: Evergreen, 1969). Another translation is found in '*The Blind Owl' and Other Hedayat Stories,* compiled by Carol L. Sayers (Minneapolis: Sorayya Publishers, 1984). However, Costello's translation remains the most widely circulated version in English.

[18] Numerous articles exist in English on *The Blind Owl.* A relatively recent in-depth book-length study of this work is Michael Beard, *Hedayat's "Blind Owl" as a Western Novel* (Princeton: Princeton University, 1990). See also: Iraj Bashiri, *The Fiction of Sadeq Hedayat* (Lexington, KY: Mazda Publishers, 1984).

[19] Kubičková and Kamshad both use the term "renaissance" to describe the literary events of this period. I have termed this change as a "literary revolution" in M. R. Ghanoonparvar, *Prophets of Doom: Literature as a Socio-Political Phenomenon in Modern Iran* (Lanham, Maryland: University Press of America, 1984).

[20] In poetry, Nima Yushij (1895-1960), now known as the father of "new poetry" in Iran, initiated the break with traditional verse in 1921. For a discussion of "new poetry," see Ahmad Karimi-Hakkak, *Recasting Persian Poetry: Scenarios of Poetic Modernity in Iran* (Salt Lake City: University of Utah Press, 1995), and Majid Naficy, *Modernism and Ideology in Persian Literature: A Return to Nature in the Poetry of Nima Yushij* (Lanham, New York, and Oxford: University Press of America, 1997). For sample translations of Persian "new poetry" in English and an introductory background, see Ahmad Karimi-Hakkak, *An Anthology of Modern Persian Poetry* (Boulder, Colorado: Westview Press, 1978).

[21] Jazayery, p. 12.

[22] *Nakhostin Kongereh-ye Nevisandegan-e Iran*, p. 184.

[23] This book has been translated into English by John O'Kane as *Her Eyes* (Lanham, Maryland: University Press of America, 1989) as a part of the Modern Persian Literature Series sponsored by Bibliotheca Persica.

[24] This novel has been translated into English by John K. Newton: Jalal Al-e Ahmad, *The School Principal* (Minneapolis and Chicago: Bibliotheca Islamica, 1974).

[25] Translations of this work include: Jalal Al-e Ahmad, *Plagued by the West*, trans. Paul Sprachman (New York: Caravan Books, 1982), and Jalal Al-e Ahmad, *Weststruckness*, trans. John Green and Ahmad Alizadeh (Lexington, Kentucky: Mazda Publishers, 1982).

[26] Baraheni, p. 465.

[27] See the review of Sadeq Chubak's *Kheymehshabbazi* in *Sokhan* 11-12 (December 1945-January 1946):913; and *Nakhostin Kongereh-ye Nevisandegan-e Iran*, p. 165; also, Henry D. G. Law, "Introductory Essay: Persian Writers," *Life and Letters and the London Mercury* 63, No. 148 (December 1949):199.

[28] For an overview of the works of these writers, see: Ghanoonparvar, *Prophets of Doom* and *In a Persian Mirror: Images of the West and Westerners in Iranian Fiction* (Austin: University of Texas Press, 1993); and Kamran Talattof, *The Politics of Writing in Iran: A History of Modern Persian Literature* (Syracuse: Syracuse University Press, 2000).

[29] For a discussion of the present generation of writers, see: Talattof, *The Politics of Writing in Iran*, and Mohammad Mehdi Khorrami, *Modern Reflections of Classical Traditions in Persian Fiction* (Lewiston, New York: The Edwin Mellen Press, 2003). For samples of English translations of contemporary Iranian writers, see: Trans. and ed., Shouleh Vatanabadi and Mohammad Mehdi Khorrami, *Another Sea, Another Shore: Persian Short*

Stories of Migration (Northampton, Massachusetts: Interlink Books, 2004).

[30] Sadeq Chubak, "Ah-e Ensan," *Kheymehshabbazi*, 4th ed. (Tehran: Javidan, 1972). "The Sigh of Mankind," though apparently written much earlier, replaced a short story in the 3rd ed. of *The Puppet Show* published in 1967.

[31]The biographical information is taken from: Mahnaz Abdollahi, "Salshomar-e Zendegi-ye Sadeq Chubak," and Sadeq Chubak, "Zendegi-ye Man," published in Ali Dehbashi, ed., *Yad-e Sadeq Chubak* (Tehran: Nashr-e Sales, 2001), and also from my personal conversations with Sadeq Chubak as well as a short biography in a personal letter to me, which appears in the Appendix.

[32] For a discussion of this novel, see "Chapter Three: The Fate of the Victims."

[33] These two short story collections are discussed in "Chapter Three."

[34] Concerning the particular interests of Jamalzadeh and Hedayat, mention should be made of Jamalzadeh's *Farhang-e Loghat-e Amiyaneh* [A Dictionary of Colloquial Words] (1962/63) and Hedayat's various works on Persian folklore, including *Osaneh* [Legend] (1931) and *Neyrangestan* [Land of Trickery] (1933).

[35] Mas'ud Zavarzadeh, "The Persian Short Story Since the Second World War: An Overview," *The Muslim World* 58 (1968):311.

[36] Kamshad, p. 127.

[37] Kubičková, p. 415.

[38] Chubak, *Kheymehshabbazi*, p. 234. This translation is my own.

[39] *Nakhostin Kongereh-ye Nevisandegan-e Iran*, pp. 183-184.

[40] See, for example: Abdolali Dastgheyb, *Naqd-e Asar-e Sadeq Chubak* (Tehran: Pazand, 1974), which is an elaboration of a series of articles he published in *Ferdowsi* magazine from 1969-1970; also, Hushang Golshiri, "Si Sal Romannevisi," *Jong-e Esfahan* 5 (Summer 1967):187-229; and Mahmud Kiyanush, *Barrasi-ye She'r va Nasr-e Farsi-ye Mo'aser* (Tehran: Mani, 1974/75), pp. 186-197.

[41] See Alavi's remarks quoted earlier in this chapter.

[42] For a discussion on the incarceration of writers during this period, see: Leo Hamalian and John D. Yohannan, eds. "Persian Literature," *New Writings From the Middle East* (New York: Mentor, 1978), pp. 274-275.

[43] Hafez F. Farmayan, "Observations on Sources for the Study of Nineteenth- and Twentieth-Century Iranian History," *International Journal of Middle East Studies* 5 (January 1974):3.

[44] Dastgheyb, p. 93.

[45] Sadeq Chubak, *The Patient Stone*, trans. M. R. Ghanoonparvar (Costa Mesa, California: Mazda Publishers, 1989), p. 11.

[46] Notable examples of these female characters are found in Ali Dashti's *Fetneh* (1949), *Jadu* (1952), and *Hendu* (1955); and also in Mohammad Hejazi's *Parichehr* (1927) and *Ziba* (1931), among others.
[47] Sa'id Nafisi, "A General Survey of the Existing Situation in Persian Literature," *Bulletin of the Institute of Iranian Studies*, No. 1 (1957):21.
[48] Kiyanush, p. 195.
[49] William James, *Pragmatism* (New York: Longman, Greens and Co., 1907), pp. 60-61.
[50] Hasan Nekuruh, "Dastanha-ye Sadeq Chubak: Ra az Shenakht Besu-ye Andisheh," *Negin* 11, No. 126 (October 1975):34.

Chapter 2: Social Puppets

[1] Sadeq Chubak, *Kheymehshabbazi* [The Puppet Show], 4th ed. (Tehran: Javidan, 1972). The most recent edition of this collection was published in the United States by Sherkat-e Ketab in Los Angeles, 1990. All quotations and references are from the latter edition. After the first edition, the subsequent printings in Iran replaced "Insolence" with "The Sigh of Mankind." The Los Angeles addition includes both selections.
[2] See the review of Sadeq Chubak's *Kheymehshabbazi* in *Sokhan* 11-12 (December 1945-January 1946):913.
[3] "Nafti" [The Kerosene Man], *Kheymehshabbazi*, pp. 9-21. This translation is taken from "The Kerosene Man," trans. Carter Bryant, in "Major Voices in Contemporary Persian Literature," *Literature East and West* 20 (1976):81.
[4] Ibid. For a discussion of this story, see Ali Ferdowsi, "Jame'ehshnakhti-ye Kheyr-o Sharr dar Qessehha-ye Sadeq Chubak," in *Yad-e Sadeq Chubak* [In Memory of Sadeq Chubak], ed. Ali Dehbashi (Tehran: Nashr-e Sales, 1991), p. 193.
[5] Ibid., p. 82.
[6] "Golha-ye Gushti," *Kheymehshabbazi*, pp. 23-41. A translation of this story by John Limbert is found in *Iranian Studies* 1 (Summer 1968):115-119.
[7] Ibid., pp. 26-27.
[8] Ibid., p. 41.
[9] Ibid., p. 38. For a discussion of this and other stories in this collection see: Abdolali Dastgheyb, *Naqd-e Asar-e Sadeq Chubak* (Tehran: Pazand, 1974).
[10] "Adl," *Kheymehshabbazi*, p. 45.
[11] "Zir-e Cheragh Qermez," *Khemehshabbazi*, p. 65. This story is discussed in Dastgheyb, pp. 47-48.

[12] Ibid., p. 71.
[13] "Akher-e Shab," *Kheymehshabbazi*, p. 84. This story is briefly discussed in: Reza Baraheni, *Qessehnevisi* (Tehran: Ashrafi, 1969), pp. 566-567.
[14] Ibid., p. 85.
[15] "Mardi dar Qafas," *Kheymehshabbazi*, pp. 89-137.
[16] Ibid., p. 126.
[17] Ibid., p. 124.
[18] Ibid., p. 137.
[19] "Pirahan-e Zereshki," *Kheymehshabbazi*, p. 141. For a discussion of this story, see Jahangir Dorri, "Tanz dar Asar-e Chubak" in *In Memory of Sadeq Chubak*, pp. 69-77.
[20] Ibid., p. 152.
[21] Ibid., pp. 150-151.
[22] "Musiyu Elyas" [Monsieur Elyas], *Kheymehshabbazi*, pp. 181-198. This story is translated by William Hanaway, *The Literary_Review* 18 (Fall 1974):61-68; also reprinted in *Sadeq Chubak: An Anthology*, ed. F. R. C. Bagley (Delmar, New York: Caravan Books, 1982), pp. 233-240. The two published versions differ slightly.
[23] The quoted version here is from *Sadeq Chubak: An Anthology*, pp. 233-234.
[24] *Korsi* is a traditional apparatus for heating in the winter. It consists of a square table the height of a coffee table around the four sides of which mattresses and cushions are placed, with a large quilt covering the table and the mattresses. The heat source is from thoroughly burned crushed charcoal that does not emit poisonous fumes and that is placed under the table.
[25] "Monsieur Elyas," *Sadeq Chubak: An Anthology*, pp. 236-237.
[26] "Ba'd az Zohr-e Akhar-e Pa'iz," *Kheymehshabbazi*, p. 205. For an analysis of this story, see: Azar Nafisi, "Barrasi-ye Adabi-ye Dastan-e 'Ba'd az Zohr-e Akher-e Pa'iz'" in *In Memory of Sadeq Chubak*, pp. 211-223.
[27] Ibid., p. 209.
[28] "Yahya," *Kheymehshabbazi*, pp. 223-225. A translation of this story by H. D. Law appears in *Life and Letters and the London Mercury* 63 (December 1949):228-229.
[29] "Esa'eh-ye Adab" appeared in the 3rd edition of *Kheymehshabbazi*, 1967. It is also included in the reprint of the collection in the United States. The quotes from the story are from the latter edition, p. 261.
[30] Ibid.
[31] "Ah-e Ensan" appears in the American edition of *The Puppet Show*, pp. 227-252. A translation of the poem by Leonard Bogle is published in "Major Voices in Contemporary Persian Fiction."

Literature East and West 20 (1976):73-80. The translation in this chapter is my own.
[32] *Kheymehshabbazi*, p. 252.
[33] For an analysis of this poem, see: Heshmat Moayyad, "Negahi Ah-e Ensan," in Ali Dehbashi, ed., *Yad-e Sadeq Chubak* (Tehran: Nashr-e Sales, 1991), pp. 317-323.

Chapter 3: The Fate of the Victims

[1] Sadeq Chubak, *Antari keh Lutiyash Mordeh Bud* (Los Angeles: Sherkat-e Ketab, 1990). All references in this book are to this edition.
[2] "Chera Darya Tufani Shodeh Bud," *Antari keh Lutiyash Mordeh Bud*, pp. 7-57.
[3] For an analysis of this story, see Abdolali Dastgheyb, *Naqd-e Asar-e Sadeq Chubak* (Tehran: Pazand, 1974), p. 48.
[4] "Chera Darya Tufani Shodeh Bud," p. 11. All translation passages of this story are my own.
[5] Ibid., p. 34.
[6] Ibid., pp. 33-34.
[7] Ibid., p. 52.
[8] Ibid., p. 53.
[9] Ibid., p. 57.
[10] "Qafas," *Antari keh Lutiyash Mordeh Bud*, pp. 59-65.
[11] For a brief discussion of this story, see Abdolali Dastgheyb, "Dastannevisi-ye Sadeq Chubak" in *Yad-e Sadeq Chubak* [In the Memory of Sadeq Chubak], ed. Ali Dehbashi (Tehran: Nashr-e Sales, 1991), p. 424.
[12] "Qafas," p. 60-61. The translated passages of this story are my own. A translation of the entire story is available by V. Kubičková and I. Lewit, published in *New Orient* 4 (1965):151-152.
[13] "Qafas," p. 62.
[14] "Antari keh Lutiyash Mordeh Bud," *Antari keh Lutiyash Mordeh Bud*, pp. 67-111.
[15] This story has been analyzed and discussed by many critics, among them Mohammad San'ati, "Barrasi-ye Ravanshenakhti-ye Asar-e Sadeq Chubak" pp. 162-167; Morio Fujei, "Arzeshyabi-ye 'Antari keh Lutiyash Mordeh Bud,'" pp. 263-265; and Abdolali Dastgheyb, "Dastannevisi-ye Sadeq Chubak," pp. 424-426, in *Yad-e Sadeq Chubak.*
[16] "Tup-e Lastiki," *Antari keh Lutiyash Mordeh Bud*, pp. 113-187. This play has been partially translated by Gertrude Elizabeth Nye, in "The Phonemes and Morphemes of Modern Persian: A Descriptive Study," PhD Dissertation, University of Michigan, 1955. A

complete translation of the play by F. R. C. Bagley is included in *Sadeq Chubak: An Anthology*, ed. F. R. C. Bagley (Delmar, New York: Caravan Books, 1982), pp. 241-282.

[17] For an analysis of this play see Hasan Mir'abedini, "Sadeq Chubak:Neveshtan az A'maq-e Mardom," in *Yad-e Sadeq Chubak*, p. 528, and Mahmud Enayat, "Taha'-ye Sadeq Chubak," in *Yad-e Sadeq Chubak*, pp. 238-239.

[18] "The Rubber Ball," trans. F. R. C. Bagley, in *Sadeq Chubak: An Anthology*, p. 274.

[19] Ibid.

[20] *Sadeq Chubak: An Anthology*, p. 8.

[21] Sadeq Chubak, *Tangsir* (Tehran: Javidan, 1963). A translation of this novel by Marziya Sami'i and F. R. C. Bagley entitled *One Man and His Gun* is included *Sadeq Chubak: An Anthology*, p. 13-181. A short story about the same incident, "Shir Mohammad" [Lion Mohammad], was published in the prestigious literary journal at the time, *Sokhan*, and later was included in a collection of short stories by the same author entitled *Shalvarha-ye Vaslehdar* [Patched Pants] (Tehran: Ketabha-ye Parastu, 1966).

[22] Observations on *Tangsir* by Abd al-Ali Dastgheyb, *Naqd-e Asar-e Sadeq Chubak*, such as that Chubak portrays the protagonist of this novel who is an ordinary human being as "an unrealistic champion and has promoted him to the status of the fist-fighting characters of Hollywood films" (p. 24), and also comments by Mahmud Kiyanush, 3rd ed. *Barrasi-ye She'r va Nasr-e Farsi-ye Mo'aser* (Tehran: Mani, 1974/75), p. 189, are typical of critics' views. Another critic who had criticized *Tangsir* and stated that it "more resembles the short story called 'Shir Mohammad' by Rasul Parvizi" and did not consider it a novel, in an article entitled "Puzeshi Agarcheh Dir" [An Apology, Though Late] published in *Yad-e Sadeq Chubak*, pp. 325-329, expressed his regrets for having expressed his earlier harsh views.

[23] "Darazna-ye Seh Shab-e Porgu," *Ayandegan*, 24 January 1970, p. 6, quoted in Hasan Nekuruh, "Dastanha-ye Sadeq Chubak: Rahi az Shenakht Besu-ye Andisheh," *Negin* 11, No. 126 (October 1975):31. This interview by Nosrat Rahmani also appears in *Yad-e Sadeq Chubak*, pp. 267-295.

[24] For an enlightening analysis of this novel see: Mohammad Mehdi Khorrami, "*Tangsir*, Bazsazi-ye Osturehguneh-ye Dastan-e Vaqe'i" [*Tangsir*, Mythological Reconstruction of a True Story], *Iranshenasi*, Vol. V, No. 2 (Summer 1993):283-291. Among other articles discussing this novel, see: Ehsan Tabari, "Roman-e *Tangsir,* Manzelgahi dar Adabiyyat-e Mo'aser," pp. 313-316; K. Tina, "Dar Bareh-ye *Tangsir*," pp. 345-356; Gholamhoseyn Yusefi, "Naqd-e Roman-e *Tangsir*," pp.

465-474; and Nasrin Rahimiyeh, "Sadeq Chubak dar Adabiyyat-e Jahan," pp. 337-343, in *Yad-e Sadeq Chubak.*
[25] Khorrami, "*Tangsir*, Bazsazi-ye Osturehguneh-ye Dastan-e Vaqe'i," p. 284.
[26] For example, see: Tina, "Darbareh-ye *Tangsir,*" pp. 345-355.
[27] Sadeq Chubak, *Ruz-e Avval-e Qabr* (Los Angeles: Sherkat-e Ketab, 1990). All quotations are from this printing unless otherwise indicated.
[28] Ibid., "Gurkanha," pp. 8-27.
[29] Ibid., pp. 13-14.
[30] Ibid., pp. 26-27. This story has been discussed Ali Ferdowsi, "Jame'ehshenasi-ye Kheyr va Sharr dar Qessehha-ye Sadeq Chubak," pp. 189-190, and Abdolali Dastgheyb, "Dastannevisi-ye Sadeq Chubak," pp. 441-442, in *Yad-e Sadeq Chubak*; and Abdolali Dastgheyb, *Naqd-e Asar-e Sadeq Chubak*, p. 59.
[31] "Cheshm-e Shisheh'i," *Ruz-e Avval-e Qabr*, pp. 29-34.
[32] Ibid., p. 33. For a brief analysis of this story, see Debra Miller-Mostaqel, "Barrasi-ye Dastanha-ye Kutah-e Sadeq of Chubak," in *Yad-e Sadeq Chubak*, p. 81.
[33] "Dasteh Gol," *Ruz-e Avval-e Qabr*, pp. 35-76.
[34] Ibid., p. 44.
[35] Ibid., p. 39.
[36] For varied analyses of this story, see Ali Ferdowsi, "Jame'ehshenasi-ye Kheyr va Sharr dar Qessehha-ye Sadeq Chubak," pp. 179-184; Fariborz Ebrahimpur, "Naqd va Barrasi-ye Dastani az Chubak," pp. 368-405; and Abdolali Dastgheyb, "Dastannevisi-ye Sadeq Chubak," pp. 442-443 in *Yad-e Sadeq Chubak.*
[37] "Yek Chiz-e Khakestari," *Ruz-e Avval-e Qabr*, pp. 75-80.
[38] Ibid., p. 79.
[39] "Pacheh Khizak," *Ruz-e Avval-e Qabr*, pp. 81-92.
[40] Ibid., p. 82.
[41] Ibid.
[42] For an analysis of this story, see: Dastgheyb, "Dastannevisi-ye Sadeq Chubak," *Yad-e Sadeq Chubak*, pp. 443-444. He considers this story one of Chubak's best.
[43] "The First Day in the Grave," *Ruz-e Avval-e Qabr*, pp. 93-144.
[44] This novel has been translated by G. M. Wickens as *Haji Agha: Portrait of an Iranian Confidence Man* (Austin: Center for Middle Eastern Studies, The University of Texas at Austin, 1979).
[45] "The First Day in the Grave," *Ruz-e Avval-e Qabr*, pp. 134-135.
[46] Ibid., p. 135.
[47] "Hamrah," *Ruz-e Avval-e Qabr*, pp. 145-148. The second version appears later in the collection and is called "Hamrah, Shiveh'i Digar" [Companion, Another Method], pp. 181-186.
[48] For an analysis of this story, see "Jame'ehshnasi-ye Kheyr va Sharr dar Qessehha-ye Sadeq Chubak," *Ruz-e Avval-e Qabr*, pp. 185-187.

[49] "Arusak-e Forushi," *Ruz-e Avval-e Qabr*, pp. 149-172.
[50] Dastgheyb briefly discusses this story in "Dastannevisi-ye Sadeq Chubak," p. 446.
[51] "Yek Shab-e Bikhabi," *Ruz-e Avval-e Qabr*, pp. 173-179.
[52] Ibid., p. 178. Abdolali Dastgheyb considers this story to be "even more artificial" than "A Doll for Sale." See: "Dastannevisi-ye Sadeq Chubak," p. 446.
[53] "Hafkhat," pp. 187-238.
[54] A translation of this play by Shireen Aghdami, Jeff Bloxsome and Caryn Hodge is available in: M. R. Ghanoonparvar and John Green, *Iranian Drama: An Anthology* (Costa Mesa, California: Mazda Publishers, 1989), pp. 133-151.
[55] Chubak himself regarded this play as having deserved more attention than it had gotten (personal conversation with the author in 1989).
[56] Sadeq Chubak, *Cheragh-e Akher* (Los Angeles: Sherkat-e Ketab, 1990). All translated segments refer to this edition, unless otherwise indicated.
[57] For an analysis of this story, see: Abdolali Dastgheyb, "Dastannevisi-ye Sadeq Chubak," p. 430, and Hasan Mir'abedini, "Sadeq Chubak: Neveshtan az A'maq-e Mardom," pp. 536-537, in *Yad-e Sadeq Chubak.*
[58] "The Hubcap Thief," *Cheragh-e Akher*, pp. 75-80.
[59] Ibid., p. 77.
[60] Ibid., p. 80. For an analysis of this story, see: Peter Chelkowski, "Sadeq Chubak va Dastan-e Kutah-e Farsi," in *Yad-e Sadeq Chubak*, pp. 43-47.
[61] "Kaftarbaz," *Cheragh-e Akher*, pp. 81-97.
[62] This story has been analyzed by Mohammad Ali Sepanlu, "Darbareh-ye Dastan-e Kaftarbaz," in *Yad-e Sadeq Chubak*, pp. 505-515.
[63] In his "Dastannevisi-ye Sadeq Chubak," pp. 431-432, Abdolali Dastgheyb finds this to be a "weak story in which no new social meaning is found."
[64] "Bacheh Gorbeh'i keh Chesmanash Baz Nashodeh Bud," *Cheragh-e Akher*, pp. 99-109.
[65] Ibid., p. 109.
[66] "Asb-e Chubi," *Cheragh-e Akher*, pp. 111-131.
[67] This story is analyzed in: Dastgheyb, "Dastannevisi-ye Sadeq Chubak," pp. 438-441.
[68] For a discussion of this story in the context of the portrayal of Westerners in Persian literature, see: M. R. Ghanoonparvar, *In a Persian Mirror: Images of the West and Westerners in Iranian Fiction* (Austin: The University of Texas Press, 1993), pp. 97-98.
[69] "Atma, Sag-e Man," *Cheragh-e Akher*, pp. 133-197.
[70] Ibid., pp. 184-185.
[71] Ibid., 196-197.

[72] "Rahavard," *Cheragh-e Akher*, pp. 199-210.
[73] Reza Baraheni discusses this story in *Qessehnevisi*, pp. 647-648.
[74] "Parizad va Pariman," *Cheragh-e Akher*, pp. 211-229.
[75] In pre-Islamic times and in Persian mythology there are examples of marriage between brothers and sisters.
[76] "Rahavard," *Cheragh-e Akher*, pp. 266-267.
[77] Ancient Iranians believed that there is a supernatural, mysterious force, *farr*, from which stems the victory of kings and with which they engaged in great feats. This story is briefly discussed in: Baraheni, *Qessehnevisi*, pp. 648-649.
[78] "Dust," *Cheragh-e Akher*, pp. 231-256.
[79] See: Baraheni, *Qessehnevisi*, pp. 649-651, for a brief discussion of this story.

Chapter 4: On The Patient Stone

[1]Stendhal, *The Red and the Black*, trans. Lloyd C. Parks (New York: New American Library, Signet Classic, 1970), p. 85. A summary of part of this chapter was used in my translation of *The Patient Stone*.
[2]Henry James, "The Art of Fiction," in *Henry James*, ed. Lyon N. Richardson (Urbana and London: University of Illinois Press, 1966), p. 77.
[3]Paul de Man, *Blindness and Insight* (New York: Oxford University Press, 1971). See especially p. 17.
[4] Hushang Golshiri, "Si Sal Romannevisi," *Jong-e Esfahan* 5 (Summer 1967) :217.
[5]Abdoalali Dastgheyb, *Naqd-e Asar-e Sadeq Chubak* (Tehran: Pazand, 1974), p. 96.
[6] Mahmud Kiyanush, *Barrasi-ye She'r va Nasr-e Farsi-ye Mo'aser*, 3rd ed. (Tehran: Mani, 1974/75), p. 196. Similar views were also expressed by Najaf Daryabandari in his article, "Az Natayej-e Neveshtan bara-ye Nevisandeh Budan," reprinted in *Yad-e Sadeq Chubak*, pp. 379-389.
[7] Hasan Nekuruh, "Dastanha-ye Sadeq Chubak: Rahi az Shenakht Besu-ye Andisheh," *Negin* 11, no. 126 (October 1975):34.
[8] Reza Baraheni, *Qessehnevisi* (Tehran: Ashrafi, 1969), pp. 680-681.
[9] Golshiri, p. 216.
[10] Opinions of critics have changed in recent years, particularly since the death of Chubak in 1998. Numerous positive analytical articles on Chubak and *The Patient Stone* have been published, including Faridoun Farrokh, "Didgah-e Nafsgarayaneh-ye Sadeq Chubak dar *Sang-e Sabur*," in *Iranshenasi*, Vol. V, No. 2 (Summer 1993):276-282; Mahmud Enayat, "Tanha'i-ye Sadeq Chubak," pp. 237-244; Kinka Markush, "Alam-e Sehramiz-e *Sang-e Sabur-e* Chubak," pp. 245-256;

and Mohammad Ali Sepanlu, "Darbabareh-ye *Sang-e Sabur*," pp. 391-394 in *Yad-e Sadeq Chubak.*

[11] Sadeq Chubak, *The Patient Stone*, trans. M. R. Ghanoonparvar (Costa Mesa, California: Mazda Publishers, 1989), p. 2.

[12] E. M. Forster, *Aspects of the Novel* (New York: Harcourt, Brace and World, Inc., 1955), p. 25.

[13] Abdolali Dastgheyb, *Naqd-e Asar-e Sadeq Chubak* (Tehran: Zaman, 1974), p. 79; and Mahmud Kiyanush, *Barrasi-ye She'r va Nasr-e Farsi-ye Mo'aser*, 3rd ed. (Tehran: Mani, 1974/75), p. 192, are among the critical commentaries that refer to the "technique" of the novel as stream of consciousness. Hushang Golshiri, "Sad Sal Romannevisi," *Jong-e Esfahan*_5 (Summer 1967):225-226, believes that the novel is an unsuccessful attempt at the technique of interior monologue (mistranslated into Persian as "interior dialogue"). In a similar vein, in the longest and most detailed critical piece devoted to *The Patient Stone*, Reza Baraheni, in *Qessehnevisi*, 2nd ed. (Tehran: Ashrafi, 1969), briefly describes the technique of the novel as "interior monologue."

[14] William James, "The Stream of Thought," *The Principles of Psychology*, 20th ed., ed. Robert Maynard Hutchins (Chicago: Encyclopaedia Britannica, Great Books of the Western World, 1975), pp. 146-187.

[15] Rene Wellek and Austin Warren, *Theory of Literature*, 3rd ed. (New York: Harcourt, Brace and World, Inc., 1970), p. 92.

[16] Robert Humphrey, *Stream of Consciousness in the Modern Novel*, 8th ed. (Berkely: University of California Press, 1972), p. 2. Humphrey points out that there is no stream of consciousness technique, rather several techniques which present stream of consciousness.

[17] Erich Auerbach, *Mimesis: The Representation of Reality in Western Literature*,_4th ed., trans. Willard R. Trask (Princeton, New Jersey: Princeton University Press, 1974), p. 538.

[18] *The Patient Stone*, p. 13.

[19] Ibid, pp. 17-20.

[20] Humphrey, *Stream of Consciousness in the Modern Novel*, (see note 16); Leon Edel, *The Modern Psychological Novel* (New York: Grosset and Dunlap, Universal Library Edition, 1964); Melvin Friedman, *Stream of Consciousness: A Study in Literary Method* (New Haven: Yale University Press, 1955).

[21] Humphrey, p. 24.

[22] Ibid., p. 25.

[23] Ibid., p. 27.

[24] Ibid., pp. 33-34.

[25] Ibid., pp. 35-36. Friedman does not clearly distinguish between "interior monologue" and "soliloquy" (see pp. 20, 253); Edel, on the other hand, does not seem to consider soliloquy as a technique of stream of consciousness novels. In fact, he distinguishes soliloquies as "organized monologues in which the mind presents reasoned and ordered thought, 'the end-product' of stream of consciousness, not the disordered stream itself" (p. 17).
[26] *The Patient Stone*, p. 2.
[27] Humphrey, p. 36.
[28] *The Patient Stone*, p. 101.
[29] Ibid. p. 138.
[30] In general terms, I am using the notions of convention and literary competence as Jonathan Culler discusses them in his *Structural Poetics* (Ithaca, New York: Cornell University Press, 1975), pp. 113-130.
[31] Humphrey, p. 43.
[32] *The Patient Stone*, p. 39.
[33] Ibid., pp. 119-120.
[34] Ibid., pp. 123-124.
[35] Ibid., pp.124-125. [36] Ibid., p. 13.
[37] Ibid., p. 43.
[38] Ibid., p. 138.
[39] Ibid., p. 133.
[40] The Persian text of *The Patient Stone* uses two print fonts, a larger and a smaller one. The smaller one I have rendered into English script as italics in my translation of the novel.
[41] *The Patient Stone*, pp.7-8.
[42] Golshiri (see note 13) uses the term "internal dialogue"; however, he refers to the general technique of the novel as a whole, and his use of the term indicates that it is a Persian mistranslation of the English "interior monologue" or French *monologue interieur*.
[43] *The Patient Stone*, pp. 3-4.
[44] Ibid., p. 4.
[45] Ibid.
[46] These exceptions include two doggerel rhymes (pp. 136, 142) that seem to function to soften the intensity of the moment.
[47] *The Patient Stone*, p. 110.
[48] Ibid., p. 22.
[49] Ibid., p. 92.
[50] Ibid., p. 101.
[51] Ibid., p. 119.
[52] Ibid., p. 120.
[53] Ibid.
[54] Ibid., p. 85.

[55] Kiyanush, *Barrasi-ye She'r va Nasr-e Farsi-ye Mo'aser*, p. 192 (see note 2), notes that Chubak is not "innovative" in his use of small print (italics), citing others who have employed the device, such as Faulkner in *The Sound and the Fury*; however, the critic seems oblivious to the function of the device in either novel.
[56] Humphrey, p. 54.
[57] *The Patient Stone*, pp. 85-86, 87.
[58] Ibid., p. 96.
[59] Ibid., pp. 34-38.
[60] Friedman, p. 253.
[61] *The Patient Stone*, pp. 36, 38.
[62] Humphrey, p. 59.
[63] See, for instance, Baraheni, pp. 680-681; and Golshiri, pp. 226-227.
[64] Humphrey, p. 39.
[65] *The Patient Stone*, p. 22.
[66] Ibid., pp. 61-73.
[67] Ibid., pp. 142-144.
[68] Ibid., pp. 45-51.
[69] Ibid., p. 106.
[70] For a translation and discussion of this poem, see: Reza Saberi, *The Poems of Hafez* (Lanham, New York, London: University Press of America, 1995), pp. 20-21.
[71] A linguistic study of the idiolects contained in *The Patient Stone* deserves more detailed attention. However, since such a study should be conducted on the original Persian text, it is beyond the scope of the present analysis.
[72] Humphrey, p. 85.
[73] *The Patient Stone*. p. 116.
[74] Ibid.
[75] The "patient stone" is a folkloric symbol representing an ear or a friend, as it were, which listens to the grieving, lonely person. For a version of this story see: Sadeq Hedayat, "The Patient Stone," *Neveshtehha-ye Parakandeh*, 2nd printing (Tehran: Enteshart-e Amir Kabir, 1965), pp. 131-138.
[76] *The Patient Stone*, pp. 4-6.
[77] Edel, pp. 25-26.
[78] Nosrat Rahmani, "Darazna-ye Seh Shab-e Porgu," *Yadnameh-ye Sadeq Chubak* (Tehran: Nashr-e Sales, 2001), p. 289.
[79] *The Patient Stone*, p. 1.
[80] Ibid.
[81] Ibid.
[82] Ibid., p. 2.
[83] Ibid.
[84] Ibid., pp. 3-4.

[85] Ibid., p. 18.
[86] Ibid., pp. 18-19.
[87] Georg Lukacs, *The Theory of the Novel*, 3rd ed., trans. Anna Bostock (Cambridge: MIT Press, 1977), pp. 30-31. I am using Lukacs' description of "the age of the epic" in general terms as it seems to apply here to the epic world of the *Book of Kings*.
[88] *The Patient Stone*, p. 45.
[89] Ibid., p. 48.
[90] Georg Lukacs, *The Theory of the Novel*, p. 29.
[91] *The Patient Stone*, p. 94.
[92] Ibid., p. 7.
[93] Georg Lukacs, *The Theory of the Novel*, p. 44. Again, Lukacs' observation applies here: "Every figure...is related at his deepest roots to every other figure; all understand one another because all speak the same language...be it as mortal enemies."
[94] *The Patient Stone*, p. 25.
[95]Reza Baraheni, *Qessehnevisi*, p. 696.
[96] *The Patient Stone*, p. 10.
[97] Ibid., p. 23.
[98] Ibid., p. 12.
[99] Ibid., p. 10.
[100] Ibid., p. 77.
[101] Ibid., p. 114.
[102] Ibid.
[103] Ibid., p. 39.
[104] Ibid., p. 117.
[105] Ibid., p. 57.
[106] Ibid., pp. 117-118.
[107] Ibid., p. 42.
[108] Ibid., pp. 23, 42.
[109] Ibid., p. 23.
[110] Ibid., p. 109.
[111] Ibid., p. 100.
[112] Ibid., pp. 130-131.
[113] Perhaps in Seyf ol-Qalam there is a reflection of Rostam Farrokhzad's prediction: "From Persians, Arabs, and Turks will appear/ A race so mingled and so queer," *The Patient Stone*, p. 49.
[114] *The Patient Stone*, p. 13.
[115] Ibid.
[116] Ibid., p. 60.
[117] This legend has been recorded in: Amirgoli Amini, "Dastan-e Sang-e Sabur," *Si Afsaneh* (Isfahan, Iran: Owliya, n.d.), pp. 27-30; and Sadeq Hedayat, "Sang-e Sabur," *Neveshtehha-ye Parakandeh*, p. 131-138. The latter has been translated into English

by Stephen McFarland in "Major Voices in Contemporary Persian Literature," *Literature East and West* 20 (1976):45-49.

[118] *The Patient Stone*, p. 19.

[119] Ibid., p. 154.

[120] Ibid., p. 172, 175. Although in the translation Mashya and Mashyaneh are used, in the original Persian, in these two instances Chubak uses Adam and Eve, perhaps inadvertently.

[121] R. C. Zaehner, *The Teachings of the Magi: A Compendium of Zoroastrian Beliefs* (New York: Oxford University Press, 1976), p. 18.

[122] For a discussion of Zervan and Zervanism, see R. C. Zaehner, *Zurvan: A Zoroastrian Dilemma* (Oxford: The Clarendon Press, 1955).

[123] Zaehner, *The Teachings of the Magi*, p. 18.

[124] Ibid.

[125] For a similar perception about creation also see: Sadeq Hedayat, *Afsaneh-ye Afarinesh*, translated as *The Myth of Creation* by M. R. Ghanoonparvar (Costa Mesa, California: Mazda publishers, 1998).

[126] *The Patient Stone*, p. 33.

[127] Ibid., p. 172.

[128] Ibid., p. 178.

[129] Ibid., p. 183.

[130] Baraheni, *Qessehnevisi*, pp. 681-682; Hasan Nekuruh, p. 34; Abdolali Dastgheyb, *Naqd-e Asar-e Sadeq Chubak*, p. 89; and Hushang Golshiri, "Si Sal Romannevisi," p. 224.

Chapter 5: Conclusion and Reassessment

[1]Mohammad Ali Jamalzadeh, *Yeki Bud Yeki Nabud*, 4th ed. (Tehran: Ebn-e Sina, 1954).

[2] Sadeq Hedayat, *Buf-e Kur*, 14th ed. (Tehran: Amir Kabir, 1973).

[3]Zeynolabedin Maragheh'i, *Siyahatnameh-ye Ebrahim Beyg*, 3rd ed. (Tehran: Andisheh, 1975). A translation of this work has been completed by James Clark and will be published by Mazda Publishers in 2005.

[4] This book has been translated into English by John O'Kane as *Her Eyes* (Lanham, MD: University Press of America, 1989) as a part of the Modern Persian Literature Series sponsored by Bibliotheca Persica.

[5] For an enlightening discussion of Bahram Sadeqi's work see Hasan Abedini, *Sad Sal Dastannevisi Dar Iran*, Vol.1, second printing, 1989, and Vol. 2, 1990, (Tehran: Nashr-e Tandar).

[6] Personal conversation with the author in 1994.
[7] *Gavkhuni* has been translated as *The Marsh* by Afkham Darbandi (Costa Mesa, California: Mazda Publishers, 1996); and a translation of *Kalleh-ye Asb* by Ali Anooshahr is in press and will be available in 2005 by Mazda Publishers.
[8] Not only to this author, but to many people who visited Chubak, in conversations Chubak often mentioned that he was writing his memoirs. On one occasion he took this author to his home office and showed him the manuscript.
[9] For a discussion of the image of Jews in modern Persian literature see: Jaleh Pirnazar, "Chehreh-ye Yahud dar Asar-e Seh Nevisandah-ye Motajadad-e Irani," *Iran Nameh* Vol. 13, No. 4 (Fall 1995):483-502.
[10] See: Amnon Netzer, ed., *Padyavand*, Judeo-Iranian and Jewish Studies Series, published under the auspices of the Graduate Student Foundation (Costa Mesa, Califormia: Mazda Publishers, Vol. 1, 1996; Vol. 2, 1997; Vol. 3, 1999).
[11] See: Joya Blondel Saad, *The Image of Arabs in Modern Persian Literature* (Lanham, Maryland: University Press of America, 1996).
[12] For example see the essays in a collection entitled *Arab-Iranian Relations*, edited by Khair el-Din Haseeb (Beirut: Centre for Arab Unity Studies, 1998). It should be pointed out that perhaps what I have referred to as an anti-Jewish attitude should not be confused with the anti-Semitism that was prevalent in Europe and the West in general. Atrocities against Jews certainly took place in Iran, but they were generally incited by fanatical clerics and their zealous followers. This was also true in regard to the Baha'is. The general public, in particular the educated classes, however, did not widely share such sentiments.
[13] Appendix No. 1. At that time I was teaching at the University of Virginia in Charlottesville.
[14] Appendix No. 2.
[15] These comments appear in personal letters to this author not included in the Appendices.
[16] Appendix No. 3.
[17] Appendix No. 4.
[18] Appendix No. 5.
[19] Appendices Nos. 6 and 7.
[20] Appendix No. 8.
[21] Despite Chubak's expressed wish, later on with the efforts and encouragement of Farzaneh Milani, his papers and memoirs were given by his family to the library of the University of Virginia in Charlottesville.
[22] The short biography of Chubak, Appendix No. 9.
[23] Appendix No. 10.
[24] Appendix No. 11.

[25] This is despite the fact that he had already expressed his approval of my translation. He also expressed his approval of the translation in an interview with Sadroddin Elahi, "Ba Sadeq Chubak dar Bagh-e Khaterehha" in Ali Dehbashi, *Yad-e Sadeq Chubak* (Tehran: Nashr-e Sales, 2001), p. 110.

[26] Appendix No. 12.

[27] He had also made similar statements to Dr. Ahmad Jabbari, the president of Mazda Publishers, which eventually published *The Patient Stone*.

[28] Appendix No. 13.

[29] Appendix No. 14.

[30] Given all that had occurred before, I took notes of the telephone conversation with Mr. Chubak on June 4, 1988, when I had moved to Austin, Texas. He informed me that he was supposed to be hospitalized in two days for kidney problems. Having sent several pages of notes to me earlier, he told me that he had a few other notes that he would send me. I told him that I had been told that he had asked someone else to write the introduction to the translation. He said that he had not talked to that person for over a year. He described the contract with Mazda Publishers as the Turkmanchay Treaty (of 1828, according to which Iran was cheated out of major territories).

[31] Francis William Bain, *A Digit of the Moon*, translated by Sadeq Chubak as *Mahpareh* (Tehran: Nilufar, 1991).

[32] See two articles by Kaveh Gowharin, "Mahpareh'i az Nasr," in *Yad-e Sadeq Chubak*, pp. 331-335 and 475-482.

[33] The scholar was Liora Hendelman-Baavur and the title of her presentation was "Vital or Volatile? Gendered Bodies in Two Iranian Novels."

Appendix

UNIVERSITY OF VIRGINIA
ORIENTAL LANGUAGES
302 CABELL HALL
CHARLOTTESVILLE, VIRGINIA 22903

October 17, 1979

TEL. (804) 924-715.

Mr. Frank Bagley
School of Oriental Studies
University of Durham
Elvet Hill, Durham DH1 3TH
England

Dear Mr. Bagley,

I have just completed a translation of Sādeq Chūbak's Sang-e Sabūr (my translation is part of a larger work, which includes a critical study of The Patient Stone and was submitted to The University of Texas at Austin as my doctoral dissertation), and Mr. Ehsan Yarshater of the Persian Heritage Series has informed me that they are interested in including it in their new series in Modern Persian Literature.

I am writing to you on the advice of Mr. Yarshater, hoping to get in touch with Mr. Chūbak through you. During the last three years which I have been engaged in this project of translation and critical study, I have tried by various means and through different persons, including Professor Michael C. Hillmann of The University of Texas, to get in touch with Mr. Chūbak. Unfortunately, however, I have thusfar been unsuccessful. For the publication of my translation I would like very much to have Mr. Chūbak's permission. I understand that this is not legally necessary; however, I feel I have a moral obligation to secure it.

No financial benefit from this publication can be expected as the publication of the book requires a subvention, which, Mr. Yarshater has been kind to inform me, may be provided by Bibliotheca Persica. Their primary interest is, I am told, in affording better recognition to modern Persian literature.

If you could inform me of how to get in touch with Mr. Chūbak, or of how I might go about gaining his permission to publish my translation, I would be very grateful.

Thank you for your time and attention.

Sincerely,

Mohammad R. Ghanoonparvar

Mohammad R. Ghanoonparvar

University of Durham School of Oriental Studies

Elvet Hill, Durham DH1 3TH
Telephone: Durham 64371 (STD code 0385)

Mr. Mohammad R. Ghanoonparvar,
Department of Oriental Languages,
University of Virginia,
302 Cabell Hall,
Charlottesville,
Virginia 22903,
U.S.A.

2nd November, 1979.

Dear Mr. Ghanoonparvar,

Thank you for your letter of 17 October 1979. After receiving it, I telephoned Mr. Sadeq Chubak, who is at present in London. He authorized me to give you his address: 25 Collingwood House, 99 New Cavendish Street, London W.1., England (Telephone 01 580 8160). He also told me that he intends to travel to the U.S.A. at the end of November and would like to meet you.

A series of translations entitled "Modern Persian Literature Series" is being prepared under the auspices of the Encyclopaedia Persica and the general editorship of Professor E. Yarshater's colleague Dr. Robert C. Eng. One of the books is to consist of translations of Chubak's works including Tangsir (tr. by Dr. Marziye Sami'i and myself, Monsieur Elias (tr.b Prof. Hanaway), Chashm-e Shishe'i (tr. by Mr. Babak Chubak), and probably also Cherāgh-e Ākhar and Tup-e Lāstīkī.

Mr. Sadeq Chubak's son Bābak has also translated part of Sang-e Sabur which he has entitled "The Zoo of Eden". Now I learn that you have translated the whole of Sang-e Sabur.

On account of the local colour and the background elements from classical Persian literature, Sang-e Sabur must have been very difficult to translate into intelligible English for non-Iranologist readers.

At Mr. Sadeq Chubak's request, and with Dr. Robert C. Eng's permission, I have checked the translations by other contributors and have offered suggestions for making the English more idiomatic and for adding explanatory footnotes. Dr. Eng has in turn checked my suggestions and eliminated my anglicisms and British (i.e. un-American) spellings.

With regard to your translation of Sang-e Sabur, I suggest that you consult (1) Mr. Sadeq Chubak, (2) Dr. Robert C. Eng, (3) Mr. Babak Chubak. Dr. Eng's address is 167 East 67 Street, New York, N.Y. 10021, U.S.A. The address of Mr. Babak Chubak, who has an American wife and is now domiciled in the U.S.A., was formerly 3440 North 84th Street, Milwaukee, Wisconsin 53222 9624385 (Telephone 414 4422635 [home] or 414 6786283 [office]; but Mr. Sadeq Chubak told me that Mr. and Mrs. Babak Chubak have recently moved house.

Inclusion of a translation Sang-e Sabur would probably make the first Chubak volume for the Modern Persian Literature Series too long. Since you have translated the whole of Sang-e Sabur and Mr. Babak Chubak has translated a part of it, I suggest that you and Mr. Babak Chubak agree on a text to be described as your joint translation and then propose to Dr. Eng that it be published in a second Chubak volume in The Modern Persian Literature Series.

contd...

...contd

I have taken the liberty to make copies of your letter and of this reply and to send the copies to Mr. Sadeq Chubak and to Dr. Robert C. Eng for their information and comments.

If you and all concerned agree to my suggestion, I request that you will kindly let me check the translation of Sang-e Sabur and (if necessary) make the English more idiomatic and add explanatory footnotes.

With good wishes,

Yours sincerely,

F.R.C. Bagley

F.R.C. Bagley,
Lecturer in Persian Studies.

21 March, 1979.

Dr. Robert W. Eng,
167 East 67 Street,
New York, N.Y. 10021,
U.S.A.

Dear Mr. Eng,

I am glad to have received your letter of 5 March 1979, and i hope I am right in inferring from it that your organization is able to continue its work. Having learnt by telephone that Mr. Sadeq Chubak is still in London (at the same address), I informed him of what you said.

I possess copies of the manuscripts which I sent you with the exceptions of "The Zoo of Eden," "The Glass Eye", and "Monsieur Elias". My copy of "One Man and his Gun" is uncorrected. I think that it will be unnecessary for you to return the manuscripts to me, and that checking of the galley proofs against the Persian texts will suffice. I hope that your copy-editor will not make further changes of vocabulary, spelling, and punctuation.

After consultation with Mr. Chubak, I request that the copyright may be held by him alone. I can make this request also on behalf of Dr. Marziye Sami'i (Qannadan), who authorized me to act for her; and Mr. SadeqyChubak said on the telephone that I may make it on behalf of Mr. Babak Chubak. Dr. William L. Hanaway Jnr. teaches Persian at a U.S. university, I understand Pennsylvania. Last year I tried hard to find the whereabouts of Mr. Maurice Left, but without success. Neither Mr. Chubak nor I know the present whereabouts of Mr. John Limbert. Mr. W. Graves Law died many years ago.

I amended the translations at Mr. Sadeq Chubak's request and did not seek the approval of the translators for my amendments. Mr. Sadeq Chubak on behalf of his son Babak authorized me to amend the latter's translations. The amendments which I made to Dr. Hanaway's translation (of "Monsieur Elias") are very slight and mainly concerned with transliteration, but the amendments, including insertions of omitted passages, which I made to those of Mr. John Limbert and the late W. Graves Law are substantial.

In principle, agreement ought to be obtained from all the translators to (1) the publication, (2) the amendments, (3) the assignment of the copyright (to Mr. Chubak), and (4) the division of the royalties (on the basis of half to Mr. Chubak and half to be apportioned among the translators in proportion to the lengths of their contributions).

In regard to the apportionment and payment of the translators' royalties, I must (as I said before) request that you or the publishers kindly do this, so as to save me trouble with the British tax authorities.

I see no solution to the problem of obtaining agreement from Mr. John Limbert, who is an American, and Mr. Maurice Left. I have given Dr. Hanaway's address above. Mr. Babak Chubak is now living in the U.S.A. at 3440 North 84th Street, Milwaukee, Wisconsin 53222, Telephone (414) 4422635 (home) or 414 6786283 (office). I suggest that perhaps you may send to Dr. Hanaway and Mr. Babak Chubak copies of the galley proofs of their contributions and request them to state their formal agreement to the above four points.

Mr. Sadeq Chubak asked me to convey his gratitude for your help, and I wish to repeat my own thanks.

Yours sincerely,

جناب آقای چوبک

بعد از مکالمه تلفنی منیژه هم بار دیگر خوشحالی خودم را از صحبت با جنابعالی و نیز مژده دیدار با شما را در آینده نزدیک در آمریکا به عرض برسانم. همانطور که قبلاً به اطلاع رسانده‌ام سه سال گذشته کار مدام شد و روز و شب با آثار جنابعالی بخصوص سنگ صبور بوده است. در این سه سال باز همانطور که عرض کردم سعی کرده بودم به طرق مختلف با شما تماس بگیرم ولی همان سال گذشته که شنیدم شما در آمریکا بودید این کار عملی نشد. بهر حال این گذشته است و امیدوارم آشنائی تلفنی اخیر سرآغازی نوید بخش برای آشنائی بیشتر در آینده باشد.

فکر کنم بیجا نباشد (و امید است این امر حمل به خودستائی نشود) که چند کلمه از خودم بنویسم. بنده متولد اصفهانم و تحصیلات ابتدائی و متوسطه خود را در همان شهر به پایان رسانده‌ام. در سال ۱۹۵۵ پس از دریافت لیسانس در رشته زبان و ادبیات انگلیسی عازم خارج شدم. پس از یک سال در دانشگاه هایدلبرگ آلمان (فوق لیسانس در ادبیات و جامعه شناسی) به آمریکا آمدم و تا سال ۱۹۷۳ در دانشگاه‌های مختلف در رشته ادبیات انگلیسی به تحصیل پرداختم. ولی در تمام این مدت کم و بیش با ادبیات معاصر ایران سروکار داشته‌ام. در سال ۱۹۷۴ به ایران رفتم

Translation of Appendix 4)
[November 1979]

Dear Mr. Chubak,

Following our telephone conversation, once again I would like to express my pleasure in talking with you as well as the good news of being able to meet with you in the near future in the United States. As I mentioned before, I have spent the past three years working day and night on your work, especially *The Patient Stone*. In these three years, as I mentioned to you, I tried to contact you in various ways, but I was unable to do so even last year, when I heard that you were in the United States. In any case, this is in the past, and I hope that our recent telephone acquaintance will be a promising start to getting to know each other better in the future.

I think it would be proper (I hope that you will not consider this self-praise) for me to write a few words about myself. I was born in Isfahan and completed my elementary and high school education in the same city. In 1966, after receiving my bachelor's degree in English Language and Literature, I came abroad. After studying for one year at the University of Heidelberg in Germany (in the master's degree program in literature and sociology), I came to the United States, and up to 1973, I studied English literature in various universities. Nevertheless, during all these years, I also studied the contemporary literature of Iran. In 1973, I went to Iran and for three

و مدت سه سال تا ۱۹۷۶ در دانشگاه اصفهان ادبیات انگلیسی و نیز
درسهائی در فن ترجمه و نثر تدریس کردم. در تابستان ۱۹۷۶ به آمریکا
برگشتم و در دانشگاه تگزاس تحصیلات خود را در رشته ادبیات
تطبیقی ادامه دادم. البته از ابتدای کار تصمیم داشتم رساله دکترای
خود را درباره آثار او بخصوص سنگ صبور بنویسم. با داستان نویسی
اروپائی و آمریکائی آشنائی کامل دارم و البته در زمینه ادبیات
فارسی بخصوص ادبیات معاصر تحقیق کرده‌ام و مقالاتی در این زمینه
چاپ کرده‌ام.

درباره ترجمه سنگ صبور و رساله دکترای اینجانب که راجع به همین رمان
است وقتی به آمریکا تشریف آوردید مفصلاً صحبت خواهم کرد.

به امید دیدار در آینده نزدیک

محمدرضا قانون پرور

years until 1976 taught English literature courses, including translation, among others. In the summer of 1976, I returned to the United States and continued my education in the field of comparative literature at the University of Texas. Of course, from the beginning I had decided to write my Ph.D. dissertation on your work, especially *The Patient Stone*. I am quite familiar with European and American fiction, and of course I have conducted research in Persian literature, especially contemporary literature, and I have published articles in this field.

We will discuss the translation of *The Patient Stone* and my Ph.D. dissertation, which is about the same novel, when you come to the United States.

Hoping to meet you in the near future,

M. R. Ghanoonparvar.

جناب قانون پرور دوست گرامی

امیدوارم همیشه شادکام و تندرست باشید.

نامه شریف رسید و کاملاً معلوم است تا چه حد سرکار در کار چاپ
سنگ صبور کوشیده اید و شک نیست نتیجه بردوام آن الی منتظر چاپ آن
به انگلیسی بوده ام. از نسخه پیش از انتشار بسیار و دلالهای
که برای خود دارم به این نتیجه رسیده ام که چاپ و انتشار سنگ صبور
فعلاً متعذر است. خواهشمندم جنابعالی بیش از این در این کار وقت نگذرانید.
بنده کتاب دیگری ترجمه را دارم میدانم در آمریکا سرکار از
لابلای سطور آن پیداست. کار ما که به نظرم می آید درباره سرکار
صدور نامه قرارداد بوده. البته در دسترسی سرکار خواهم گذاشت. باشد
روزی به یک اصلاحات کنم و روزنامه ها مطالبی را به ... کنم.

با تقدیم سلام خدمت خانم

ارادتمند

صادق چوبک

ال سوبرانته

۲۳ مرداد ۱۳۵۹

(Translation of Appendix 5)

Dear Friend, Mr. Ghanoonparvar,

I wish for your health and happiness.

I received your letter, and it is quite clear that you have worked hard to publish *The Patient Stone*, and there is no doubt that both of us would like to publish it in English. But after much thought and for personal reasons, I have come to the conclusion that *The Patient Stone* should not be printed and published at the present time, and please do not waste your time on this effort.

I am reading the translation once more and your hard work is evident in every line. About the points that I think you should reconsider, I will, of course, provide them to you. Perhaps one day we will meet and examine the issue together.

My greetings to your wife.

Sincerely,

Sadeq Chubak
El Cerrito, 23 Khordad 1359 [12 June 1980]

UNIVERSITY OF VIRGINIA
ORIENTAL LANGUAGES
302 CABELL HALL
CHARLOTTESVILLE VIRGINIA 22903

21 May 1980

TEL. (804) 924-7157

Three Continents Press
1346 Connecticut Ave., NW
Washington, D. C. 20036

To Whom It May Concern:

Having seen your publications of Middle Eastern literature in translation, in particular the recent collection of Persian short stories translated by Minoo Southgate, I thought to contact you concerning the possible publication of a Persian novel, Sādeq Chūbak's Sang-e Sabūr [The Patient Stone], which I have translated.

As you may know, Chūbak is perhaps the most prominent living writer of Persian fiction, and The Patient Stone is his latest and by far most important work. Given present circumstances, recent events, and as a result the new-found interest in Iranian culture and literature, the pertinence to today's Iran of a work such as The Patient Stone with its totally relevant political, social, cultural, and psychological overtones is unquestionable. I do believe that the publication of this important work promises immediate success, and I hope that Three Continents Press is interested in the undertaking.

The typed manuscript consists of 375 pages including a list of characters, a glossary of Persian words, and cultural and historical explanatory notes and is part of a larger work which was my PhD dissertation at The University of Texas at Austin. Enclosed is one chapter which I feel is somewhat indicative of the tone of this rather complex work.

I am interested to know what sort of offer Three Continents Press would be prepared to make and how soon the publication might be out. I hope to hear from you soon as others have expressed interest in publishing the work.

Sincerely,

Mohammad R. Ghanoonparvar

Mohammad R. Ghanoonparvar

Enclosure

THREE CONTINENTS PRESS, INC.

1346 Connecticut Avenue, N. W.
Suite 1131
Washington, D. C. 20036 U.S.A.
Tel: (202) 457-0288 or (202) 387-5809

3CP

May 27, 1980

Mohammad R. Ghanoonparvar
University of Virginia
Oriental Languages
302 Cabell Hall
Charlottesville, Va. 22903

Dear Mr. Ghanoonparvar:

Thank you for your letter and manuscript offer of May 21, 1980. 3CP is, unfortunately, all booked up with contracts for the next two or three years and consequently, we are unable to consider "The Patient Stone" at this time.

If your manuscript is still available in 18 months time, please contact us again.

Sincerely,

Robin A. Roosevelt
Editor

11 June 1982

Professor Ehsan Yarshater
450 Riverside Dr. no. 4
Columbia University
New York, NY 10027

Dear Professor Yarshater,

After two weeks of revising, *The Patient Stone* is completed. Since you mentioned that you would like to have the manuscript within a week or two, I did not wait to receive a copy you were going to send me and I am sending you my own original copy.

I have changed the apostrophes which seemed burdensome to reviewers and have accordingly "standardized" the substandard dialectical variations to a degree which I feel does not interfere with the original tone of the novel. I have tried to be consistent; hopefully I have not overlooked any inconsistency. One additional change I have made which was not mentioned by the reviewers is in the gender of Ahriman from female to male, which was done since Mr. Chubak, after reading the translation, specifically pointed out that he intended Ahriman to be male, despite the feminine characteristics ascribed to him in the novel. I have also made the appropriate changes in the "Explanatory Notes."

I have conscientiously tried to provide a clear copy and I feel that the printer should have no problem reating the changes that I have made.

Please let me know if there is anything else that I can do to help.

Sincerely,

M. R. Ghanoonparvar

M. R. Ghanoonparvar

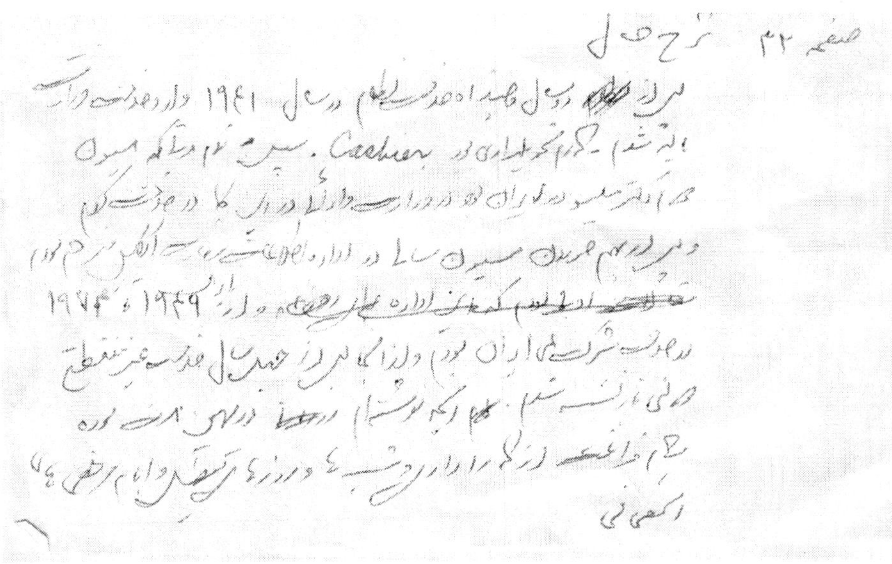

(Translation of Appendix 9)

Biography

After two years and a few months of military service, in 1941 I was employed by the Ministry of Finance. I worked as a cashier. Then during the entire time that the second mission of Dr. Millspaugh was in Iran, I worked in the Ministry of Finance in that position, and after the mission fell apart, I worked as a translator for a year in the Information Department of the British Embassy. From 1949 to 1970 [1974] I worked for the National Iranian [Oil] Company, and after continuous government service for four years, I retired. All I have written has been during that time in my leisure hours and during the nights and days of holidays and vacations.

۳ ژوئن ۱۹۸۰

جناب آقای چوبک

پس از عرض سلام امیدوارم حال خودتان و خانم خوب باشد.
چند هفته است که تلفنی مزاحم شدم باز هم مشغول ناشر دیگری
برای انتشار ترجمه سنگ صبور بوده‌ام.

پس از تماس‌های تلفنی و کتبی از طریق دوستان دانشگاهی
و دیگران متاسفانه باید به عرض برسانم که تمام جواب‌ها منفی بوده‌اند.
Bibliotheca Islamica فقط از طریق عکس‌برداری از نسخه تصحیح شده کتاب چاپ
می‌کند و در نتیجه این صورت خرج حروف‌چینی و تصحیح را باید داد. این موسسه
انتشاراتی هیچگونه حقی هم به ما نمی‌دهد و فعلاً نمی‌تواند این کتاب را
چاپ کند. انتشارات دانشگاهی منجمله دانشگاه ویرجینیا و
تگزاس هم گرفتارند که بودجه انتشارات را دولت کم کرده و وضع
انتشارات دانشگاهی خراب شده و مثل سابق نیست. تنها ناشری
که امید بیشتری به آن داشتیم و منتظر جوابش بودیم Three Continents Press
بود که پس از دو هفته نامه‌ای فرستاده و اظهار تاسف کرده است
که تا اوایل سال دیگر اصلاً کتابی قبول نمی‌کند

(Translation of Appendix 10)
3 June 1980

Dear Mr. Chubak,

Greetings. I hope that you and your wife are well. During the few weeks that I did not trouble you with a telephone call, again I was busy trying to find another publisher for the translation of *The Patient Stone*.

After telephone contacts and correspondence through university friends and others, unfortunately, I must inform you that all the answers have been negative. Bibliotheca Islamica only publishes books by photocopying the typed manuscript; otherwise, we will have to pay for typesetting, etc. This publisher will not give us any rights, and it cannot publish this book at the present time. Academic publishers, including the University of Virginia and the University of Texas, say that the government has reduced the publication budget and academic publishers are in a bad situation, which is not like in the past. The only publisher that I had set my hopes on and was waiting for its reply was Three Continents Press, which after two weeks has sent a letter expressing regret that it is not accepting any manuscripts for the next three years.

مطمئن ام که قبول می کنید که با وضع کنونی نشر هر چه زودتر سنگ صبور به انگلیسی هم لازم و هم از نظر زمانی اهمیت خاصی دارد. با در نظر داشتن آنچه به عرض رسید فکر می کنم Bibliotheca Persica به دلایل زیر بهترین ناشر آن می باشد

اولاً Bibliotheca Persica و Persian Heritage Series

که با یونسکو کتاب چاپ می کنند به هیچ وجه در آمریکا با رژیم سابق ایران ارتباطی نداشته. هیئت مشاورین شامل اساتیدی از دانشگاههای کلمبیا و هاروارد و غیره هستند و با رژیم گذشته ارتباطی نداشته اند

Persian Heritage Series چاپخانه مخصوص ندارد و معمولاً به چاپخانه های مختلف سفارش چاپ می دهد. از این لحاظ هر بار مسئله امنیت دیگر یا نظر کنترلی در مطالب ندارند و هر نوع کتاب از اشکال مختلف به چاپ رسیده اند

پیشنهاد بنده این است که موسسه Bibliotheca Persica که توافق کرده است چاپ کتاب را در اسرع اوقات شروع کند این کتاب را چاپ کند.

فکر می کنم باید هر چه زودتر در این مورد تصمیم گرفت

با احترام

محمدرضا قانون پرور

I am certain that you will agree that, given the present situation, the publication of *The Patient Stone* in English is both necessary and especially important time-wise. Considering what I said above, I think that Bibliotheca Persica is the best choice for the following reasons.

Firstly, Bibliotheca Persica and the Persian Heritage Series that publish books with a grant from UNESCO are not affiliated in any way in the United States with the previous regime. Their advisory board, including professors from Cambridge, Hamburg, and Rome Universities, has had no affiliation with the previous regime. The Persian Heritage Series does not have its own special print shop and usually sends its orders to various print shops. In this respect as well there is no problem, and Dr. Yarshater does not control the material, and they have published all sorts of books from various individuals. My suggestion is to have the Bibliotheca Persica Institute that has agreed to start the process of publication in October this year publish the book. I think the decision must be made in this connection as soon as possible.

Respectfully,

M. R. Ghanoonparvar

SADEQ CHUBAK,
15 COLLINGWOOD HOUSE,
99 NEW CAVENDISH STREET,
LONDON W1Y 1FQ.

لندن ۴ مرداد ۱۳۶۱ – ۲۶ ژوئیه ۱۹۸۲

آقای دکتر محمدرضا قانون‌پرور

اخیراً که آقای مایکل هیلمن در لندن بودند به من گفتند شما به دعوت و به وسیلهٔ [illegible]. آقای دکتر یارشاطر مشغول
چاپ کتاب سنگ صبور من هستید. با اینکه من کراراً به شما گفته بودم و نیز به شما نوشته بودم که از چاپ ترجمهٔ [illegible]
[illegible] سنگ صبور [illegible] حالا معلوم شد [illegible] که شما از وقتی که در سال ۱۹۸۰ که من در [illegible]
[illegible] من برخوردار بودید با اینکه [illegible] مشغول چاپ این کتاب بودید. و با اینکه
به شما گفته بودم که این ترجمه دارای [illegible] اشتباه و غلط ترجمه است که باید با هم بنشینیم و آنها را اصلاح کنیم شما ترتیب اثر
نداده و باز آن ترجمهٔ غلط را به چاپ سپرده‌اید و اصلاً مرا مطلع نساختید. حالا [illegible] خودتان [illegible]
این کار را چه می‌گذارید؟ آیا لازم نبود که [illegible] ترجمهٔ خود [illegible] بگیرید که [illegible] خود
[illegible] نویسنده [illegible]
[illegible] متعلق به او است باز به این کار دست زدید. خودتان
[illegible] مجبور [illegible]

معمولاً مترجم [illegible] وقتی که [illegible] ترجمه دارد [illegible] نویسنده نخستین کسی است که [illegible]
[illegible]
[illegible] سنگ صبور [illegible]
[illegible]
[illegible]
[illegible]

(Translation of Appendix 11)
London, 4 Mordad, 1361/26 July 1982

Dr. Mohammad Reza Ghanoonparvar,

Recently Mr. Michael Hillmann was in London. He told me that you have been trying for some time to publish *The Patient Stone* through the organization of Dr. Yarshater. Even though I have told you repeatedly, and also written to you that I do not wish to publish the translation that you have done of *The Patient Stone*, now I have learned that at the time in January 1980 when you came to my house in El Cerrito and enjoyed my friendship and hospitality without telling me what you were doing, sneakily you have been engaged in trying to publish this book. And even though I had told you that this translation has more than fifty mistakes and we must sit together and correct them, you paid no attention and you have sent the same translation with the mistakes to the printers, without informing me at all. Now, between us, what would you call this? Was it not enough for you to take advantage of this book to write your Ph.D. dissertation? Should you also take possession of this work while its writer, fit and healthy, with a body temperature of 37 degrees [centigrade], has been before your eyes and you have seen and touched him? You knew that all the rights belong to him and his heirs, and you still did it. You yourself, call this action what you will and excuse me from mentioning it here.

Usually the translator of a work because of his in-depth precision during translation, after the writer, is the first person that understands the depth of the work and its intricacies; and if he understands it, the value and the status of the writer becomes clear to him, and certainly you are no exception to this general rule. Did you not realize to what extent the writer of *The Patient Stone* is weary of lies, untruthfulness, bullying, injustice, dirty tricks, and deception, and how he has fought them? Was it right for Dr. Ghanoonparvar to sell me for a fistful of dollars and play a dirty trick on me?

I think I have said too much so far, and it would have been fair to summarize my letter as follows:

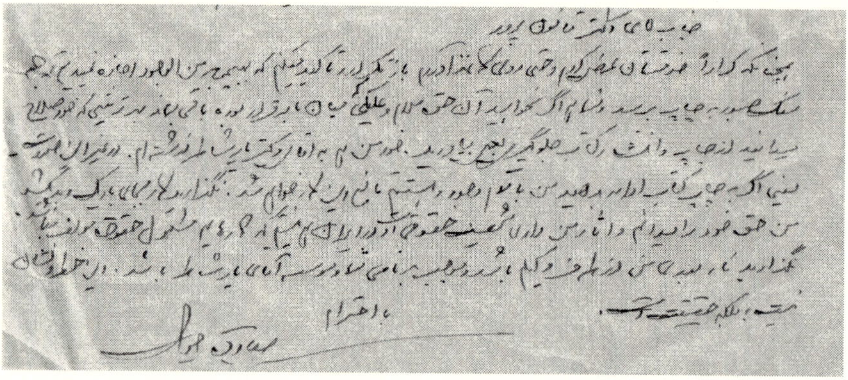

با احترام

صادق هدایت

Dear Dr. Ghanoonparvar,

As I have told you repeatedly and even put it on paper, once again I repeat and emphasize that I will not allow by any means the translation of *The Patient Stone* to be published, and if you want to have the friendly relations that we have had to remain in place, prevent the printing and publication of the book in any way that you think. I have myself written to Dr. Yarshater. Otherwise, that is, if you continue your efforts to publish this book, I will do everything in my power to prevent it. Do not let this end in a nasty situation. I know my rights, and my works are legally protected, and I am not in Iran where my work would not be protected by the writers' rights. Do not allow my next letter to come from my attorney and cause you and the establishment of Mr. Yarshater to be discredited. This is not a threat, but a fact.

Respectfully,

Sadeq Chubak

۲۵ اوت ۱۹۸۲

حبیب عزیز صادق چوبک

نامه مورخه ۴ مرداد ۱۳۶۱ شما از لندن را که گویا چند هفته پیش
رسیده است من دیروز دریافت داشتم چون چند هفته در مسافرت بودم
و از تأخیر در پاسخ پوزش می‌خواهم.

نامه جنابعالی حاوی مطالبی است که من اصلاً انتظار آنها را از آقای صادق
چوبک نداشتم. شاید در مطالب زائد سوء تفاهم یا سوء تفاهماتی است
و من واقعاً امیدوارم که این طور باشد. اگرچه به هیچ وجه اهل نیستم مکدر کنید مطالبی
که در این هذیان مسلم بعنوان در نامه مشخص است – چون آن در این صورت فرمودها
برای خواهد شد که من خطائی مرتکب شده‌ام که چنین کنم – فکر میکنم هذیان
کردن آنها با دیگران گرچه شما آنها را متذکر شده‌اید بیجا باشد

اولاً در مورد "پیغام بلطف ترجمه‌ای" که فرموده بودید من جواب از جنابعالی
خواهش کردم بسته شده آنها را برای من بنویسید و نه بود صدوقی از آنجا رامین بدهید.
شما گفتید که با هم بنشینیم و درباره آنها صحبت کنیم. متأسفانه چون
امکان آن بی وقت محدود من یک کنفرانس میسر نشد سعی کردم از طرق مختلف
منجمله دعوت کردن دعوت بیشتر از جنابعالی برای آمدن به دانشگاه و برطبق این امکان را
بوجود بیاورم که شما دعوت ما را رد کردید.

(Translation of Appendix 12)

25 August 1982

Dear Mr. Sadeq Chubak,

Yesterday I received your letter dated 4 Mordad 1361 [26 July 1982] which had apparently arrived several weeks ago. I apologize for the delay in responding because I was traveling for a few weeks.

Your letter contains statements that I did not expect from Mr. Sadeq Chubak at all. Perhaps these statements stem from a certain misunderstanding or misunderstandings, and I truly hope that this is the case. Even though by no means do I wish you to think that what I will say here is a personal defense—because in that case it would be assumed that I have committed an error to do so—I think expressing it will be proper, considering what you have written.

Firstly, regarding the "fifty translation mistakes" that you had mentioned, I frequently asked you to send me the corrections and you were supposed to send me a list of them. You told me that we should sit together and talk about them. Unfortunately, because I was unable to travel once again to California, through various means including inviting you officially and unofficially to the University of Virginia, I tried to facilitate our meeting, but you declined all those invitations.

مرقوم فرموده‌اید که من در سال ۱۹۸۰ از حمایت و پذیرائی شما برخوردار
شده‌ام ولی بعد بدون اطلاع شما "زیر ذره‌بین" مشغول چاپ‌های کتاب بودم.

من و همسرم بارها از حمایت و پذیرائی شما و خانواده گرامی تشکر کرده‌ایم و شخصاً من از
فرصتی که با شما آشنائی شد ولی چون کسی که با شما تفاوت‌ها را به صفت حضوری
متهم می‌کند باید عرض کنم که اینجانب ادعا دارم این سند کتاب هم پیش‌نویس نبوده با شما از اینکه
با شما بودم تا آنجا که وقت اجازه میداد سعی کردم از شما پذیرائی کنم

مطلبی که باید اضافه کنم اینست که همانطور که شاید بارها گفته شده تنها هدف
از سفر من و همسرم به کالیفرنیا دیدار با شما بود. بعد از اینکه در آن موقعیت
مخصوص ایام کریسمس با سفر دیگری چشم پوشیدیم این آرزوئی بود که همسر من
تازه از بیمارستان آمده بود و از ناراحتی روحی و جسمی به واسطه از دست دادن بچه رنج میبرد.
با این وجود وقتی من اصرار کردم که برای دیدن شما به کالیفرنیا بیائیم به واسطه
علاقه‌اش به شما از طریق نوشته‌هایتان و به واسطه علاقه‌ای که به نسبت من به شما دارم
قبول کرد. باز هم باید اضافه کنم که سفر با کشورهای دیگر هتلها و خانه‌ها
که با تصمیم برای آمدن به کالیفرنیا و دیدار از شما بود و نه کمک خود
من به نوعی داشته باشید. حال نمیدانم اگر من میخواستم کتاب را "زیر ذره‌بین"
چاپ کنم چه احتیاجی بود با وجود مشکلات به شما در لندن تماس بگیرم و اطمینان

You had written that I had enjoyed your friendship and hospitality in January 1980, but without informing you, I have been trying to publish the book "sneakily." My wife and I have frequently thanked you for your and Mrs. Chubak's friendship and hospitality and have especially been thankful for the opportunity to make your acquaintance. But because the tone of your letter accuses us more or less of freeloading, I must say that I hope there will be no misunderstanding, because even though we were traveling, we tried to entertain you as much as our limited time would allow.

What I should add here is that, as you realized, the only purpose for my wife and I traveling to California was to visit you, in addition to the fact that during that time, especially over the Christmas holidays, we had to cancel another trip. This was the time when my wife had just recently been hospitalized and was suffering from psychological and physical problems because of the loss of a child. Nevertheless, when I insisted that we should go to California to visit you, because of her fondness for you through your work and because she knew my fondness for you, she agreed. Once again, I should point out that Dr. Hillmann and his wife decided to come along after learning about our decision to come to California to visit you, and I think you knew about this. Now, tell me, if I wanted to publish the book "sneakily," why would I contact you in London, despite all the difficulties, and then come and visit you? If I wanted to do this "sneakily," like hundreds of other translators, I would not need to contact you.

به دو ناشر هم بنویسم. اگر نخواستند این کار را "زیراکسی" انجام دهم، باید چند ماهی صبر کردن نیازی نداشته، بنویسید تا تماس بگیرم.

باز نظر شما در خصوص "زیراکسی" چاپ کردن کتاب چه بود؟ شاید هم دیگر پیش آمده باشد. من بخوبی بخاطر دارم که در همان روز و وقتی در مکالمات تلفنی مان از این راجع به چاپ کتاب با ناشران صحبت کرده بودیم. ابتدا گفتید که می‌خواهید تا کسی پارت‌ها کتاب را چاپ کنند و به فکر دنبال ناشر دیگری گشت. گفتید من با ناشرین دیگر تماس گرفتم و جواب‌های منفی آنها را با اطلاع شما رساندم. شما گفتید که باشد، ولی تمام حقوق باید برای نویسنده یعنی شما محفوظ باشد. پس از مدتی در اواخر ۱۹۸۱ من به شما تلفنی عرض کردم که مؤسسه Persian Heritage Series یعنی Bibliotheca Persica حاضر است کتاب را چاپ کند و عرض کردم که بعقیده من از نظر اعتبار علمی و کیفیت کار این ناشر بهترین است. شما گفتید که باشد ولی مرا مطلع، از کار این پارت‌ها گاه گاه خبر کنید و پول بیشتری مطالبه کن. بنده عرض کردم پول زیادی نمی‌دهند و من فقط این کار را از نظر علاقه‌ام به کتاب و ادبیات فارسی ایران کردم و چشم داشتی هم نداشتم. اینکه به شما هم چشم داشت ندارم را باید توضیح

Again, I think that regarding publishing the book "sneakily," there must have been another misunderstanding. I remember very well that on the same day of our visit, and even during telephone conversations prior to it, I had talked to you about the publication of the book. Initially, you said that you did not want Mr. Yarshater to publish the book and that we should look for another publisher. Afterwards, when I contacted other publishers and informed you of their negative responses, you said that it would be fine, but all the rights must be given to the writer, that is, you. After a while, in late 1981, I told you over the telephone that the Persian Heritage Series, that is, Bibliotheca Persica, would like to publish this book, and I said that in my opinion the work of this publisher is the best in terms of academic credibility and the quality of their work. You told me that that was fine, but I should be careful not to be duped by Mr. Yarshater, and that I should demand more money. I said that money was not what I had in mind and that I only did that because of my interest in the book and modern Persian literature, and that I did not expect anything. I must explain what I mean by saying that I do not expect anything. Firstly, financially, I have not "pocketed money," as you say, but when we add up various costs of typing, copying, and so on, it has been a financial loss for me, and this is without taking into consideration the translation fees, regarding which of course, I have not had and do not have any expectations.

مترجم. اولاً از نظرهایی در ترجمهٔ این کتاب بنده با ترازوی «پول عجیب» کرده‌ام
بلکه واقعاً معنای جملات مختلف ناشی مؤلف، گاهی و گاهی را جمع زده‌ام. از نظرهای متفاوت هم
شده‌ام و تمام این موارد در نظر گرفتن حق انتخاب ترجمه را به‌کار برده‌ام که البته من
در این مورد انتقادی نداشته و ندارم.

در این اجازه دهید موضوعی که چنین کتابی را از دیدگاه مترجم بیان کنم.
اولاً اطلاع دارید که از نظر اعتبار دانشگاهی ترجمه کتاب نمایند. ثانیاً
وقتی چنین کتابی به چاپ رسید همگی که گفت که این انتخاب مترجم است
بلکه آن کتابی است از مؤلفی که به زبان دیگری ترجمه داده‌اند شده. حال
مهم است بپرسید چرا من بین آن مترجم دست بچنین کاری زده‌ام. قبلاً عرض کرده‌ام
که انگیزه اصلی من حسی است که بیانش مهم است. برای آدمهای جاطلب و
پول پرست مشغول باشد و این علاقه من به ادبیات معاصر فارسی است و شناساندن آن
به دیگر مردم دنیا. انگیزه دوم برای این کار تدریسی است که چون در تدریس
ادبیات معاصر فارسی من اغلب به دانشجویان رشته ادبیات تطبیقی سر و کار دارم
که زبان فارسی را نمی‌دانند، خوب شما باید متوجه گردید فرق آنها ترجم
آثار نوشته‌های فارسی شده وصل کرده‌ام منوبه خود همراه، اینگونه ترجمه‌ها

Here allow me tell you about the publication of such a book from the perspective of a translator. Firstly, you know that translations are not taken into account in terms of academic credit. Secondly, when such a book is published, no one would say that the book belongs to the translator, but it is a book by its author that has been rendered into another language. Now, you might ask why as a translator I would become involved in this endeavor. I have explained previously that my main motive is a sense that might seem ridiculous to ambitious and money worshiping individuals, and that is my interest in contemporary Persian literature and introducing it to other people in the world. My second motive concerns my teaching. Because in my teaching of contemporary Persian literature, often I work with comparative literature students who do not know Persian or do not know it well, I have become aware of the extraordinary dearth of translations of modern Persian works and have tried, as much as I have been able to, along with others, to provide translations in English of Persian works. Of course, the larger project that I had been working on is basically the complete translation of all your works, but of course, with your opinion as a writer of those works regarding my work and the accusations that you made against me such as worshiping money, I will have to stop all this and burn all that I have finished so far and toss it away, and write about the works of others who have asked me to write about their works and have not accused me of money worshiping and lying.

۵

از آثار ایشان را به انگلیسی ترجمه کنم. البته پروژه بزرگتری که روی آن کار

میکرده‌ام اصولاً یک ترجمه کامل از تمام آثارشان بوده که البته با نظر آقای

که جنابعالی بعنوان نویسنده آن آثار از کار منصرف دارید و امکاناتی که برای چاپ نوشته‌ها

و شعرها میسر نیست مجبورم این کار را متوقف کنم و برخی را هم که تا حال تمام کرده‌ام

بسوزانم و بدور بریزم و روی کارهای دیگران که از من خواهش کرده‌اند و به‌جای ایشان

در زمینه‌ای دیگر هم متمم این گذشته کار کنم.

من واقعاً نمیدانم در جواب نامه‌تان چه بنویسم. فقط عرض میکنم که نه انتظار پول

دارم و نه میخواهم کارشان را "تصاحب" کنم. درباره حقوق نویسنده من

دو سال پیش حضور شما را اطلاع دادم و ناشرشان حضور رسانده‌ام. تماماً حقوق ترجمه

مال مترجم و ناشر است ولی باز من این حقوق را نخواهم و تا وقتی که اطلاع

دارم یک ناشرشان هرگز اعتراضی ندارند که این حقوق برای نویسنده تنها محفوظ

بماند. اگر واقعاً این مطلب باعث نگرانی شما شده من دوباره با ایشان

تماس خواهم گرفت و سرمشقی را هم از آن میگیرم. "جاهای تاریک" همه آن

مطالبی که در آن نامه خود را هم "دلیل" و

میشد، ایده را من نمیدانم چگونه ترجمه کنم. مثلاً "شعر" را که دیده هم روح و به

و کلی خودش نگاه کند بیاید، با وکیل شما بگذارند؟ من بخاطر اقدام و علاقه‌ای که

به ادبیات چپ دارم، خواهم داشت همیشه چنان کنم. امیدوارم منظورم را

Indeed, I do not know what to write in response to your letter. I will only say that I neither expect any money nor want to "take possession" of your work. Regarding the rights of the writer, two years ago I informed Mr. Yarshater about what you had said. Generally speaking, the rights of the translation belong to the translator and the publisher, but again, I do not want these rights, and as far as I know, Mr. Yarshater does not have any objections to giving the writer, that is, you, all these rights. If this issue is in fact the cause of concern, please let me know and I will contact him once again and discuss the issue.

I do not know how to explain to myself the statements that you have written at the end of your letter regarding "attorney" and "nasty situation." Are you telling me, for example, that I should go and ask my attorney to fight your attorney? Because of my respect for and interest in Sadeq Chubak, I do not want and would not consent to do so. I hope what you mean by "nasty situation" is not such a situation as I described.

6

از «...های بادبک» چنین وضعی نباشد.

در آینده وضعیت من احساس دروغ و ذلیل
باز هم شد همیشه میخواهم عرض کنم که
برای دلبستم و نادرو ... زدهن هم درکار نیست. داستان «مشتی دلاور» که فرموده بودید
اگر من دنبال پول بودم تا حال بعد از ۳۰ سال کار دو سه تا ساختمان و ...
برای خودم بهم زده باشم که چنین نیست و با زندگی ساده معلمی ... گذرانم و نه
کاخ دارم و نه کوچی و هرگز هم دنبال چنین چیزها نبوده و نیستم.

در خاتمه دلم پر غم است و استنکار هم نداشتم مجبور شدم چنین نامه‌ای به شما
بنویسم و ... امید دارم این نامه را فقط بعد از روشن شدن ... توقعات
تلقی بکنید.

با آرزوی خوشی و موفقیت برای شاه و خانواده
و با احترام

محمدرضا قاضی‌زاده ...

As always, again I would like to say that in acquaintance and friendship, I have not been and I am not a liar and a trickster, and I do not "play dirty tricks." Concerning "a fistful of dollars" that you had mentioned, if I were after money, after 20 years of working and teaching, I should have by now improved my living conditions, which is not the case, and I live the simple life of a teacher, and neither do I have a mansion nor own a small shack to live in, and I have never pursued such things.

In conclusion, I did not want and did not expect to be forced to write such a letter to you, and now as well, I hope that you will regard this only as a letter for clarifying certain misunderstandings.

Wishing you and your family happiness and success,

Respectfully,

M. R. Ghanoonparvar

UNIVERSITY OF VIRGINIA
ORIENTAL LANGUAGES
302 CABELL HALL
CHARLOTTESVILLE, VIRGINIA 22903

TEL. (804) 924-

جناب آقای چوبک

پس از عرض سلام باز هم تاسفم که نتوانستم خدمت برسم ولی امیدوارم که جبران شود
و نیز امیدوارم که کسالت شما برطرف شده باشد

همانقدر که خدمتتان عرض کردم از حرکات زشت رهبران مذهبی ایران
یکی اینست که دانشگاهها علاقه چندانی به ادامه برنامه‌های فارسی و ادبیات و فرهنگ
فارسی نشان نمی‌دهند که البته عوارض آن تنها کلاسها محروم می‌شود ولی در کوتاه مدت
عوارض این رفتار متوجه ما هاست. در هر صورت باید هر نوع فرصتی که وجود دارد
از دست نداد و باز هم فرهنگ و ادبیات ایران ادامه داد
دو کتاب انگلیسی که با این نامه می‌فرستم [illegible] ناقابل است برای کتابخانه چوبک و کتاب
دیگر هم کار من است که در چند سال گذشته کرده‌ام و امیدوارم مورد پسند باشد
در هر صورت بنده منتظر یادداشتهائی که بطور کلی درباره ترجمه سنگ صبور که
مرقوم [illegible] خواهم بود
با آرزوی موفقیت و [illegible] شما
قربان شما
محمدرضا قانون پرور

(Translation of Appendix 13)

[1988]
Dear Mr. Chubak,

Greetings. Again I regret that I could not come to visit you, but I hope that I will make up for it in the future, and I also hope that your health has improved.

As I told you, one of the blessings of the behavior of the present leaders of Iran is that the universities are not very much interested in continuing Persian language and literature and culture programs, the effects of which, of course, will become clear in the future, but in the short term, we are suffering the consequences of this behavior. In any case, we should not lose any opportunity and should continue promoting Iranian culture and literature.

I am sending two cookbooks with this letter, which are an inadequate gift for Mrs. Chubak. The other book is what I have been working on for the past few years and I hope you will like it.

In any case, I am waiting for your notes regarding the translation of *The Patient Stone*, which you had written that you would send me.

Wishing you greater success and good health,

M. R. Ghanoonparvar

انتشارات مزدا

mazdā publishers

۲۵ مه، ۱۹۸۸

آقای صادق چوبک گرامی :

در تاریخ ۲۰ آوریل، نامه ای به سرکار در مورد چاپ کتاب سنگ صبور به زبان انگلیسی ارسال گردید. چونکه برنامهٔ کار موسسه ما بسیار فشرده است، بنابراین از سرکار درخواست میشود که تصمیم خود را در اسرع وقت به اطلاع این موسسه برسانید.

با احترام

احمد جباری

ا ج /

رونوشت : دکتر قانون پرور

P.O. Box 2603 / Costa Mesa, CA 92626
Tel. (714) 751-5252

• *Publisher* • *Importer* • *Bookseller*

(Translation of Appendix 14)
Mazda Publishers
25 May 1988
Dear Mr. Chubak,

On April 20th a letter was sent to you regarding the publication of The Patient Stone in English. Because of the tight work schedule of our establishment, I am requesting of you to inform us of your decision as soon as possible.

Respectfully,
Ahmad Jabbari
cc: Dr. Ghanoonparvar

BIBLIOGRAPHY

Sadeq Chubak's Major Works

1945. *Kheymehshabbazi* [Puppet Show], 4th ed. Tehran: Javidan, 1972.

"Nafti" [The Kerosene Man]. Translated by Carter Bryant. In "Major Voices in Contemporary Persian Literature." *Literature East and West* 20 (1976).

"Golha-ye Gushti" [Flowers of Flesh]. Translated by John Limbert. In *Iranian Studies* 1 (Summer 1968):115-119.

"Adl" [Justice]. Translated by John Limbert. In *Iranian Studies* 1 (Summer 1968): 113-114. Also translated as "Inquest" by H. D. Law. In *Life and Letters and the London Mercury* 63 (December 1949):230-232.

"Zir-e Cheragh Qermez" [Under the Red Light].

"Akher-e Shab" [Late at Night].

"Mardi dar Qafas" [A Man in a Cage].

"Pirahan-e Zereshki" [The Purple Dress].

"Musiyu Elyas" [Monsieur Elias]. Translated by William L. Hanaway, Jr. In *The Literary Review* 18 (Fall 1974):61-68. Also included with some changes in *Sadeq Chubak: An Anthology*. Edited by F. R. C. Bagley. Pp. 233-240.

"Ba'd az Zohr-e Akher-e Pa'iz" [An Afternoon in Late Autumn].

"Yahya" [Yahya]. Translated by H. D. Law. In *Life and Letters and the London Mercury* 63 (December 1949):228-229.

"Ah-e Ensan" [The Sigh of Mankind]. Translated by Leonard Bogle. In "Major Voices in Contemporary Persian Literature." *Literature East and West* 20 (1976). "Ah-e Ensan" replaced a satirical short story called "Esa'eh-ye Adab" [Insolence] in the 3rd ed. of *Puppet Show*, 1967.

1949. *Antari keh Lutiyash Mordeh Bud* [The Baboon Whose Buffoon Was Dead], 5th ed. Tehran: Javidan, 1973/74.

"Chera Darya Tufani Shodeh Bud" [Why the Sea Was Stormy].

"Qafas" [The Cage]. Translated by Vera Kubičková and I. Lewit. In *New Orient* 4 (1965):151-152.

"Antari keh Lutiyash Mordeh Bud" [The Baboon Whose Buffoon Was Dead]. Translated by Peter Avery. In *New World Writing* 11 (May 1957):14-24.

Tup-e Lastiki [The Rubber Ball] (a one-act play). Translated by F. R. C. Bagley in *Sadeq Chubak: An Anthology*. Pp. 241-282.

1963. *Tangsir*. Tehran: Javidan, 1963. Translated by Marzieh Sami'i and F. R. C. Bagley. In *Sadeq Chubak: An Anthology*.

1965. *Ruz-e Avval-e Qabr* [The First Day in the Grave], 2nd ed. Tehran: Javidan, 1968.

"Gurkanha" [The Grave Diggers].

"Chashm-e Shisheh'i" [The Glass Eye]. Translated by Babak Chubak. In *Sadeq Chubak: An Anthology*. Pp. 231-232.

"Dasteh Gol" [The Bouquet of Flowers].

"Yek Chiz-e Khakestari" [Something Gray].

"Pachehkhizak" [Fireworks].

"Ruz-e Avval-e Qabr" [The First Day in the Grave].

"Hamrah" [Companion].

"Arusak-e Forushi" [A Doll for Sale].

"Yek Shab-e Bikhabi" [A Sleepless Night]

"Hamrah, 'Shiveh-ye Digar'" [Companion, "Another Style"].

Haftkhat [Sly] (a play). Translated by Shireen Aghdami, Jeff Bloxsome, and Carolyn Hodge. In *Iranian Drama: An Anthology*. Compiled and edited by M. R. Ghanoonparvar and John Green. Costa Mesa, California: Mazda Publishers, 1989. Pp. 133-151.

1966. *Cheragh-e Akhar* [The Last Alms]. Tehran: Javidan.

"Cheraq-e Akhar" [The Last Alms]. Translated as "The Last Offering" by G. L. Tikku. In *Sadeq Chubak: An Anthology*. Pp. 183-225.

"Dozd-e Qalpaq" [The Hubcap Thief]. Translated by F. R. C. Bagley. In *Sadeq Chubak: An Anthology*. Pp. 227-232.

"Kaftarbaz" [Pigeon Flyer].

"Omarkoshun" [Omar-Killing].

"Bacheh Gorbeh'i keh Chashmanash Baz Nashodeh Bud" [The Kitten Whose Eyes Had Not Opened].

"Asb-e Chubi" [The Wooden Horse]. Translated by Vera Kubičková and I. Lewit. In *New Orient* 4 (1965):148-152.

"Atma, Sag-e Man" [Atma, My Dog].

"Rahavard" [Souvenir].

"Parizad va Pariman" [Parizad and Pariman].

"Dust" [Friend].

1966. *Sang-e Sabur* [The Patient Stone], 3rd ed. Tehran: Javidan, 1976. Translated by M. R. Ghanoonparvar. Costa Mesa, California: Mazda Publishers, 1989.

Sources in Persian:

Abedini, Hasan. *Sad Sal Dastannevisi*, Vol. 1. Tehran: Tandar, 2nd ed., 1989; Vol. 2, Tehran: Tandar, 1990.

Amini, Amirqoli. "Dastan-e Sang-e Sabur." *Si Afsaneh az Afsanehha-ye Mahalli-ye Esfahan*. Isfahan: Owliya, n.d. Pp. 27-30.

Baraheni, Reza. *Qessehnevisi*, 2nd ed. Tehran: Ashrafi, 1969.

Daftar-e Honar, Vizheh-ye Sadeq Chubak, Vol. 2, No. 2, March 1995.

"Darazna-ye Seh Shab-e Porgu: Goftogu'i ba Sadeq Chubak." *Ayandegan*, 23, 24, 28 (January 1970).

Dastgheyb, Abdolali. "Antari keh Lutiyash Mordeh Bud." *Rahnema-ye Ketab* 18 (1962):904-906.

_____. "Cheragh-e Akher." *Negin* 7 (December/January 1966/67):22-25.

_____. "Dowreh-ye Sevvom-e Nasr-e Mo'aser-e Parsi." *Negin* 55 (November/December 1970):24-27.

_____. "Honar-e Tanz dar Neveshtehha-ye Chubak." *Payam-e Novin* 7 (March/April 1962):1-11.

_____. *Naqd-e Asar-e Sadeq Chubak*. Tehran: Pazand, 1974.

Dehbashi, Ali, ed. *Yad-e Sadeq Chubak*, Tehran: Nashr-e Sales, 2001.

Ebrahimi, Nader. "Bazdid-e Qesseh-ye Emruz." *Payam-e Novin* 7 (February 1967):89-95; 8 (March 1967):78-83; 9 (April 1967):66-72; 10 (May 1967):64-75; 11 (June 1967):98-106; 12 (July 1967):85-98; 13 (August 1967):119-126, 131.

_____. "Mafhum-e Qesseh az Didgah-e Man." *Khaneh'i Bara-ye Shab*, 3rd ed. [Tehran]: Amir Kabir, 1969.

Este'lami, Mohammad. *Adabiyyat-e Dowreh-ye Bidari va Mo'aser*. Tehran: Entesharat-e Daneshgah-e Sepahiyan-e Enqelab-e Iran, 1976.

_____. *Barrasi-ye Adabiyyat-e Emruz*, 4th ed. Tehran: n.p., 1964.

Golshiri, Ahmad. *Dastan va Naqd-e Dastan*. 2nd printing. Tehran: Negah, 1992.

Golshiri, Hushang. *Bagh dar Bagh*. Vols. 1 and 2. Tehran: Entesharat-e Nilufar, 1999.

_____. "Si Sal Romannevisi." *Jong-e Esfahan* 5 (Summer 1967):187-229.

Hedayat, Sadeq. *Buf-e Kur*, 14th ed. Tehran: Amir Kabir, 1973.

_____. *Neveshtehha-ye Parakandeh*, 2nd ed. Tehran: Amir Kabir, 1965.

Iranian, Jamshid M. *Vaqe'iyyat-e Ejtema'i va Jahan-e Dastan*. Tehran: Amir Kabir, 1979.

Jamalzadeh, Mohammad Ali. *Yeki Bud Yeki Nabud*, 4th ed. Tehran: Ebn-e Sina, 1954.

Kasma'i, Ali Akbar. *Nevisandegan-e Pishgam dar Dastan-nevisi-ye Emruz-e Iran*. Tehran: Kaviyan, 1984.

Kiyanush, Mahmud. *Barrasi-ye She'r va Nasr-e Farsi-ye Mo'aser*. Tehran: Mani, 1972.

Maragheh'i, Zeynolabedin. *Siyahatnameh-ye Ebrahim Beyg*, 3rd ed. Tehran: Andisheh, 1975.

Mirsadeqi, Jamal. *Ababiyyat-e Dastani: Qesseh, Dastan-e Kutah, Roman*. 2nd printing. Tehran: Mahvar, 1986.

_____. *Anasor-e Dastan*. Tehran: Shafa, 1985.

_____. "Negahi Kutah be Dastannevisi-ye Mo'aser-e Iran." *Sokhan* 26 (August/September 1978): 913-931.

_____. *Qesseh, Dastan-e Kutah, Roman*. Tehran: Agah, 1981.

Mo'azzen, Naser, ed. *Dah Shab: Shabha-ye Sha'eran va Nevisandegan dar Anjoman-e Farhangi-ye Iran va Alman*. Tehran: Amir Kabir, 1978.

Mohammadzadeh-Saddiq, Hoseyn. *Masa'el-e Adabiyyat-e Novin-e Iran*. Tehran: Donya, 1978.

Nakhostin Kongereh-ye Nevisandegan-e Iran. Tehran: Anjoman-e Ravabet-e Farhangi-ye Iran va Ettehad-e Jamahir-e Showravi-ye Sosiyalisti, 1947.

Nafisi, Sa'id, ed. *Shahkarha-ye Nasr-e Farsi-ye Mo'aser*. Tehran: Ma'refat, 1951.

Nekuruh, Hasan. "Rahi az Shenakht Besu-ye Andisheh." *Negin* 11 (October 1976):15-18, 51-52; 11 (November 1976):27-35.

Razmju, Hoseyn. *Ravesh-e Nevisandegan-e Bozorg-e Mo'aser*. Mashhad: n.p., 1962.

Sepanlu, Mohammad, comp. and ed. *Bazafarini-ye Vaqe'iyyat*. Tehran: Zaman, 1970/71.

_____. *Nevisandegan-e Pishrow-e Iran*. Tehran: Ketab-e Zaman, 1983.

Yunosi, Ebrahim. *Honar-e Dastannevisi*. 2nd ed. Tehran: Amir Kabir, 1973.

Sources in English

Al-e Ahmad, Jalal. *The School Principal*. Translated by John K. Newton. Minneapolis and Chicago: Bibliotheca Islamica, 1974.

_____. *Plagued by the West*. Translated by Paul Sprachman, New York: Caravan Books, 1982.

_____. *Weststruckness*[Gharbzadegi]. Translated by John Green and Ahmad Alizadeh. Lexington, Kentucky: Mazda Publishers, 1982.

Alavi, Bozorg. *Her Eyes*. Translated by John O'Kane. Lanham, Maryland: University Press of America, 1989.

_____. "From Modern Persian Literature." *Yadname-ye Jan Rypka*. The Hague/Paris: Mouton, 1967. Pp. 167-172.

Aryanpur, Manoochehr. "Retrospect and Progress: A Short View of Modern Persian Literature." *Books Abroad* 46, No. 2 (Spring 1972):200-210.

Auerbach, Erich. *Mimesis: The Representation of Reality in Western Literature*, 4th ed. Translated by Willard R. Task. Princeton, New Jersey: Princeton University Press, 1974.

Avery, Peter W. "Developments in Modern Persian Prose. *The Muslim World* 45 (1955):313-323.

Banani, Amin. *The Modernization of Iran (1921-1941)*. Stanford, California: Stanford University Press, 1961.

Baraheni, Reza. *The Crowned Cannibals: Writings on Repression in Iran*. New York: Vintage Books, 1977.

Barthes, Roland. *S/Z*. Translated by Richard Miller. New York: Hill and Wang, 1974.

_____. *The Pleasure of the Text*. Translated by Richard Miller. New York: Hill and Wang, 1975.

Blondel Saad, Joya. *The Image of Arabs in Modern Persian Literature*. Lanham, Maryland: University Press of America, 1996.

Booth, Wayne. *The Rhetoric of Fiction*, 10th ed. Chicago: University of Chicago Press, 1973.

Borecky, Milos. "Persian Prose Since 1946." *Middle East Journal* 7 (1953):235-244.

Boyle, J. A. "Notes on the Colloquial Language of Persia as Recorded in Certain Recent Writings." *Bulletin of the School of Oriental and African Studies* 14 (1952):451-462.

Culler, Jonathan. *Structuralist Poetics: Structuralism, Linguistics, and the Study of Literature*. Ithaca, New York: Cornell University Press, 1975.

Dargahi, Haideh. "The Shaping of the Modern Persian Short Story: Jamalzadih's 'Preface' to *Yiki Bud, Yiki Nabud*." *The Literary Review* 18 (1974):18-24.

Edel, Leon. *The Modern Psychological Novel*. New York: Grosset and Dunlap, The University Library Edition, 1964.

Elwell-Sutton, L. P. "The Influence of Folk-tale and Legend on Modern Persian Literature." *Iran and Islam, in Memory of the Late Vladimir Minorsky*. Edited by C. E. Bosworth. Edinburgh: Edinburgh University Press, 1971. Pp. 247-254.

Farzan, Masud. "Modern Persian Literature: How Good Is It?" *University of Pennsylvania-Pahlavi University Lecture Series*: Spring 1966. N.p., n.d. Pp. 9-25.

Forster, E. M. *Aspects of the Novel*. New York: Harcourt, Brace and World, 1955.

Friedman, Melvin. *Stream of Consciousness: A Study in Literary Method*. New York: Yale University Press, 1955.

Frye, Northrop. *Anatomy of Criticism*, 3rd ed. Princeton, New Jersey: Princeton University Press, 1973.

Ghanoonparvar, M. R. *In a Persian Mirror: Images of the West and Westerners in Contemporary Iranian Fiction*. Austin: University of Texas Press, 1993.

_____. *Prophets of Doom: Literature as a Socio-Political Phenomenon in Modern Iran*. Lanham, Maryland: University Press of America, 1984.

_____. *Translating the Garden*. Austin: University of Texas Press, 2002.

Girard, Rene. *Deceit, Desire, and the Novel*. Translated by Yvonne Freccero. Baltimore: Johns Hopkins University Press, 1965.

Halliday, Fred. *Iran: Dictatorship and Development* (New York: Penguin, 1979).

Hamalian, Leo, and John D. Yohannan, eds. "Persian Literature." *New Writing From the Middle East*. New York: Mentor, 1978. Pp. 271-400.

Hedayat, Sadeq. *The Blind Owl*. Translated by D. P. Costello. New York: Evergreen, 1969.

_____. *Haji Agha: Portrait of an Iranian Confidence Man*. Translated by G. M. Wickens, Austin: Center for Middle Eastern Studies, 1979.

Humphrey, Robert. *Stream of Consciousness in the Modern Novel*, 8th ed. Berkeley: University of California Press, 1972.

Iranshenasi, Vol. 5, No. 2 (Summer 1993).

Jazayery, M. A. "Recent Persian Literature: Observations on Themes and Tendencies." *Review of National Literatures* 2 (Spring 1971):11-28.

Kamshad, Hassan. *Modern Persian Prose Literature*. Cambridge: Cambridge University Press, 1966.

Karimi-Hakkak, Ahmad. *Recasting Persian Poetry: Scenarios of Poetic Modernity in Iran.* Salt Lake City: University of Utah Press, 1995.

Khorrami, Mohammad Mehdi. *Modern Reflections of Classical Traditions in Persian Fiction.* Lewson, Queenston, Lamper: The Edwin Mellon Press, 2003.

Law, Henry D. C. "Introductory Essays: Persian Writers." *Life and Letters and the London Mercury* 63 (December 1949):196-209.

Lukacs, Georg. *The Theory of the Novel*, 3rd ed. Translated by Anna Bostock. Cambridge, Massachusetts: MIT Press, 1977.

Mashiah, Yaakov. "Once Upon a Time: A Study of *Yaki Bud Yaki Nabud.*" *Acta Orientalia* 33 (1971):109-143.

Mostafavi, R. "Fiction in Contemporary Persian Literature." *Middle Eastern Affairs* 2, Pts. 8-9 (1951):273-279.

Naficy, Majid. *Modernism and Ideology in Persian Literature: A Return to Nature in the Poetry of Nima Yushij.* Lanham, Maryland: University Press of America, 1997.

Nafisi, Sa'id. "A General Survey of the Existing Situation in Persian Literature." *Bulletin of the Institute of Islamic Studies,* No. 1 (1957):15-16.

Netzer, Amnon, ed. *Padyavand.* Costa Mesa, California: Mazda Publishers, Vol. 1, 1996; Vol. 2, 1997; Vol. 3, 1999.

Panichas, George A., ed. *The Politics of Twentieth Century Novelists.* New York: Thomas Y. Crowell, 1974.

Pirnazar, Jaleh. "Chehreh-ye Yahud dar Asar-e Seh Nevisandeh-ye Motojadded-e Irani," *Iran Nameh*, Vol. XIII, No. 4 (Fall 1995):483-502.

Rahman, Manibar. "Social Satire in Modern Persian Literature." *Bulletin of Islamic Studies* 2-3 (1958-1959):63-91.

Ricks, Thomas M. "Contemporary Persian Literature." *The Literary Review* 18, No. 1 (Fall 1974):4-17.

_____, ed. *Critical Perspectives on Modern Persian Literature.* Washington, D.C.: Three Continents Press, 1984.

Robbe-Grillet, Alain. *For a New Novel*, 4th ed. Translated by Richard Howard. New York: Grove Press, 1965.

Rypka Jan. *History of Iranian Literature*. Edited by Karl Jahn. Dordrecht, Holland: Reidel, 1968.

Talattof, Kamran. *The Politics of Writing in Iran: A History of Modern Persian Literature*. Syracuse: Syracuse University Press, 2000.

Tikku, Girdhari L. "Some Socio-Religious Themes in Modern Persian Fiction." *Islam and Its Cultural Divergence*. Edited by Girdhari L. Tikku. Urbana: University of Illinois, 1971. Pp. 165-179.

Vatanabadi, Shouleh, and Mohammad Mehdi Khorrami. *Another Sea, Another Shore: Persian Stories of Migration*. Northampton, Massachusetts: Interlik Books, 2004.

Weisstein, Ulrich. *Comparative Literature and Literary Theory*. Bloomington: Indiana University Press, 1973.

Wellek, Rene, and Austin Warren. *Theory of Literature*, 3rd ed. New York: Harcourt and World, 1970.

Wickens, G. M. "Persian Literature as an Affirmation of National Identity." *Review of National Literatures* 2, Pt. 1 (Spring 1971):29-60.

Wilbur, Donald N. *Iran: Past and Present*, 8th ed. Princeton, New Jersey: Princeton University Press, 1976.

Yarshater, Ehsan, ed. *Iran Faces the Seventies*. New York: Praeger, 1971.

_____. "Persian Letters in the Last Fifty Years." *Middle Eastern Affairs* 9 (1960):298-306.

Zaehner, R. C. *The Teachings of the Magi: A Compendium of Zoroastrian Beliefs*. New York: Oxford University Press, 1976.

_____. *Zurvan: A Zoroastrian Dilemma*. Oxford: The Clarendon Press, 1955.

Zavarzadeh, Mas'ud. "The Persian Short Story Since the Second World War: An Overview." *The Muslim World* 58 (1968):310-311.

Index

About the Author

M. R. Ghanoonparvar is Professor of Persian and Comparative Literature at the University of Texas at Austin. His books include *Prophets of Doom: Literature as a Socio-Political Phenomenon in Modern Iran* (1984), *In a Persian Mirror: Images of the West and Westerners in Iranian Fiction* (1993), and *Translating the Garden* (2001). He has edited several volumes including *Iranian Drama: an Anthology* (1989), *In Transition: Essays on Culture and Identity in Middle Eastern Societies* (1994), Gholamhoseyn Sa'edi's *Othello in Wonderland* and *Mirror-Polishing Storytellers* (1996), and Moniru Ravanipur's *Satan Stones* (1996) and *Kanizu* (2004). His translations include Jalal Al-e Ahmad's *By the Pen* (1988), Sadeq Chubak's *The Patient Stone* (1989), Simin Daneshvar's *Savushun* (1990), Ahmad Kasravi's *On Islam* and *Shi'ism* (1990), and Sadeq Hedayat's *The Myth of Creation* (1998).